150 NOT OUT
HAMPSHIRE COUNTY CRICKET 1863–2013

Compiled and Edited by Dave Allen
with Stephen Saunders

Preface by Mark Nicholas
Foreword by Jimmy Adams

Typeset in UK by Solent Design Studio Ltd
Production Managed by Jellyfish Solutions

Copyright © 2013 Dave Allen

All rights reserved. No part of this publication may be reproduced, stored in a retrieval system, or transmitted, in any form or by any means, electronic, mechanical, photocopying, recording, or otherwise, without the prior written permission of the publisher.

ISBN: 978-1-909811-10-2

All the photographs used in this book are from Hampshire Cricket's Archive. We would like to acknowledge in particular the help of Patrick Eagar, Dave Vokes (LMI Photography) and local newspapers the *Daily Echo* (Bournemouth and Southampton) and the *News* (Portsmouth). We would be pleased to learn the identity of photographers who are responsible for any other photographs in the book. We are always pleased to hear from anyone able to contribute relevant photographs to our archive.

Front Cover: the Ageas Bowl and the grounds at Bournemouth, Portsmouth, Broadhalfpenny Down and Southampton
Back Cover: the 'Hambledon' (Hampshire) team on the Memorial Stone Broadhalfpenny Down in September 1908

CONTENTS

Acknowledgements	1
Preface: Mark Nicholas	2
Foreword: Jimmy Adams	4
Introduction	6
Hambledon, Hampshire by Stephen Saunders	7
Hampshire in First-Class Cricket	9
Appendix One Cricket in Hampshire in the Eighteenth Century	141
Appendix Two Hampshire Cricket: 1800–1863	143
Appendix Three Hampshire's Cricketers	147
Appendix Four Presidents of Hampshire & MCC	150
Bibliography	152
Index	153

ACKNOWLEDGEMENTS

In 1999 I organised an exhibition at Portsmouth City Museum to celebrate the first *recorded* cricket match in Hampshire, played at Milldam, Portsmouth exactly 250 years earlier. A few years later the Association of Cricket Statisticians (ACS) published an earlier date of 1733 for a match in Stubbington.

But of course history is like that and this book, which is full of historical 'facts' will probably be amended, corrected and updated when Hampshire celebrates the 200th anniversary of the formation of the club in 2063. I became aware of Hampshire's proud cricketing history in my early years as a junior member through the first official history by Harry Altham, Desmond Eagar, John Arlott and statistician Roy Webber (1957). For this publication I describe myself as the compiler and editor, not author, precisely because its production has required me to trawl through that publication and quite a few others, plus averages minutes and balance sheets, to get as close to an accurate account as might be possible in the messy business of writing history. Any errors are entirely mine.

I am indebted in my work to the efforts of all those men and others such as Lieut-Col John May and FS Ashley-Cooper, and their successors, including all the editors of Hampshire's Guides and Handbooks. Following the 1957 publication there was a new history, thirty years, later from Peter Wynne-Thomas and various statistical publications, notably by Hampshire's statistician Vic Isaacs and his successor Bob Murrell. I have mentioned the ACS and thank them again for the invaluable assistance that they and the on-line Cricket Archive provide to those of us engaged on this kind of research. They have literally transformed the field over the past thirty years.

More recently, my shift from loyal supporter to committee member and Hon Archivist has benefited from the support of many friends on the Committee and staff at Hampshire – not least Members' Chairman Terry Crump, who has supported the idea of this publication from the outset. In the business of compiling and writing histories, four men, all authors, have been informative and supportive friends for some years; between them they provide a wealth of knowledge, which has informed much of what you will find within. Stephen Saunders has contributed specific sections to this book and commented on others, Alan Edwards cast a careful eye and offered some amendments, Andrew Renshaw, my predecessor as Handbook editor, is a regular help and Neil Jenkinson, the previous Hon Archivist, supported me from my first formal involvement in Hampshire County Cricket Club about 20 years ago. I thank them all and add Bob Elliott and others who have spotted amendments needed to the first draft, which, in the modern way, was displayed on the Hampshire Cricket History 'Blog'.

I am grateful to our captain Jimmy Adams for his delightful Foreword – it feels very right that Hampshire's first official 'home-grown' post-war captain should introduce this volume. Finally, the book is a testament to the unfailing efforts of succeeding generations, including all members and supporters, who, both on the field and behind the scenes, created, sustained and developed our club. In that context, I choose to single out one man here although many others' tales are told within. Over the past decade, Rod Bransgrove has ensured that we would survive some very challenging times to reach this historic anniversary and I record my thanks and appreciation to him on behalf of everyone who cares about Hampshire Cricket.

Dave Allen
Hon Archivist, Hampshire Cricket

PREFACE: MARK NICHOLAS

The first time I walked into the old county ground at Northlands Road, Barry Richards was batting. He stood tall and elegant and, from his back foot, drove Jeff Thomson through the covers. It was a stroke so difficult and so magical that a love affair began there and then. Mesmerised, I took every opportunity to see him in person and came to accept the pain that went with his failure as an inevitable part of the addiction from which I was suffering. Sometimes, he would make a hundred and get himself out immediately – an act so selfish that I would swear to cut back on the devotion and treat him with a colder, more dispassionate eye. But it never worked. Barry drew me to Hampshire cricket and almost 40 years on I am still there: if not so often in body, always in spirit.

That year was 1975 and the match was against the Australians. To a schoolboy, the occasion was irresistible, an affirmation of the dreams that formed the early time of my life. There was a romance to Hampshire cricket, first inspired by Colin Ingleby-Mackenzie and then made good by the brilliance of the overseas players who created a legend of their own. My next visit was in 1977, an eager kid hounding down a place on the groundstaff. The young pros used to help run the scoreboard and I sneaked in with Tim Tremlett, who spent a memorably hectic afternoon posting Mike Procter's incredible hat-trick in the semi-final of the Benson and Hedges Cup.

Procter was another truly heroic figure who had grown up with Richards in Durban, South Africa. His flamboyant fast bowling was one of the game's most thrilling spectacles and at Southampton in the late June of 1977 he did for Gordon Greenidge, Richards himself, Trevor Jesty and John Rice in the space of five balls. He had Nigel Cowley plumb LBW off the sixth too but Umpire Tommy Spencer froze in the headlights of the moment and gave Cowley the benefit of very little doubt. That evening we went into the bar of the old Pavilion and hoped to rub shoulders with the men who had cornered our affection. Hampshire might have lost the match but our ambition to wear the blue and gold colours of the club that is now 150 years old had not dimmed.

There is, for reasons that are not necessarily tangible, something special about Hampshire cricket. The game's greatest have been drawn to it, perhaps because a sense of adventure remains at the core. Results have not always reflected talent but this has been because an inherent commitment to entertain has overridden the more hard-nosed pragmatism that brings lesser lights their brighter days.

The balance between an amateur "feel" and a professional performance is the holy grail of Hampshire cricket and many a team has found it. Think Lionel Tennyson with Phil Mead, Jack Newman and Alec Kennedy; Dick Moore with Neil McCorkell and Stuart Boyes; Desmond Eagar, Derek Shackleton and Vic Cannings; Ingleby-Mackenzie alongside Leo Harrison, Jimmy Gray and Butch White; Richard Gilliatt with Peter Sainsbury, David Turner and Gordon Greenidge; this writer with Malcolm Marshall, Paul Terry and Chris Smith; Robin Smith with Shaun Udal and Nic Pothas and the men of today, led by Jimmy Adams and supported by Dimi Mascarenhas, Michael Carberry and Sean Ervine.

So much has changed and yet so much stays the same. At a new ground, new names wear new clothes in various formats of the game but the simple battle between bat and ball and Hampshire's lifelong attempt to make that attractive for their supporters lives on. It is a legacy worth protecting. Indeed, it is an ideal worth pursuing for all time.

And a final thought...my Hampshire greatest team (based on performances for the county rather than elsewhere): Barry Richards, Gordon Greenidge, Roy Marshall, Robin Smith, Phil Mead, Colin Ingleby-Mackenzie (capt), George Brown, Malcolm Marshall, Shane Warne, Andy Roberts, Derek Shackleton. 12th man, Peter Sainsbury. Go Sains!

Mark Nicholas
Hampshire County Cricket Club, 1978-1995
Captain 1985-1995

FOREWORD: JIMMY ADAMS

Mum, Dad and Robin Smith. It's highly likely that without the influence of the aforementioned triumvirate I would not have been as privileged as I have been over the last 25 plus years, to have seen, played and supported cricket at this wonderful club. Dad's love of the game rubbed off on my brothers and I and marathon sessions of garden cricket were commonplace. Perhaps the one drawback could have been dad's Kentish roots … fortunately mum's Winchester roots were firmly embedded and my brothers and I grew up in the Hampshire camp.

Robin Smith was the cricketing spark that ignited our enthusiasm for the game to the next level. His performances for Hampshire, particularly in the limited-overs finals and in the international arena, only served to heighten the cricket fever.

While 'The Judge' stole the headlines, visits to Northlands Road over the following decades brought us closer to other Hampshire players and there are plenty of fond and slightly random memories – Tony Middleton's fantastic year in 1992, Will Kendall's double hundred against Sussex in 1999, Jon Ayling's upper cut in the 1991 NatWest Final, Paul Whitaker's stance, Adi Aymes standing miles back to Nixon McLean, Jason Laney and Derek Kenway putting on 200 against Lancashire in 1999. I remember reading the scorecard of 'Dimi's' debut wickets against Glamorgan and my brother pleading with Dad to get an Axa, Equity & Law one-day shirt with Thursfield on the back.

As the 1990s drew to a close I had some games for the 2nd XI, a few runs followed and I managed to earn a contract for the last season of cricket at Northlands Road. It coincided with the more headline-grabbing signing of Shane Warne – aside from his obvious cricketing prowess, one of my abiding memories is of bringing 'Warnie' his lunch, standard 12th man duties, and being a little taken aback as the man who was arguably the current world's best cricketer tipped the cheese from the baguette onto his chips, added enough ketchup to get one of his 5-a-day and washed it down with that well-marketed energy drink. I doubt it'll surprise you to find out he rounded it off with a Benson & Hedges.

Another character of the time, Alex Morris, sticks in my mind for his accuracy, not just with the ball but with a mini pork pie on the balcony at Basingstoke, dropped straight into a supporter's pint down below – I didn't hang around to assess the reaction. Among other things, it's a reflection of how some things have changed in the game – you wouldn't find chips or a pork pie on the lunch or tea menu now.

On a personal level, those initial years proved a real struggle and a stint at university followed. Even so, in that time I was lucky to face (and survive) the first ball bowled at the Rose Bowl. I made my championship debut at Hove and was still in when RA Smith strode out, which remains one of my fondest moments in cricket.

Things began to pick up and slowly the county's patience started to bear fruit. The vision of Rod Bransgrove combined with Warne's captaincy brought renewed belief to us all and my own game started to click too. Our first trophy in 13 years duly arrived in 2005; Sean Ervine's hundreds in the semi and final are obvious stand-outs, though Kevin Latouf's catch to dismiss Nick Knight in the final sits at the forefront of my mind. We pushed hard in the Championship too, falling just short in 2005 and 2006. Changing next to John Crawley was a blessing, as his run scoring proved infectious. My maiden hundred for the county arrived better-late-than-never in a fantastic run chase at Headingley 2006 and I started to feel worthy of my place in the dressing room. Others must have felt the same, as my county cap followed soon after.

There are always ups and downs, cricket is a great leveller, but generally it's been good going since. I've experienced more playing highlights in the past five years than most are lucky to get in a career – two Lord's finals wins and two T20 Finals Day wins, the first of which was at our home ground. I had the honour of being offered the captaincy leading into 2012 and we managed to cap a wonderful season ('Dimi' had led us to the T20 title a month earlier) with a last ball win at Lords – it's hard to better lifting a trophy at the home of cricket.

The ground's progress has seemingly mirrored the team's successes and has developed into a world-class arena – perhaps strangely, it's been something that I've set goals for. I wanted to be on the staff for the start of our time at the Rose Bowl, I hoped to still be around for the development of the new stands; the same applies now for the finishing of the hotel and golf course and eventually what will surely be the arrival of regular Test cricket. With the ground nearing completion and a squad with a strong nucleus of young players hungry for more success, the future of the club looks bright.

There are too many fond times and memories to mention and hopefully a few more to come; not just the games played and the matches won but, more importantly, the people I've met and played with (and against), the friendly faces around the ground, the camaraderie and support of teammates, coaches and support staff, the time in the changing room after those wins and everyone about the place which I'm very lucky to call my home ground. I hope this book helps stir your own memories of past glories, good times and perhaps, too, some more random moments.

It would be remiss of me to pass up this chance to thank my wife, my brothers and sister and all my friends for their ongoing support, to the many coaches who have helped me over the years, but most of all Giles White and Tony Middleton for their faith and patience, to Rod, for all he's done for our great club, the players for all their efforts on the pitch and for making the changing room such a hard place to leave and finally all the supporters for their continued support. Oh, and, of course, Mum, Dad and Robin Smith.

Jimmy Adams
Hampshire's Captain, 2013

INTRODUCTION

This book is published to celebrate the 150th anniversary of the formation of Hampshire County Cricket Club at two meetings in the late summer of 1863. It traces that history, but also sets out some of the essential features of cricket in the county during the century and more, prior to those important meetings.

There may be references to cricket in and around Hampshire before 1700, but more useful in terms of the 'modern' club and the organised game are references to Hampshire cricketers and/or cricket *in* Hampshire between 1729–1749, all of which precede and lead to the formation of what is usually known as the famous Hambledon Club. There has never been an indisputably precise date for that formation and today's historians distinguish between the wealthy social 'club' called Hambledon and the side they raised and 'sponsored' which took the field and which is increasingly known as Hampshire. We have evidence of a match played in Hambledon in 1753 (see *The Cricket Statistician* no 154, Summer 2011), and cricket played there, elsewhere in the county and by that team *outside* the county, through the following decades. This is explained more fully below by Stephen Saunders.

We do, however, have clear evidence in the form of contemporary minutes of the two meetings held late in the season of 1863, which led to the formation of Hampshire County Cricket Club – specifically at the first General Meeting held in Southampton on 11 September 1863. This book records through a year-by-year chronology the development of that club and the many changes in its organisation over the subsequent century-and-a-half. The chronology focuses on the performances of the players and teams but notes also some significant off-field events that have taken Hampshire from a modest 'shire' club to the side which has won a dozen major titles in the past 40 years and moved from a cramped Victorian headquarters to a purpose-built international stadium. The stadium implies an exciting future but, in its semi-rural setting, also offers views towards Hambledon, reminding us of our long, proud place in any history of English cricket.

HAMBLEDON, HAMPSHIRE by STEPHEN SAUNDERS

All cricket enthusiasts have heard of Hambledon, which has been termed, by some, as the 'cradle of cricket' and was considered for a time to be the centre of the game in Hampshire. However, there is confusion between the Hambledon Club and the village that is the location of Broadhalfpenny Down and Windmill Down. There is also a misconception that the Hambledon Club was the precursor to the Hampshire County Cricket Club.

Several clubs in several counties played cricket before the first recorded game at Hambledon in August 1753 when Hambledon beat Surrey by 113 runs (reported in the *Salisbury Journal*). A further match is known to have been played at Hambledon against Dartford in August 1756 *(Reading Mercury)*. The earliest reference to Hampshire as an individual county team is a match against Sussex played at Racedown, Hampshire in June 1766. Subsequently all major games played in the County were played at Hambledon from 1767 to 1792, so it can rightly be claimed to be the centre of the game in the County during that period.

G. B. Buckley, in his book *Fresh Light on 18th Century Cricket*, records a match between Hampshire and Sussex played on Broadhalfpenny Down in 1767. This match is also mentioned by H. F. & A. P. Squire in *Pre-Victorian Sussex Cricket*. (Waghorn's *Cricket Scores 1730–1773* reports a similar match the previous year but does not give a date or venue.) Also, F. S. Ashley-Cooper's *Kent Cricket Matches* records Hampshire playing Kent in a two-day game in 1768. So we have three separate erudite sources informing us that Hampshire played cricket before the Hambledon Club was formed.

The *Salisbury Journal* of 27 April 1772 stated that "The first meeting of the Gentlemen of The Hambledon Club will be held at Broad-Halfpenny on Tuesday, the 5th of May next, at which every subscriber is requested to attend". This was the formation of the Club, which lasted until 1796 when the last minute famously recorded "No Gentlemen".

The Hambledon Club was never referred to as the Hambledon Cricket Club and, although involved with cricket, it never was a cricket club, but a Gentlemen's Club, as referred to in the *Salisbury Journal*. Looking through the minute books and the membership you find titled gentlemen, military officers and clerics, but none of the players. The members were well-to-do persons who organised and laid bets on matches and enjoyed lavish dinners at the Bat and Ball. The Club was logically based at Broadhalfpenny as this was, as stated, the centre of the game in Hampshire.

Many matches are recorded as Hampshire during the time of the Hambledon Club. Indeed there is one in 1774 against Hambledon and two, in this period, against Hambledon Town. Cricket Archive records 83 first-class matches by Hampshire between 1772 and 1796 (the period of the Hambledon Club). So a Hampshire team existed in addition to, and indeed prior to, any Hambledon team.

The last first-class match on Broadhalfpenny Down was played in 1781 (Hampshire v Kent). Matches then moved to Windmill Down until 1792 but were also played at Stoke Down (4 miles North-East of Winchester) from 1778–1798. Hampshire played one match in 1806 at Stoke Down and did not play again in the County till 1823 when one match was played at Bramshill Park, owned by Sir John Cope. A further two matches were played there in 1825.

For record purposes, Hampshire played 24 matches between 1803 and 1828, mainly at Lord's, after which (with the exception of one 'odd' fixture against Stonehenge in 1839) they did not play again until 1842 when Day's Antelope Ground in Southampton was in use. Cricket Archive records a further 17 first-class matches by Hampshire before the formation of the County Cricket Club in 1863, making a total of 128 matches played by Hampshire from 1772.

Returning to the gentlemen of Hambledon, these gentlemen had a keen interest in the game of cricket and often had country estates where the game was played. They also formed a separate team called the Gentlemen of Hampshire. This implies that the Hampshire side were the professionals and it was on them that they laid their bets. It is known that the Gentlemen of Hampshire played two games in 1771 against the Gentlemen of Sussex, the first of these on Broadhalfpenny Down eight months before the announcement in the *Salisbury Journal*: further evidence of formalising a Gentlemen's Club? Their next recorded game was in 1830 and between then and the last recorded game in 1889, 106 games were played.

H. T. Waghorn mentions in *The Dawn of Cricket* a report dated August 17, 1795 stating, "The members of the Hampshire County Club will please take notice that the anniversary meeting will be held at the White Hart Inn, Winchester on Wednesday the 26th. Dinner at 3 o'clock". This he interprets as being the Hampshire County Cricket Club, but this is a misconception that has persisted and is even quoted in *Hampshire County Cricket: the Official History* (Altham et al., 1957), which describes it as "the first recorded meeting of the Hampshire County Cricket Club" (p. 23).

The club being referred to was instituted on 30th March 1789 and among the resolutions of the General Meeting on 28th September that year were: "that one General Meeting to be held each year on the Monday preceding the full moon in the month of August" (hence the anniversary meeting in August in the above notice); "that the committee for considering of such measures as shall be necessary to preserve the Independence of the County in future …" and "that the Chairman be desired to express to Mr. Thistlethwayte the earnest wish of this meeting for the continuance of his services in Parliament as one of the Representatives of the County". Waghorn and subsequent authors are incorrect. This was a political club.

The pre-eminence of the gentlemen of the Hambledon Club in the game of cricket is evidenced first by Thomas Chamberlayne who led the Gentlemen of Hampshire and, when he succeeded to Cranbury Park, had a cricket pitch laid and formed his own team. His prominence in the game led to him being nominated President of MCC in 1845. Similarly, another stalwart of the Gentlemen of Hampshire, Sir Frederick Hervey-Bathurst, was nominated President in 1857. It was these two gentlemen, along with Sir John Barker-Mill of Mottisfont Abbey, who financed the development of the Antelope Ground in Southampton, in 1839, and then in 1842 installed Daniel Day in the Antelope Hotel, thereby heralding the formalisation of cricket in the County.

Mention should also be made of The South Hants Cricket Club. This club was formed in 1842 and comprised many members of The Gentlemen of Hampshire. Their home ground was Day's Antelope Ground in Southampton and in the period up to the formation of the County Club in 1863 they had played 19 matches. H. G. Green mentions that this club had a "dinner dress, consisting of a blue cloth swallow tail coat, ornamented with gilt basket buttons; a white, rolled-back waistcoat, knee breeches, with black stockings and shoes with steel buckles" and that he has seen such dress at a dinner that he attended. Another club whose priority is dining! He also suggests that the South Hants is "the most important local Cricket club in existence prior to the formation of the Hampshire County Cricket Club". The same players also played on the same ground as South Hampshire, for whom Arthur Conan-Doyle played one match.

On July 3, 1878 a meeting was held to form the Hambledon Cricket Club and it was resolved that "the Clubhouse be The George Inn". On July 8 a committee meeting was held "to frame the Bye Laws for the Hambledon Cricket Club" and on July 15 a general meeting, with 26 members present, passed the Bye Laws. Now we have the Hambledon Cricket Club, but it is after the foundation of the Hampshire County *Cricket* club in 1863.

HAMPSHIRE IN FIRST-CLASS CRICKET

It was not until 1947 that the Imperial Cricket Conference formulated "an exact definition of a first-class match". It was, most simply, "a match of three or more days duration between two sides of eleven players officially adjudged first-class" (Association of Cricket Statisticians (ACS), 1982, p. 4).

In Hampshire's earliest history, Ashley-Cooper (1924, p. 22) described "Hampshire's elevation to first-class rank", having been admitted to the County Championship in 1895. Similarly, Altham *et al.* (1957, p. 41) describe the advocacy of Lord Harris at the end of the 1894 season leading to Hampshire's "promotion" to "the first-class counties".

Wynne-Thomas (1988) offers a more subtle interpretation of Hampshire as a first-class county, but he was also Secretary of the ACS Committee that, in 1982, published the second edition of *A Guide to First-class Cricket Matches Played in the British Isles*. The ACS drew principally on the publications of the time such as *Lillywhite's* (Green and Red), *Fred's*, *Cricket* and *Wisden*.

The ACS, drawing on such evidence, "considers the county first-class from 1864" but also cites from 'Green Lilly' 1869 that by then it had "collapsed as a first-class county". As a consequence, 1868 is not considered as a first-class season but, immediately afterwards, the single matches played in 1869 and 1870 were "treated as first-class by the contemporary Annuals". The ACS noted that from 1875 "regular Hampshire matches were resumed" and therefore the county "was again considered first-class".

There was another single season, 1879, with only a minor match v MCC, but first-class cricket resumed the following season and was recorded in 'Red Lilly' of 1881. However, during the early 1880s, while the annuals continued to report Hampshire's matches as first-class, they expressed doubts about their status and from 1886 "The Cricket Reporting Agency brings about a unanimity amongst the annuals and Hampshire is excluded from first-class status".

This seems clear and the dates referred to above are those used by Victor Isaacs, the club's scorer and statistician, when he published their updated "First-class Records 1864–1996" in a pamphlet.

The ACS, having described the situation above, continued by saying, "in this booklet the county is given as first-class from 1864–1885 inclusive". This is not quite clear then, given the gaps identified above. The precise years are as follows: 1864–1867, 1869–1870, 1875–1878, 1880–1885 and from 1895 when Hampshire were admitted to the County Championship – *except* for the war years (1915–1918 and 1940–1945) when the Championship ceased.

Today we have other competitions between first-class sides, which are not first-class. 'One-day' or, rather more precisely, limited-overs single innings matches have been played in major competitions since 1963 and at various times innings have lasted 65, 60, 55, 50, 45 and 40 overs. These are all now known generically as 'List A'. In 2003 we added Twenty20 matches and their records, which are separate from List A.

1863

A variety of Hampshire sides played matches during the season (see Appendix 1) then, on 12 August and 11 September 1863, two meetings were held which led to the formation of the Hampshire County Cricket Club.

In the club's minute book, the meeting held at the Antelope Inn, Southampton on Wednesday 12 August 1863 was "for the purpose of making the preliminary arrangements for the formation of a County Cricket Club". The aim was that "annual contests with Surrey, Sussex etc can be received and an organisation for the furthering and encouraging of games of cricket provided".

Thomas Chamberlayne of Cranbury Park near Eastleigh was elected President and GM Ede Secretary. The Committee would include Col Hervey-Bathurst, EL Ede, A Dyer, H Lees, Col Tyson, GM Ede and HG Green. They would draw up Rules and Regulations and "submit the same to a General Meeting to be held at the Antelope Inn on Friday 11 September 1863".

On Friday 11 September 1863, in accordance with Resolution Number 4 from the Meeting of 12 August, a very fully attended General Meeting was held at the Antelope Inn Southampton at 10 am. Colonel Tyson took the Chair and among those present were Captain Eccles, Captain Quinton, Captain GF Day and Messrs GE George, H Stewart, EL Ede, GM Ede, H Frere, E Hall, JW Lowe, J Frederick, WH Pearce, AS Thorndike, J Hunt, T Wells, F Lanchester, M Batchelor, A Dyer and RN Bernard, the Secretary of Surrey CCC. That meeting was held during a three-day match v Surrey on the ground and it was the September date that was celebrated in 1963 as marking the precise centenary with the start of the three-day match v MCC All-England.

Thomas Chamberlayne was elected President, John Hunt Treasurer and GM Ede Hon Secretary. The Chairman read and proposed the rules and two Vice Presidents were elected: the Earls of Portsmouth and Uxbridge. The first match played by the newly formed Hampshire County Cricket Club would follow in the summer of 1864. GM Ede was a famous amateur jockey who won the Grand National in 1868 but was killed in a racing accident at the same meeting, two years later. EL Ede was his twin brother and became the club's secretary, scorer and editor of the early annual *Hampshire Cricket Guides*, which eventually became the *Hampshire Handbook*.

1864 *(First-class)*

The first match as *Hampshire County Cricket Club* came in the season following the formation, on 7, 8 July v Sussex at Day's Antelope Ground, Southampton:

Hampshire 63 (Ridding 13, Lillywhite 5-22) & 122 (Case 48, Lillywhite 5-58), Sussex 185 (Smith 47, Fillery 35) & 1-0. Sussex won by 10 wickets.

The Hampshire XI was: CF Lucas, JC Lord, H Holmes, GM Ede (captain), HT Frere (w/kpr), CH Ridding, EL Ede, W Humphrey, G Ubsdell, S Tubb, GH Case.

After the defeat v Sussex, there were three more three-day first-class matches:

Middlesex v Hampshire at Islington, 11, 12 July: Middlesex won inns & 38 runs.
Sussex v Hampshire at Hove, 11, 12, 13 August: Sussex won by 10 wickets.
Hampshire v Middlesex at Southampton, 29, 30 August, Middlesex won by 10 wickets.

Despite this disappointing start for the new county club in major matches, they did travel to Kennington Oval immediately following the match at Islington, where they beat Surrey by 86 runs. Since Hampshire were playing with 14 men, this match was *not* first-class, but Walton, with match figures of 9-111, was a key performer for Hampshire.

In the first-class matches, only two men, H Holmes (71) and GM Ede (52), passed 50 in an innings, although J StJ Frederick was overall top scorer with 122 runs in his four innings. EL Ede took nine wickets at 27.88 but no bowler managed five wickets in an innings. The best bowling was by Frederick again, 4-45. Overs consisted of four balls in this period.

In June, Southampton Union beat the English XI in a three-day match at Day's Antelope Ground although the home side had the advantage of fielding 22 men. In the four innings, no batsman reached 30. In August, South Wilts beat the South Hants Club at day's Antelope Ground. GM Ede top-scored with 53 and Southerton took seven wickets in the match.

1865

Hampshire's first win in a first-class match came v Surrey at Antelope Ground (24, 25 August) on the second day of three-day match. This was their third and final match of the season. They had lost previously to Middlesex and Surrey by an innings in 1865, so they had lost all of their first six first-class matches before this first victory.

Surrey 87 (Tubb 7-32) & 101 (Jupp 39, Southerton 7-45) lost to Hampshire 96 (Lucas 43, Humphrey 5-26) & 93-2 (Lucas 58*) by 8 wickets.

Hampshire's Southampton-born wicket-keeper, George Ubsdell, dismissed six Surrey batsmen in one innings, five of them stumped. The latter figure remains a county record. Southerton ended the season with 21 wickets at 12.85 in his three first-class appearances. In the match v Middlesex at Islington, AJA Wilkinson (8-69) and T Hearne (10-84) bowled unchanged in the match – the first instance against Hampshire. The next came in the following season by J Grundy and G Wootton for MCC at Lord's and there have been four subsequent instances, although none since Rhodes and Haig for Yorkshire in 1904. There was much disappointment that Middlesex failed to raise a side for the return match at Southampton and, following some bitter exchanges, Hampshire did not play Middlesex again until 1907.

Hampshire frequently struggled because their best men were not always available. They played and lost two matches against Buckinghamshire that were not first-class.

1866

This was a season of steady improvement over four matches. Hampshire began on 4 June with an innings defeat at Lord's v MCC. In that game James Southerton bowled just five overs (0-13) but in the next three matches he took 32 wickets at 13.59. It is strange to note that in 1864 he had not bowled but executed three stumpings. E Hemsted and S Tubb both took five wickets in an innings, although, with the exception of one important innings by CF Lucas, the batting was weak – no one else reaching 50.

Hampshire lost to Surrey at the Oval by 59 runs (9 July) after Surrey had followed-on, then, in the return match v MCC at Day's Ground a week later, they lost by just 11 runs. Finally, from 16–18 August, they met Surrey again at Day's Ground and dismissed them for 85 (Southerton 7-49), after which Hampshire scored 281 with CF Lucas, 135, recording Hampshire's first first-class century. Surrey made 216 second time around and Hampshire's 21-0 gave them a victory by 10 wickets. This would be their last first-class victory until 1875.

The South Hants Club played what appears to be their last nineteenth century match, an exciting one innings game v Winchester College in which the students, pursuing 106 to win, finished at 79-9. Lipscomb scored 54 and Thresher took four wickets.

Around this time, the Committee agreed that the pay of the professionals "was not to exceed £5 a match" and the secretary was required to make arrangements with them "according to their expenses".

1867

The appropriately named Charles Young made his debut for Hants v Kent at Gravesend in June at 15 years 130 days. Until 2011, it was an English first-class record and it remains a record for the youngest debutant in a first-class match between two counties. Young appeared in three matches v Kent that season, after they were added to the small group of mainly southern counties that Hampshire played against in the mid-19th century. Young played in three matches, averaging 11.60 with the bat and taking six wickets at 19.83. H Holmes and H Soames both scored half-centuries and led the batting averages and, although Southerton played in only two first-class matches, he was leading wicket taker with 10 at 18.70.

Young played for Hampshire against Kent in 1885 at Tonbridge, his final first-class match, as Hampshire was thereafter regarded as 'second class' until admitted to the Championship in 1895. Young played his final game for the county at the relatively new Northlands Road headquarters in 1890. He died in Lancashire in 1913.

1868 *(Not first-class)*

An Australian Aboriginal side toured England through the summer and into autumn, playing many games. They played three matches in Hampshire. The first was in Southsea at the East Hants Cricket Ground against East Hampshire on 15 & 16 June. The hosts won by an innings and there was a sad element in that one of the tourists, known as 'King Cole', contracted a lung infection and died in London before playing another match.

The tourists returned to that ground on 5 & 6 October and won by an innings and 61 runs before moving on to Daniel Day's Antelope Ground on the following two days where the match against the Gentlemen of Hampshire was drawn. For the visitors "Twopenny" took 9-17 while, after two days, the Aboriginals were 49-3, just 29 short of victory. The two sides bowled 234 overs in the two days.

In 1867 Hampshire had played just three first-class matches, all against Kent, but in 1868 they played none – indeed we have no record of any matches played by a full Hampshire side although some Hampshire cricketers participated in the matches against the Aboriginals. WWB Beach was elected President, succeeding Thomas Chamberlayne, and in the following year AH Wood took over from Captain WH Eccles after his one year as Secretary.

1869

The Dean Park Ground was first laid out in Bournemouth (then in Hampshire). Two first-class matches were played against MCC and lost. There were no first-class inter-county matches.

Southerton was no longer playing for Hampshire and in those two matches, P Thresher's 47* was the highest score of the season while Henry W Tate took eight wickets (at 13.37) and, Henry Misselbrook led the averages with six wickets at 6.50.

1870

The early 1870s were a bleak period for the newly formed Hampshire County Cricket. There were frequent resignations, changes of officers and poorly attended meetings.

Hampshire played just two first-class matches in 1870, both, curiously, against Lancashire (home and away). They had not played them previously and did not meet them again until 1897. Hampshire lost by 10 wickets at Old Trafford in July and the northern county won again next month in Southampton in a low-scoring match. In the first match, Lancashire's W Hickton took 10-46, the only instance of 10 wickets in an innings on either side by one bowler in any of Hampshire's county matches until Ottis Gibson for Durham in 2007.

No batsman reached 40 in an innings, or 100 overall in the two matches. Fred Tate took 13 wickets at 10.69

1871 *(Not first-class)*

Gentlemen of Hampshire v Gentlemen of Devon at the Torquay Cricket Festival

1872 *(Not first-class)*

An amateur side played Gentlemen of Sussex at Winchester College. Haygarth's *Scores and Biographies* reported that Hampshire played MCC at Catisfield near Fareham in July.

1873 *(Not first-class)*

In 1873 Hampshire played against 18 players representing 'Hampshire Colts' but the match was not first-class. That is the only recorded Hampshire match of any kind from 1871–1874 inclusive found on *Cricket Archive*.

The Gentlemen of Hampshire played home and away v Sussex. They beat Sussex away, but only having borrowed OE Winslow to make up their numbers and he scored the only half-century. There was also an end-of-season trial match Gentlemen v Players, on the Antelope Ground.

1874 *(Not first-class)*

XVI of Hampshire v Yorkshire United at Lyndhurst. A meeting considered whether the club "shall be dissolved or not".

1875

W Beach continued as President for the next decade and the Club's official history (1957) records how the appointment of Clement Booth as captain and secretary "provided the first element of rescue". He had won his Cambridge blue in the 1860s and organised the county side in his native Lincolnshire. In the early 1870s he moved near to Alresford and contributed to the revival of his new county. May (1906) recorded Booth as arriving in 1874.

In 1875, Booth arranged four matches, home and away against Kent and Sussex. The two home matches were played on separate Winchester grounds – the College's Ridding Field and the St Cross/Greenjackets' Ground – rather than Southampton, where the Antelope Ground was now called Southampton Cricket Ground. Hampshire's total of 34 v Kent at Winchester College was then their lowest innings, although the 'record' lasted only for three years.

There were three defeats by an innings but victory at Hove, where Arthur W Ridley came from Oxford University to make his county debut. He top-scored with 54, took 6-35 & 6-38, finishing the match with a hat-trick and four wickets in five balls. Sussex collapsed from 83-4 to 93 all out, losing by 28 runs. Sadly, business meant that he played only ten matches for the county – he played his last inter-county match for Hampshire two years later and once against MCC in 1878. Later he played for Middlesex.

1876

Hampshire lost the first match of the season at Derby but won the other three. At Southampton, Penn took 14 wickets in the match for Kent but they lost by 236 runs. Hampshire then beat Derbyshire at Southampton in late July, even though William Mycroft had match figures of 17-103 for Derbyshire. Of the two other Hampshire wickets to fall, Mycroft caught one. He was a left-arm bowler who apparently bowled fast but also spun the ball – an interestingly dangerous combination. He enjoyed considerable success that year with Derbyshire and MCC.

By coincidence, in 1895 Walter Mead took 17 wickets for Essex against Hampshire and these are the only two occasions when a bowler has taken 17 wickets in a first-class match and finished on the losing side. In mid-August, Ridley scored 104 as Hampshire beat Kent by innings at Faversham and Ridley also took 10-113 – the first Hampshire player to score a century and take 10 wickets in the same match. In his century he did not score one boundary – there were 14 threes. Henry W Tate supported him with 9-121 in the match; he and his brother Fred, who also played for Hampshire in this period, were both from Lyndhurst. With three victories in four matches, this was Hampshire's best season before they entered the Championship in 1895.

1877

The first-ever Test Match was held between Australia and England at Melbourne in mid-March. In a timeless match, Australia won by 45 runs on the fourth day. Bannerman scored 165 (retired hurt) in Australia's first innings of 245.

Hampshire's season began early, but with a two-day defeat at Lord's v MCC on 3 & 4 May. They dismissed MCC for 202 but needed nine bowlers to achieve this. Ridley took 7-46 when Derbyshire visited Southampton but Hampshire lost again; he then top-scored with 62 as they lost to Kent. There was a break of seven weeks before their next first-class match and another defeat, this time at Derby by an innings. Ridley took five wickets and top-scored – but with just 19 as Hampshire's fate was sealed.

Harry Baldwin made his Hampshire debut at the age of 16 years, six months v Derbyshire – he would not play another *first-class* match until 1895. Seventeen men bowled in the match as Kent beat Hampshire at Canterbury at the end of July. It was a very disappointing season.

1878

Hampshire started with an innings defeat in 1878 v MCC at Lord's, when they were dismissed for 24 & 65. Rylott had match figures of 14-34 and Hampshire's 24 is their third lowest first-class score ever – 15 v Warwickshire in 1922 being the lowest, then 23 v Derbyshire in 1958.

In 1878, Derby provided the only relief from defeat over the two seasons. Only 148 overs were possible and the two first innings were not completed when rain obliterated the final day. Young took 5-60 and top-scored but no batsman made 40 in the match. Hampshire's three other matches – at home to Derbyshire and home-and-away v Kent – all ended in defeat, so that in 1877 & 1878, their record was played 10, drawn one (abandoned), lost nine.

1879 *(Not first-class)*

There were no first-class matches at all, although the 'Gentlemen' of Hampshire did play against MCC again at Lord's but the fixture was second-class. There was the same fixture at Southampton in late August.

Nonetheless, an important event occurred in 1879 when Clement Booth resigned as Hon Secretary and was replaced by Russell Bencraft from Southampton. Bencraft would play a key role in the county's history, on and off the field, for many years. Cambridge University and Hampshire cricketer Lindsay Bury appeared for Old Etonians in the football Cup Final, as did EG ('Teddy') Wynyard for the Old Carthusians two years later.

1880

Russell Bencraft was captain as Hampshire's fortunes improved somewhat through the first half of the 1880s. In 1880 they played four first-class matches and won two of them – home and away against MCC. In the home match, Young took 7-34 & 6-23.

Francis E Lacey, who had been an outstanding schoolboy cricketer at Sherborne, played for Dorset in 1879 and made his Hampshire debut in 1880. He still holds the record score for Hampshire in any match *(Not first-class)* 323* v Norfolk in 1887. He was appointed Secretary of the MCC in 1898 and retained the post for 28 years.

Hampshire lost twice to Sussex and, outside first-class matches, to Devonshire and Somerset. The match against Somerset was the first home game played by Hampshire at Dean Park, Bournemouth. PA Champion de Crespigny, one of the county's more exotically named players, a naval officer, made his debut against Devon *(Not first-class)*.

The Australian tourists visited England for the first time and lost the only Test at the Oval in September. Their first match was at the Antelope Ground where they beat a team called St Luke's on 13–14 May by an innings. St Luke's fielded 18 players, a number of whom were regular Hampshire cricketers (Bencraft, Ede, etc.) and also GF Grace, brother of WG, who would die in a Basingstoke Hotel four months later, just short of his 30th birthday.

1881

After the encouragements of the previous season, Hampshire disappointed in 1881, losing three and drawing the other of their four first-class matches. An indication of the club's difficulties in developing a strong side came with the debut of Captain Francis W Lipscomb when nearly 47.

The drawn match was against MCC at Southampton. On the first two days the two teams lost 24 wickets, scoring 261 runs in 166 overs and three balls. Rain prevented any play on the final day. Hampshire also met Somerset twice in second-class matches, losing both. There would be more cheer when they won nine matches in the next four seasons.

1882

Hampshire played five first-class matches, winning three and losing two. Lacey gave an incredible all-round performance in the first first-class match of the season as Hampshire beat Sussex by 7 wickets. He scored 157 & 50* and his bowling figures were 26-13-32-4 & 75-23-149-7 – match figures of 11-181 in 101 overs. This was the second instance of a man scoring a century and taking 10 wickets in a match for the county.

On 17 August, the United Services (RN) Ground, Portsmouth staged its inaugural first-class match: Cambridge University Past & Present v Australians. The University side won by 20 runs after the visitors, chasing 208, slipped from 155-3 to 187 all out. On that ground, Major James Spens' 386 for United Services v Nondescripts is believed to be the highest individual innings ever in the county. Spens also played for the full county side in first-class matches from 1884–1899.

1883

Each season Hampshire's first-class fixtures increased, and this year they played six with two victories, one draw and three defeats. They played two matches each against Surrey, Sussex and Somerset, beating Sussex and Somerset once each, both at the Antelope Ground. In the Sussex match, fast-bowler William Dible took 4-16 & 6-50. He was born in Southampton and played for Surrey in 1882 before playing the next three seasons with Hampshire, but at 23 he left first-class cricket and died in 1894 aged just 32. He took 5-34 as Hampshire beat Somerset.

Charles Seymour carried his bat with 77* of 154 v Surrey at Southampton – the first instance for Hampshire. In addition, Hampshire fought hard for a draw at the Oval after Surrey posted the then record score for a county match of 650. Over the three days, the two sides bowled 443.3 overs.

Off the field, Hampshire established five regions and for some time elected representatives from each of them to the Committee. In addition, the secretary, Col James Fellowes, began negotiating to acquire a new ground off Banister Road in Southampton.

1884

Hampshire played eight matches, winning two but losing the other six. The season opened with defeat at the Oval where Ernest Powell, who had played briefly for Surrey, was dismissed for 99. Hampshire then lost to Kent at Gravesend with Lord Harris leading his side to victory with a century. Hampshire's first victory came in the return match, with Lacey scoring 211 & 92*. Lacey was a centurion again as Hampshire played their last major match at the Antelope Ground in August and this time Powell too reached three figures – the only time for Hampshire. They reached 645 all out, beating Somerset by an innings and 179 runs, which was their best win to date, the highest-ever score on that ground, the highest home score until 2005 and still their fourth highest score. On his county debut, Francis Bacon, a key figure in the club's development, scored 114 v Warwickshire at Birmingham, although this was not a first-class match.

Meanwhile, the new County Ground was established with eight acres of land off Bannister Road, leased at £160 pa with an agreement to build the first pavilion. In the following spring the first ever *Hampshire Cricketers' Guide*, reflecting on the 1884 season, noted the county's "steady progress" and recorded that in addition to the full county matches, the Gentlemen of Hampshire won fixtures against the Philadelphians, Devon, Dorset and Winchester College. There were also two regional Colts matches played at Portsmouth and Basingstoke. The author hoped that such fixtures would "produce that professional talent which the county so sadly needs".

1885

The 1885 *Guide* named Hampshire's officers as President, the Earl of Northesk, with Major J Fellowes (Hon Sec), Mr R Bencraft (Hon Treasurer) and AH Wood (Captain).

Hampshire played 11 first-class matches, the most ever, but won only two and lost the others. The *Guide* admitted that it was an "indifferent season" but was more optimistic about "the real resuscitation of County Cricket" following "the acquisition of permanent headquarters at Southampton". The Grand Opening occurred on 8 May and was presided over by the Countess of Northesk. The north of the county played the south in the opening match, a bazaar raised £177. 15s. 9d and the *Southampton Times and Hampshire Express* reported that "at two o'clock luncheon was served in the pavilion" and "at the termination of the day's play the Artillery band played the National Anthem". The President made a speech in which he singled out one name for special praise in the club reaching this day, Major Fellowes, and this brought "loud applause".

The two victories came in August against Sussex and Somerset but the defeats were all substantial, most by an innings, and despite the late improvement Hampshire lost their status as a first-class county at the end of that season. This was decided by the Cricket Reporting Agency and it would be a decade before they regained their place in the top flight, when they were admitted to the County Championship.

At the Oval in May, Surrey dismissed Hampshire for 32 (Lohmann 7-13) and replied on the first day alone with 404-6. This is one of the largest leads ever secured on the first day of an inter-county match and the highest instance in English county cricket of a side leading by at least 10 times their opponent's score. Surrey won by an innings in two days and in the circumstances, Lacey's 5-70 was a real 'captain's effort'.

The batting was very weak. Powell played throughout and averaged 31.36 and Seymour averaged 20 in six matches but no other batsman managed that, with Lacey third at 19.77, while in all those matches not one century was scored. Cecil Currie and Dible were the leading bowlers. In the victory against Sussex, Powell scored 42 & 73 and in beating Somerset he scored 36 & 54*. If he failed, it seemed so did Hampshire. William Cropper of Derbyshire was the first man to take a hat-trick in a Hampshire match when he visited Southampton in June and Derbyshire won by an innings. Walter Humphreys repeated the feat for Sussex in early August, although Hampshire won. Humphreys was born in Southsea.

The *Guide* listed 123 local clubs with officials and addresses in Hampshire and the Isle of Wight, adding notable performances by club cricketers.

1886 *(Not first-class)*

Hampshire lost first-class status although they still played six matches against first-class sides; sadly, six defeats confirmed the decision and the *Guide* recorded "nothing in the season's cricket to call for any special comment". Norfolk were beaten twice and Hertfordshire once and the Club & Ground and Gentlemen of Hampshire also played a number of matches. There were improvements to the ground, with a wing added to the pavilion to be used by the professionals and a concrete practice wicket laid down.

One of the season's debutants was Alfred Isaac Russell (1867–1961), a batsman and wicket-keeper who was also captain of Southampton club Deanery. He played 15 *second class* matches for Hampshire, 1886–1893 and often opened the batting, but with a highest score of 27 v Norfolk in 1887 and again v MCC in 1888.

1887 *(Not first-class)*

AH Wood had one year as President. For the first time, Hampshire met Essex ("out and home") rather than Hertfordshire, otherwise the fixtures and results were very similar. Lacey scored 323 v Norfolk, not first-class, but the highest ever innings for Hampshire and highest ever in a Minor Counties match. At the end of the season, the *Guide* observed, "never … in recent years has the want of good reliable bowling been so apparent", just as at the start of the season, the previous edition (1887) suggested the need for "another bowler who could coach at headquarters". Nottinghamshire and England cricketer Alfred Shaw recommended Tom Soar as a groundsman for the County

Ground and Soar was also a right-arm fast bowler who was to contribute greatly to Hampshire's cause over the next few years (making his debut in 1888 v MCC). He was employed initially on a year's trial at £2-5s pw plus £1 per day for matches in the summer and £1-10s in the winter. Ordnance Survey won the first Hampshire club competition.

Lieutenant EG Wynyard was awarded the DSO for distinguished service against the enemy in the Burma Expedition. He retired from military service as Major in 1919 and was awarded the OBE (military division).

1888 *(Not first-class)*

F Ricardo was President while Russell Bencraft took over as Secretary with HK Grierson. *Wisden* introduced the Second Class (i.e. Minor Counties) Competition and Hampshire finished sixth of ten teams although they won just one match, against Norfolk. Eight other teams competed in the first-class competition and in the period from 1888–1894 Surrey were the outstanding side, followed by Lancashire and Yorkshire. Following thefts from the new pavilion, a cottage was built for £200 to enable the groundsman to sleep at the ground.

1889 *(Not first-class)*

The *Guide* suggested "some improvement on the previous year" and noted bad luck with weather in two fixtures that might have been won. In addition there was the view that "want of funds has greatly handicapped the club of late". Lacey headed the batting averages and the left-armer WC Roberts was leading bowler. Bencraft scored 195 v Warwickshire in an innings of 407, the first season that Hampshire played Warwickshire. The Gentlemen of Hampshire continued to play matches – for example against the Philadelphians when they lost a thrilling game by just three runs. A donkey and mower were purchased for the ground.

From this point, we identify each year the county champions among the first-class counties. We begin with the Championship in 1890 while acknowledging that various agencies identified 'Champions' prior to that date. During the 1880s, an embryonic County Cricket Council was formed although it failed to survive and in the 1890s the counties and MCC agreed that counties would then be divided into first class and 'minor' counties – from which emerged the two competitions we have today.

From 1963, we add the winners of the various limited-overs competitions. Where possible we have avoided identifying these by sponsors' names as there have been a variety of names and formats, although some sponsors are identified in the text. The exception is the B&H Cup, which from start to finish had one sponsor and that title differentiates it from the original knock-out cup, sponsored initially by Gillette.

1890 *(Not first-class)*

First-class County Champions: Surrey.

AF Jeffreys MP was the new President and Henry William (later Lord) Forster (Eton and Oxford) was appointed captain. He became President of MCC in 1919 and, from 1925, Governor General of Australia. Sussex were beaten twice in a season that brought some encouragement and four victories were recorded against Second-Class sides. Army officer Edward ('Teddy') G Wynyard returned from overseas to play regularly and Harry Baldwin had an excellent season, taking over 50 wickets cheaply. 1890 is often considered the first year of the 'real' County Championship, won by Surrey, contested by eight teams but not including Hampshire.

At Southampton, the donkey went missing and a reward of 10/- was offered. The *minimum* annual subscription was one guinea, a telephone was installed at the ground and Mrs Tolfree was appointed in charge of catering.

1891 *(Not first-class)*

Champions: Surrey.

Somerset were admitted to the County Championship. Hampshire played 11 matches, including home and away v Leicestershire – the first time they had played each other. They won three matches, v MCC, Leicestershire and Essex.

Hampshire's batting was very poor; they did not reach 100 until the sixth innings and the captain headed the averages with 20.6, while no one passed 75 in a single innings. The bowling was stronger, with Captain Charles G Barton taking 42 wickets at 9.33 and Baldwin passing 50 wickets again.

Winchester beat Southampton Park in the County Challenge Cup Final, played over two innings per side and two days. Some "spare" part of the county ground was sought for archery.

1892 *(Not first-class)*

Champions: Surrey.

RG Hargreaves was the new President and Dr Bencraft was now sole secretary. The *Guide* listed around 400 members. Subscriptions and other donations raised around £500 and gate money from major games came to £131.16s.6d while local clubs paid ground rent of £80 to play at 'headquarters'. County match expenses, wages and labour cost the club just over £600. At various times, Lacey, Forster and Bencraft captained the side. Hampshire-born soldier Victor Barton had played first-class cricket for Kent and, during the winter of 1891–1892, he played in a game later designated as a Test Match v South Africa in Cape Town. He then returned to his native county and made his debut for Hampshire in the early matches in 1892, subsequently playing over 100 first-class matches for the county.

After Club & Ground matches against local clubs, Sussex beat Hampshire by 205 runs in a side in which Hampshire fielded eight professionals plus Barton, Soar and Baldwin (Captain Barton played also). Hampshire beat Oxfordshire and Essex (by an innings) – Victor Barton top-scoring with 89 – but they lost the return at Leyton and the second match v Sussex. There were subsequent defeats to Derbyshire and Leicestershire and another victory over Oxfordshire. Victor Barton topped the batting averages with 741 runs at 39.0 while Soar (62) and Baldwin (44) shared over 100 wickets. Hampshire finished sixth in the table of the Minor Counties.

Winchester beat Deanery in the Challenge Cup Final by two wickets and as this was their third consecutive victory the Cup became their property.

1893 *(Not first-class)*

Champions: Yorkshire.

Hampshire enjoyed August, winning four home matches against Sussex, Devonshire, Warwickshire and Essex although they also lost twice in that month to Leicestershire and Derbyshire. Earlier in the season they lost away matches at Leicester, Leyton, Birmingham and Derby and there was a drawn match against Sussex in July. The Club & Ground side met MCC, Uppingham Rovers and XXI (21) County Colts.

Wynyard and Victor Barton scored centuries, with the former topping the averages at exactly 50 per innings and Soar was easily leading wicket taker with 49 at 13.40 each. AJL (Ledger) Hill joined Hampshire at the end of his third season at Cambridge University and was an effective all-rounder, finishing second in the batting averages and third in the bowling, while Elisha Light produced some useful bowling performances.

Off the field, Hampshire made significant strides in erecting a new stand and scoreboard and, at the autumn AGM, Treasurer HK Grierson proposed the purchase of the freehold of the ground from Sir Edward Hulse for £5,400 and an additional £600 for the buildings on the ground. A separate Hampshire County Ground Company was formed and shares with a 3.5% yield were soon taken up. The ground was secure, which brought comfort throughout the 20th century and enabled its sale and relocation at the start of the 21st.

1894 *(Not first-class)*

Champions: Surrey.

The Duke of Wellington was elected President. At the start of the 1894 season, Derbyshire were among a group of counties admitted to the increased group of First-Class counties – the others were Essex, Leicestershire and Warwickshire. Because the decision was taken as late as May 1894, the matches of these four were not included in the County Championship until 1895 but their players' averages counted as First-Class.

In the last Championship before its expansion, Surrey led Yorkshire followed by Middlesex, Kent, Lancashire, Somerset, Nottinghamshire, Sussex and, at the foot, Gloucestershire. Sadly, Hampshire were not (yet) included in the list of first-class counties but they played against some of them and, as above, competed well on occasions, particularly in the last month of the season.

Before that, Hampshire played a non first-class South African side and beat MCC but struggled in the home match against Derbyshire and lost at Leicester, Birmingham and Brighton. Their fortunes turned in August, as they won five of their six matches. The first was a victory over Essex, then one by five wickets at Derby. Wynyard was playing his first match of the season, Baldwin had match figures of 12-112, and Harold Ward from Winchester made a valuable contribution. Ward would die tragically, shortly after the first match of the 1897 season during which he had suffered sunstroke.

Ward scored well again with Victor Barton as Hampshire beat Warwickshire at Southampton by two wickets, and Wynyard made a century as Sussex were beaten with three minutes to spare. Rain spoiled the next match but Hampshire concluded the season with an innings victory over Essex, helped by the performance of amateur all-rounder David Steele. Hampshire had demonstrated their strength and petitioned for inclusion in the list of First-Class and Championship counties.

1895

Champions: Surrey.

Hampshire were admitted to the expanded County Championship with Derbyshire, Essex, Leicestershire and Warwickshire. There were now 14 First-Class/Championship counties, with Worcestershire, Northamptonshire, Glamorgan and Durham to be added subsequently to make up the current 18.

Hampshire followed-on in their first Championship match v Somerset at Taunton on 30, 31 May and 1 June 1895 but won (the first of three instances, also in 1922 and 2003). Bacon scored 15 & 92 in that match, his first-class debut for the county, and his second innings score remained the highest first-class debut score by a Hampshire player for 99 years, until passed by Paul Whitaker. Wicket-keeper Marmaduke W Deane who had played for Surrey 15 years earlier, replaced the injured Charles Robson in Hampshire's second match and on debut v Derbyshire dismissed five batsmen in the second innings (4 ct 1 st). In the same match, Baldwin (8-93) and Soar (11-113) bowled unchanged, the first instance (of six) for Hampshire.

Hampshire finished 10th (of 14) in this first Championship season, winning six of their 16 matches, including a surprising victory in Sheffield against a strong Yorkshire side. In a low-scoring match

Hill passed 40 twice and Baldwin, Soar and Edward Buckland dismissed Yorkshire cheaply. Another notable victory (by three wickets) came against Leicestershire in the first Championship match ever at Portsmouth. They played the same fixture there in the following year and won again. In the final game of the season, Surrey beat Hampshire by an innings to secure the title ahead of Lancashire and Yorkshire.

Baldwin was the first Hampshire bowler to exceed 100 wickets in a season and Soar took 7-71 on Championship debut for Hampshire v Somerset at Taunton although he had played previously for Hampshire. Captain Francis WD Quinton's 178 v Leicestershire at Leicester was the first Championship century for Hants and at the time their highest maiden century. He led the season's batting averages. Hampshire won that match by 342 runs – at the time their largest margin of victory in a county match.

Four hundred new members joined for this historic season – the total approaching 1,000. Soar was now playing regularly as a professional bowler and Messrs Hillier and Holmes were working as groundsmen. Edward Martin came from the Oval as Head Groundsman. Captain EG Wynyard was the new President and at the end of the season, Bencraft – also secretary – passed the captaincy to Wynyard.

1895–1896

During the winter, an England side toured South Africa and played three matches later designated as Test Matches. They lacked many senior players, so that the side that took the field in the First Test showed 11 changes from England's previous Test, 11 months earlier and included eight Test debutants plus Sammy Woods, who had previously played for Australia.

The first England side included AJL Hill and CB (Charles) Fry, then of Sussex. England won by 288 runs after dismissing South Africa for 30 in their second innings. Hill was the first Hampshire cricketer and the first Hampshire-born Hampshire cricketer to represent England. In the latter case, the next would be Shaun Udal, more than a century later.

Hill scored 25 & 37 and in the second Test 65, as England won by an innings. His teammate Christopher Heseltine made his debut in the second Test and took 5-38 in the second innings, while British serving officer RM (Robert) Poore (born Dublin), who was stationed in the country, was selected by South Africa, scoring 20 & 10. The future Hampshire cricketer Charles B ('Buck') Llewellyn made his Test debut for South Africa in the second Test. England won the third Test, again by an innings, with Hill scoring 124 and taking 4-8. However, he stayed in South Africa after the tour, missed the 1896 English season and never played in another Test. Of that Third Test side, only Lohmann and Hayward were selected by England for the next v Australia at Lord's in June

1896

Champions: Yorkshire.

Wynyard took over leadership of the side. He had a fine season and scored the first double century for Hampshire in a First-Class Championship match, 268 v Yorkshire at Southampton. During the season, he played in one Test v Australia and the county also played their first first-class match v

Australians. Frederick G Kitchener took 5-21 on debut v Sussex in a victory for Hampshire, but in fine weather the bowling was less effective, with Soar injured and Baldwin taking fewer wickets. Lionel Palairet's 291 for Somerset at Southampton was the highest innings against Hampshire until 1920.

Hampshire won only five of their 16 matches but moved up to eighth in the table – their victories against Essex and Sussex twice and Leicestershire. Perhaps their outstanding performance was against the Champions as Yorkshire finished the match on 235-8, just 27 ahead when time ran out. Francis WD Quinton hit five consecutive half-centuries (his younger brother James played a few matches for the county) and also held five catches in one innings in the match v Yorkshire at Harrogate – a Hampshire record that has been equalled on six more occasions, most recently by Paul Terry in 1989. Barton and Ward batted well on occasions and Edward Barrett from Cheltenham College showed promise in August, but he became yet another services cricketer who could not appear regularly. There were concerns around the country with bowlers' actions and at Hampshire (Sir) Evelyn Bradford was called for throwing.

During the winter football season of 1896-7 Southampton FC played at Northlands Road and won the Southern League for the first time. In the following season they won the league again and reached the Third Round of the FA Cup, playing at home with a crowd of 15,000. After this they moved to the Dell. They had previously played at the Antelope Ground after Hampshire CCC vacated it. The United Services Ground, Portsmouth was always, and still is, used for rugby union during winter months, hosting the United Services RFC and also Combined Services and inter-county matches.

1897

Champions: Lancashire.

Hampshire made a poor start to the season and did not win a Championship match until mid-July, despite the return of Hill from South Africa. Unfortunately, Wynyard's military duties kept him away for the early part of the season and Londoner Charles Robson, who had played for Middlesex, was the usual deputy. He also kept wicket and would eventually replace Wynyard as official captain.

Hampshire played their first First-class match at Bournemouth, v Gentlemen of Philadelphia, and Spens scored the first century for Hampshire on the ground. Ward scored 40 & 39 v Lancashire at Southampton but was taken ill and died within two weeks, while Henry Bethune played v Lancashire when 52 years, 5 months – the oldest first-class cricketer to play for Hampshire. Abel and Brockwell opened with a stand of 379 for Surrey at the Oval, then a first wicket record in all first-class cricket, and all eleven Hampshire players bowled in an attempt to break the partnership and conclude the innings. Eleven men bowled again in the match v Warwickshire at Southampton. Hampshire won three matches in August and four overall, but because the poor weather led to many drawn matches they finished ninth.

Lord Aberdare was Hampshire's new President. Entry to the (second) ladies pavilion was 1/- and £1,032 was spent on building the second tier.

1898

Champions: Yorkshire.

Hampshire began with a couple of rain-affected draws before meeting Yorkshire at Southampton in Baldwin's Benefit Match. The first day was rained off and on the second, Yorkshire beat Hampshire by an innings in the county's only Championship match ever completed in one day. Hampshire were dismissed for 42, Yorkshire replied with 157 (four wickets for the beneficiary) and then Hampshire were dismissed again for 36. The match aggregate of 235 runs remains the lowest in Hampshire's history and, in four innings v Yorkshire in 1898, Hampshire's totals were 42, 36, 45 & 83. Baldwin is reported to have received £237-10s.

At Derby, four home batsmen scored centuries in one innings of 645. Hampshire played 18 matches this season but won only two and finished 12th (of 14) teams. Wynyard was often absent again, playing in just three matches, while Lacey was appointed secretary of MCC (until 1926). Hampshire played their first ever Championship match at Dean Park in mid-July, beating Somerset by 9 runs despite trailing by 115 on first innings. Captain Hedley was a first innings centurion for the visitors apart from which only Major Poore passed 50 while Ted Tate from the New Forest bowled Hampshire to victory with 8-51.

On his county debut against the same county at Bath, Poore carried his bat with 49* of 97 all out; he had played first-class cricket previously abroad. Thomas Sutherland took 6-111 v Warwickshire on debut. Edward English was caught on the boundary for 98 from the final ball of the drawn match at the Oval – his highest first-class score. He died in 1966, in his 103rd year and is the oldest-ever Hampshire cricketer. Hill scored 199 in the same drawn fixture – he took 40 wickets in the season as well as scoring 662 runs.

A scoreboard was erected at the Hulse Road end of the ground (£10) and a new printing press purchased for £20. However, there were concerns about attendances at Southampton and an extra match was given to Portsmouth, which always attracted good crowds. A drama/music benefit concert was held in Southampton.

1899

Champions: Surrey.

Major Robert M Poore enjoyed his great season, indeed one of the greatest seasons that any Hampshire player has ever experienced. He was a serving officer and began the summer taking the highest honours as a swordsman at the Military Tournament and he also played in the team that won the Army's Regimental Polo Competition. Then in mid-June he travelled to Portsmouth and scored 104 & 119* v Somerset – the only man ever to score two first-class hundreds on that ground. He followed this with 111 & 40 v Lancashire, 11 v Essex, 175 & 39* v Surrey (back at Portsmouth) and, after missing the match at Brighton, came the extraordinary performance at Taunton. His first three centuries were in successive innings, the first instance for Hampshire.

Against Somerset, Poore scored Hampshire's first triple century (304) in Hampshire's highest innings in first-class cricket (672-7 declared) until 2005. Poore and Wynyard's 411 for the sixth wicket remains a record in county cricket. Hampshire were the first side to score over 600 in a day's play in first-class cricket, while Somerset's wicket-keeper did not concede a single bye in the innings. For Poore, there was another century at Worcester, 71 v the Australians, 79 & 53* at Derby and 157 at Leicester. That match was drawn and then his season finished on 12 August, after which he returned to the Army and was soon in South Africa for the start of the Boer War. In 12 completed innings for Hampshire he scored 1399 runs (at 116.58).

While Poore and Wynyard were part of a generally strong batting side, only Baldwin with 78 wickets at 27.89 was effective with the ball and Hampshire won just four of their 20 matches, finishing 11th. Warwickshire's 657-6 declared was the highest score against Hampshire until beaten 10 years later. Captain Bradford was twice called for throwing.

The *Guide* reported that Hampshire's new President, Mr LG Bonham-Carter, was "unquestionably one of the most popular sportsmen in the county". He had played for Hampshire from 1884–1888. South African CB Llewellyn, Hampshire's first 'overseas' cricketer, took 8-132 and scored 72 & 21 on debut for Hants v the Australians while qualifying to appear in the Championship, but there were complaints that the pavilion was filled with non-members for this match. Worcestershire were the 15th side admitted to the County Championship.

1900

Champions: Yorkshire.

In Hampshire's official history (1957, p. 52), HS Altham wrote

"The first six years of the (twentieth) century were … a depressing period for the county's cricket. Of the 109 fixtures … played in those seasons, sixty-six were lost and only twelve were won and in five of the six seasons we were bottom of the Championship Table. No wonder then that the gates suffered severely, so much so indeed that in the winter of 1904 the committee were seriously discussing closing the county ground at Southampton and poor Soar's benefit match in 1900 resulted in a loss of £6!" Altham pointed out that the principal cause of this poor run was instability – for example, in 1900 alone, 41 players appeared. In the next major history, Peter Wynne-Thomas (1988) added details:

"The Boer War affected Hampshire more than any other county in 1900. Captain Wynyard's military duties meant that he resigned as captain and handed the reigns over to Charles Robson … Beside Wynyard, Hampshire lost Poore, Heseltine and for most matches Quinton as well as two or three more who had been occasionally in the side, to the military authorities …" (p. 65).

In addition, Hampshire's regular bowlers were ageing. At the start of the 1900 season Baldwin was 40 and Soar was 34, while Hill was often absent on business. Robson, who took on the captaincy, was a somewhat reluctant wicket-keeper who had begun his career at Middlesex as an attacking batsman and occasional bowler.

Hampshire lost 16 of their 22 Championship matches and most of these defeats were by considerable margins. Four were by an innings, three by more than five wickets, seven by more than 150 runs and the other two by 143 and 111 runs – their narrowest defeat. Leicestershire, who were next to bottom, won three matches.

Two men, Wynyard and the Rev George B Raikes, averaged over 40 but played just five and six innings respectively. Of the regulars, Victor Barton passed 1,000 runs but at an average below 30, although he also took 38 wickets. Baldwin took 84 wickets but at 28.85 and no one else managed 40 in the season – Soar headed the averages at 23.12 but with just 24 wickets. Hampshire-born Edward Newton had appeared in the Hampshire side of the early 1890s but in this, his only first-class season, he played in 17 matches but never for Hampshire again and he died in Scotland in 1906 at the age of 34.

Hampshire also played against the West Indians at Southampton in late July *(Not first-class)*, the visitors winning by 90 runs. Llewellyn, still qualifying, scored 93 and took 12 wickets. His regular presence might have made a considerable difference to Hampshire but he was not yet eligible to play in the Championship.

1901

Champions: Yorkshire.

Sir George Meyrick was the new President. There was a (sadly temporary) revival in Hampshire's fortunes as Hampshire won six of their 18 matches and finished level with Kent in seventh place – their best ever to that point.

Wynyard recommended Captain JG (John) Greig, who had scored regularly in military cricket in India, and in his second match he scored 119 v South Africans. In the same innings Llewellyn scored 216 against his fellow countrymen (plus six wickets in the match) as Hampshire won by an innings. Llewellyn's was the highest maiden century for Hampshire until Hayden in 1997. In the match against Somerset at Taunton, Llewellyn was the third man to score a century and take ten wickets in the match for Hampshire. Greig had a brief, poor run until at Liverpool he scored 47* & 249* in a drawn match which Hampshire saved after a deficit of 307. Robson scored 52 batting at number 11 in the first innings of 113 – at the time, a Hampshire record.

Hampshire drew extensively on cricketers from the armed services – mainly amateurs – in this period, not least Admiral Sir AG Hotham, who made his one Championship appearance v Lancashire at Portsmouth, scoring 5 & 11 and bowling one over for six runs. In two matches, v South Africans at Southampton and Somerset at Taunton, three Hampshire batsmen scored centuries in the same innings. Of the regulars, Greig, EM Sprot and Arthur S Webb averaged over 35, while Wynyard and Barrett made occasional useful contributions. Llewellyn scored 717 runs (23.90) and took 115 wickets in his first full season, although there was little support – only Barton (48) passed 30 wickets and Baldwin managed just 11 at 48.27. He retired but returned briefly in 1904 to boost a weak bowling attack. In the match at Hove, the Sussex wicket-keeper, HR Butt, set a record against Hampshire of six dismissals in an innings. It has been equalled on 10 occasions, most recently by Phil Mustard of Durham in 2006.

The bowling club next door to the county ground complained about the danger from cricket balls hit into their space. At the season's end, Dr Bencraft informed the AGM that AC MacLaren was moving south for his wife's health and had accepted the post of Assistant Treasurer and player. In the event, he remained with Lancashire.

Major CG Barton, Major AJH Luard, Captain RM Poore and Captain HW Studd were all awarded the DSO for services in the Boer War.

1902

Champions: Yorkshire.

With the war continuing in South Africa, Hampshire suffered from the loss of a number of regular amateur cricketers required on service duty, including Greig, Barrett, Wynyard and Poore, although the latter played occasionally in August. Hampshire won two matches (of 16) but finished last, losing 10 matches – they had the wooden spoon every year from 1902–1905 inclusive.

The failings were easy to spot. With their leading batters absent, no player reached 700 runs and Llewellyn, who topped the averages, managed just 626 runs at 26.08. In addition to the absentees, neither Hill nor Sprot showed good form and there was just one century – by Llewellyn at Derby. He was also the leading bowler with 94 Championship wickets (17.67) and Hesketh Vernon Heseketh-Pritchard took 38 wickets at 20.78, apart from which only Soar with 25 wickets reached double figures. Victor Barton suffered an eye problem and missed a number of matches but was awarded a benefit. Llewellyn was in an England 'squad' for the Oval Test but was not selected – he would play eventually for his native South Africa.

Bournemouth's Dean Park pavilion was opened but both matches there were lost, although it was a near thing against Warwickshire. The visitors were dismissed for 99 but after a good start, Hampshire managed a lead of just 32. They were set 121 to win but only Alec Bowell, with 30, resisted the visiting bowlers. Bowell had come down from Oxford and was the first of a group of professionals who would transform the county's fortunes over the next decade and beyond, although he started modestly in this debut season.

1903

Champions: Middlesex.

At this time the President normally served for two years and WG Nicholson succeeded Sir George Meyrick. Sprot was appointed captain and Charles Philip ('Phil') Mead, who had had trials with Surrey, joined the staff but would not be qualified to play in the Championship until 1906. Hampshire opened the season by defeating Derbyshire at Southampton but this was a false dawn in a particularly miserable season as they failed to win another match, and in a thoroughly wet summer, three of Hampshire's away matches at the Oval, Leyton and Bath were abandoned without a ball bowled – probably the worst record in any English season. Abandoned matches with no play were not included in the Championship table and so many matches were drawn that it probably helped the Champions that they played just 16 while the nearest teams played far more – Sussex 23, Yorkshire and Lancashire 26. Hampshire played 15. With such variations, the table was decided on percentages – with this system in 1974, Hampshire would have been Champions!

CB Fry of Sussex, who would move to Hampshire, scored 2,413 runs at 80.43 – far in excess of any other batsman in this poor summer. At Hampshire, the leading scorer Sprot managed 835 runs at 36.30, apart from which only Llewellyn (542) passed 500. Wynyard, Barrett, Hill and Heseltine were rarely available and Poore and Greig not at all. More tragically, ill health forced the retirement of Victor Barton and he died in 1906, aged just 38.

Llewellyn's bowling was less effective and only Hesketh-Pritchard (45) and William T Langford (42) passed 40 wickets, although Soar, aged 37, took 36 at 18.44. In September the Bournemouth Week concluded with a match between the Gentlemen of the South and the Players of the South. Llewellyn and the young Southampton wicket-keeper, James Stone, played for the latter while WG Grace, in his only playing visit to the county, captained the Gentlemen, who included a number of Hampshire cricketers. Hampshire never played against Gloucestershire during Grace's career with them.

Lunch on match days cost 2/6d. The Committee had the old black horse destroyed as it was no longer fit and a new horse was purchased in the following year. The committee allowed Southampton Hockey Club to use the ground for 15/- per match. Members were only permitted to use the telephone at the ground on match days.

1904

Champions: Lancashire.

Hampshire won two matches, both in August, but lost 12 and finished bottom of the table again. In one of their better performances Arthur Webb enjoyed a successful benefit match v Surrey at Southampton. The visitors scored 346 and Hampshire's 297-5 was built around Webb's 162*, although sadly rain prevented a conclusion. Webb's benefit realised £150 – a sign of dwindling support for a poor team. Poore returned but could not replicate his form of five years earlier, although Hill and another army officer, Alexander C Johnston, played 14 innings each with reasonable results and the captain Sprot scored 916 Championship runs at 36.64, so the batting was just satisfactory. Johnston, who was only 20, scored his first century v Worcestershire at Southampton.

Llewellyn took 40 wickets but at 37.15 each and he averaged less than 15 with the bat. Hesketh-Pritchard led the attack with 62 wickets and topped the averages at nearly 25 each. Baldwin returned, taking 33 wickets.

Hampshire played their only first-class match at Alton, v South Africans. The tourists scored 380 (Tancred 99) and won by an innings & 19 runs, although Bowell showed promise, scoring 65. In the match at Southampton, Kent collapsed from 139-4 to 142 all out. Hampshire were 4-5 at Headingley and all out for 36; they lost nine consecutive matches, a run that was equalled in 1946. Their victory at Derby by nine wickets in early August was their first in 27 matches; the previous win in June 1903 was against the same side.

That victory interrupted a run of very high scores against Hampshire – beginning with Yorkshire's 549 in July, the bowlers then conceded innings in successive matches of 410-8 declared, 510, 521, 346, then came the Derby victory followed by 508-9 declared, 517-9 declared & 552-7 declared before dismissing Kent for 115 at Tonbridge – but even there they still lost by 8 wickets as Colin Blythe took 9-30, which was the best of the English season. He took 28 wickets in four Hampshire innings.

Cecil H Palmer played for Worcestershire v Oxford University and then played three times for Hampshire. FJ Hopkins came from Birmingham to replace Mr Martin as Head Groundsman. Nine hundred and thrity-seven members paid £1087 in subscriptions – just £50 more than the annual cost of wages, labour and salaries. The best gates were the matches at Portsmouth against

Sussex (£142) and Yorkshire (£140), although the county's share of the Gents v Players match at Bournemouth was £185-12s-3d. The county also received almost £50 from staging a football match between Southampton and Portsmouth.

1905

Champions: Yorkshire.

CAR Hoare of Hamble was the new President, succeeding WG Nicholson, while FH Bacon was appointed Secretary – Dr Bencraft having performed the duties for 17 years. Hampshire, like Somerset, won just one match and drew seven but they played and lost two more than the Westcountry side and their 12 defeats consigned them to last place again. Hampshire played the first county match at Aldershot v Surrey, who returned in 1906. Mead had come from the Oval and he made his first-class debut v Australians in 1905 – he had to wait another 12 months to qualify for the Championship. Although he became Hampshire's greatest run-scorer, in his early years he was an effective slow-left-armer and in that first match he took 2-56 while the Australians amassed 620, with Victor Trumper scoring 92 and Hill, Noble and Gregory passing the century. In reply Hampshire were dismissed for 239 with Greig 66 and Mead, at number eight, 41*. He opened as Hampshire followed-on and was run out without facing as Hampshire lost by an innings.

Despite having to wait another year for Mead, the batting improved but the bowling remained weak – Baldwin was the leading wicket taker with 63 wickets at the age of 44. Greig scored centuries in both innings at Worcester while Sprot contributed 141 in a second wicket partnership of 221 – at the time, Hampshire's record for that wicket. Worcestershire beat Hampshire at Bournemouth in the final over having scored 280 in 145 minutes. Bowell confirmed his promise with 101 & 51 in the victory against Derbyshire at Southampton; Hesketh-Pritchard took 8-32.

Wicket-keeper Stone was another useful professional and he scored 174 out of 293 v Sussex at Portsmouth but the match was lost, while Llewellyn scored two centuries, at Derby in a drawn game. Guy Bignell's 109 v Kent at Portsmouth came on 15 August, almost four months before his 19th birthday. He was at that time and until Liam Dawson in 2008, the youngest man to score a first-class century for the county – the next youngest are Phil Mead, James Vince, Robin Smith, Dick Moore and Gordon Greenidge. The amateur Bignell, whose brother played briefly a few years earlier, also scored 244* for Alton v Trojans but failed to improve on his Championship century, despite playing 55 matches for Hampshire until 1925.

Northamptonshire become the 16th side admitted to the County Championship and won one, drew one v Hampshire in their first meetings. Llewellyn scored 50 for an England XI v the Australians in a thrilling finish at Bournemouth on 2 September. The Australians, requiring 159 to win, reached 153-6, lost three wickets for five runs but won by the single wicket. In his next match, Llewellyn scored a century for the Players in an innings victory over the Gentlemen. Membership stood at 974. A National Archery Meeting and then a Rose Show were held at the County Ground and gas was piped to the groundsman's cottage, while the club took over responsibility for catering at the ground. Wynyard played two Tests in South Africa in the winter.

1906

Champions: Kent.

After the years of heavy defeats, Hampshire won seven of their 20 matches and finished eighth (of 16 counties). Mead made his Championship debut and played in every Hampshire match in his first five seasons. Against Worcestershire at Portsmouth, he passed 1,000 runs for the season at 19 years and 160 days – the youngest man ever to achieve that for the county. Fast bowler John Badcock from Christchurch made his debut and took 92 Championship wickets at 24.71. While Badcock would enjoy brief success at Hampshire, a young all-rounder of greater importance, JA ('Jack') Newman from Southsea, made his debut.

Hampshire began the season losing to Surrey and Yorkshire (despite Mead's maiden century) and then the Army at Aldershot. Their opponents included a number of Hampshire players and Johnston scored 173 – he would later bat usefully for the county, as would Poore in his last season with Hampshire.

In the following match on the same ground, Surrey won by 10 wickets and Hampshire stayed in the north of the county, playing their first match at Basingstoke v Warwickshire – and another defeat. This poor start was reminiscent of the past few years, but then they beat Derbyshire (Hill 110) and the season turned. By August they enjoyed an unprecedented four wins and a draw in five matches. Hampshire's fielders were involved in all 18 Northamptonshire wickets at Southampton, 15 caught, two run out and one stumped. Kent clinched the title at Bournemouth when they put out Hampshire for 163 and replied with 610. Even then the home side fought hard, scoring 410 in their second innings (Llewellyn 158).

The Hon Secretary met the Chief Constable of Southampton to enable cabs to park outside the ground at the close of play. Members were permitted to introduce friends into the pavilion at a charge of 2/6d. Wynyard captained the first MCC tour of New Zealand but returned home early with an injury.

1907

Champions: Nottinghamshire.

Hampshire won six matches but slipped to 12th (of 16), nonetheless, the side was becoming more settled around the core of professionals – partly of necessity, since their service amateurs were still often unavailable. In his first full season, Newman took 46 Championship wickets at 27.15, figures almost identical to Badcock's, while the amateur Henry W Persse, who had not played in 1906, led the way with 60 at 23.20. Newman's future partner, Alexander ('Alec') Kennedy, who had arrived in Southampton from Scotland as a young boy, made his debut in Leicester in mid-July when he was just 16 years and 168 days old and despite an innings defeat he took four wickets and in his second match added three more to finish the season with a remarkable average of just 11.85. He had begun as a groundstaff boy in 1905 at just 15/- per week and is Hampshire's youngest Championship debutant. By 1907 he and Newman had advanced to £1 per week for playing and helping the groundsman. A young wicket-keeper from Oxford, George Brown, arrived to join them. The captain Sprot, Mead and Bowell all passed 1,000 runs and Stone had 940, while Hill averaged 44.06 in his nine matches (of 24) and represented the Gentlemen at Lord's.

Hampshire met Middlesex and Gloucestershire in the Championship for the first time. Against Middlesex, Bowell opened and scored 69 & 108* while GL Jessop reached 53* in just 15 minutes for Gloucestershire at Cheltenham and was dismissed for 92, Gloucestershire winning a low-scoring match by 83 runs. James Seymour scored 204 in 190 minutes for Kent in a total of 596 at Tonbridge; in the previous season Kent had scored 610 at Bournemouth.

After the season, Hesketh-Pritchard and Wynyard toured the USA and Canada with MCC. In addition to improved membership figures, the gate receipts passed £2,000 for the first time. The Accounts to 31 October 1906 published in The *Guide*, declared that 967 members had paid £1,119-15s-6d. One year later (October 1907) the number of members exceeded one thousand for the first time: 1045 paying £1,234-5s-9d. The *Guide* published the names and addresses of all members in alphabetical order. In later years these were organised by local areas.

1908

Champions: Yorkshire.

The President, CAR Hoare, died during the winter. In the official history (1957), HS Altham praised his full support of the club, in time and money, describing him as "the kindest of men". In 1909, he was succeeded by Sir GA Cooper.

Hampshire won seven of 22 matches and went up to ninth in the table. George Brown, the last of the four great professionals that would sustain Hampshire for years, made his debut. In the match against Northamptonshire at Southampton, Sprot's declaration created a real 'talking point'. On the third morning Hampshire were 25-1 in reply to the visitors' 203 but the declaration came at lunch still 24 behind, after which Mead (7-18) and Wyatt dismissed Northamptonshire in 90 minutes and Sprot's rapid 62* led his side to victory. This was the first occasion on which a county side declared while behind.

At Canterbury, Hampshire's last pair, Newman and Stone, needed 51 in 70 minutes to win and they got there with five minutes to spare. Generally, however, it was Newman's bowling that impressed as he took 77 wickets at 22.53, while Badcock had 67 at 26.17. He took 212 wickets for Hampshire in three seasons but was not always fit; he took over a London cinema and never played again. He took 8-44 in the second Sussex innings at Portsmouth, Newman took 8-123 in a Middlesex innings of 502 and Francis Wyatt, who played just 11 matches between 1905–1919, had match figures of 9-91 v Somerset.

In his Benefit Year, Llewellyn scored 966 runs, took 75 wickets and received £500. Hill topped the batting averages in 16 innings while Mead and Bowell passed 1,000. There was no play on the first day at Chichester and while the pitch was fit for play on the second morning, the Sussex team was not complete until mid-afternoon, by which time the rain had returned. At the County Ground, bands played on the first two days of matches in Southampton Cricket Week. The 1909 *Guide* reported that the club was operating under "a big financial cloud" although "the portents [were] on the whole reassuring".

A Hambledon team played 'An England Team' in a three-day match on Broadhalfpenny Down on 10, 11, 12 September. The match was first-class and held to commemorate the achievements of the 18th century Hambledon/Hampshire Club. CB Fry played for Hambledon and, having moved to Hampshire to work on the Training Ship *Mercury*, joined the county from Sussex for the 1909 season. A commemorative stone was unveiled – and still stands – although WG Grace, who was due to perform the ceremony, failed to appear. It is interesting, given the tendency these days to call that early team Hampshire, that the 1908 side called Hambledon consisted mainly of past and present Hampshire players: England: 124 (Newman 8-54) & 309 (Leach 80, Newman 5-66) lost to Hambledon: 277 (Jephson 114*, Killick 4-44) & 158-6 (Fry 84*) by four wickets.

1909

Champions: Kent.

Hampshire finished eighth, with seven victories. CB Fry opened in the first match at the Oval, scoring 42 & 60. He finished the season third in the national batting averages, although he could not play in every match. Unfortunately, his debut innings followed the Surrey total of 742, which remains a record against Hampshire and they won by an innings. Hobbs and Hayes both scored double centuries and their partnership of 371 also remains a record for the second wicket against Hampshire. Hampshire recovered by winning the next match against Somerset (Bowell 149, Brown 11-110) but when Surrey came to Bournemouth in June, Hobbs scored 162 in his one innings.

In early August Sussex won by 105 runs despite Llewellyn's two centuries (130 & 101*). No other Hampshire batsman passed 40 and Kennedy took nine wickets in the match.

In the match against the Australians at Southampton, two visiting batsmen were run out while Newman took 8-43 including the hat-trick – the county's first. The Australians were all out for 83 but recovered to win the match. GL Jessop scored 161 in 95 minutes and 129 in 98 minutes for Gloucestershire in the match at Bristol.

At the end of the season, *Wisden* wrote in praise of Mead and he and Llewellyn passed 1000 runs, while Captain William N White impressed again when available. Newman took 80 wickets at 22.00, Kennedy, still a teenager, had 31 at 21.96 and Harold C McDonell 43 at a fraction over 20, although he was another amateur not always available.

Members were permitted to bring cars into the ground and non-members could do so at a charge of 1/-. At the end-of-season AGM, the Treasurer reported a significant improvement in the club's finances with the debt nearly cleared. One thousand, two hundred and sixty-two members paid almost £1500 in subscriptions while the gate receipts for the final match against the Champions at Bournemouth reached £434.14s.5d – more than double all other Championship games.

1910

Champions: Kent.

Hampshire's improvement continued and they finished sixth – their highest-ever position. Llewellyn took 133 wickets, was the first Hampshire player to perform the season's 'double' and was selected as one of *Wisden's* Cricketers of the Year, but then left the county to play for South Africa in Australia during the winter and, the following summer, for Accrington in the Lancashire League. Newman was fifth highest wicket taker in the country and in nine consecutive innings during the season Newman (46) and Llewellyn (39) took all but five of 90 wickets to fall. Of the others, Mead took one and four were run out. Kennedy, improving constantly, earned a regular place.

Unfortunately, Fry played in only two matches and Bowell had a disappointing season, but Mead, Llewellyn and Johnston passed 1,000 runs each. In August, Lancashire won by scoring 404-5, a record fourth innings score to beat Hampshire. Jack Sharp led the way with a century – during the previous season he played in three Test Matches v Australia and in the final one scored a century and took three wickets, yet never played for England again.

Hampshire played their final Championship match at Aldershot v Somerset. A brick wall replaced the Northlands Road fence and new practice nets were installed. Membership stood at 1,235 and funds were improved when an Automobile Gymkhana was held on the County Ground. Brown and Johnston were selected for the MCC tour of the West Indies, although Johnston, an amateur, withdrew. Dr Bencraft took on yet another role with the club when he was elected President at the season's end, succeeding Sir GA Cooper.

1911

Champions: Warwickshire.

Fry ended the season in first place in the national averages (1299 runs at 76.41) and Mead was second with 1706 at 58.82, despite which Hampshire won just seven matches and slipped to 11th – albeit substantially ahead of the five sides below them. The simple explanation was that Llewellyn had left and Newman's wicket tally fell from 156 at 18.45 to 67 at 33.37 so, while Hampshire's batsmen made 19 centuries, they conceded many runs in the field. Brown, Kennedy and Dudley M Evans, brother of Alfred, took some wickets but not in sufficient numbers. In addition, Hampshire was inconsistent, for example beating Somerset with a score of 418, then losing to them at Bath when dismissed for 44, chasing 146 to win. In that match, Somerset's AE Lewis was the first man to record the match 'double' of 100 runs and 10 wickets against the county. Kent challenged them to score 568 to win at Southampton and Hampshire's 463-8 remains the highest fourth innings total.

At Lord's in May, MCC won a thrilling match by one wicket despite Forster's match figures of 9-92. Col-Sgt Harold T Forster was another of Hampshire's Army cricketers. He played four more times in that season but took only one more wicket. Mead and Fry both managed two hundreds in one match and the latter also scored 258* v Gloucestershire at Southampton, a third consecutive century. GL Jessop again replied with two fast centuries in the same match – 153 in 110 minutes and 123 in 100 minutes.

Against the same county at Bristol, Sprot's century in 45 minutes was the fastest ever for Hampshire and he and Albert E Fielder added 147 in 40 minutes for the tenth wicket. Comparable records do not exist for all fast innings in terms of time and/or balls faced. Bowell scored five consecutive half-centuries in June, while Mead scored a century before lunch v Sussex at Portsmouth and with Bowell he shared a first wicket stand of 163. Bowell's share was 40 and Mead finished with 194 of a total of 346 in 79 overs. Johnston and Mead added 292 for the third wicket against the Champions at Southampton – at the time a record for that wicket for Hampshire. In a drawn match against Kent at Southampton, Hampshire's 463-8 was their highest fourth innings total and the match aggregate of 1,446 the highest in a Hampshire match at that time – and in the Championship until 1995. ER (Ernest) Remnant scored 115* in that innings, his only first-class century in 121 matches for the county.

Yorkshire scored 355 at Huddersfield and Hampshire used all eleven players as bowlers. Mead's 120 was not enough to save Hampshire but in the return at Portsmouth, Hampshire won a low-scoring match by six wickets (Brown 6-48).

At the end of the season, Mead hit 223 for the Players v Gentlemen at Scarborough and 101 for the Rest v the Champions at the Oval and became the first Hampshire batsman to pass 2,000 runs in a season in all matches. In the winter, he toured Australia, playing in four Tests; Fry was invited to captain the side but declined.

Membership grew to 1,391 and a subscription list was opened to purchase a new scoreboard for £105. The *Guide* launched an appeal to support the Nursery, which had been running for three years and was reserved for "cricketers already qualified to play for Hampshire".

1912

Champions: Yorkshire.

1912 was one of the wettest of all English cricket seasons and Hampshire suffered from six 'No Result' matches, more than any other county, despite which they finished sixth as they had in 1910. Fry was top of the first-class national batting averages again although he played in only seven Championship matches as he captained England through the summer. Johnston was second and Mead third, so Hampshire's batting was very strong. In addition, Kennedy and Newman formed an effective partnership for the first time – Kennedy with 112 Championship wickets at 17.20 and Newman 86 at 22.65. In all first-class cricket Newman ended with 99 wickets. Hesketh-Pritchard hardly played but took 5-116 & 6-18 as Hampshire won at Worcester. With more bowling support Hampshire may have finished higher than sixth.

In the Championship, Johnston headed the national batting averages (55.23). He hit centuries in both innings and with Mead shared a record second wicket partnership of 250 v Warwickshire at Coventry. At the turn of the century, Johnston was a Winchester College boy and his father had played briefly for Derbyshire. His Army commitments meant that he played intermittently – 108 matches over 14 seasons – but he was often very effective, especially in 1912, when he also impressed with a top score of 89 for the Gentlemen v Players. A bad leg injury during the First World War brought his career to an end after one match in 1919.

At Southampton, Hampshire scored 599 and Kent replied with 418, as everyone except the two wicket-keepers bowled. Fry and Barrett added 246, another county record, for the fourth wicket v Yorkshire at Southampton. This match was Stone's benefit but, despite Hampshire's first innings of 441, they lost by 9 wickets – nonetheless, he received £500. Hampshire scored 453-2 declared v Oxford University. HS Altham batted in the middle order for the University. At Bournemouth in late August only Surrey's Hayward passed 20 (Kennedy 7-29).

The membership went beyond 1500 for the first time. A new dressing room was built for the professionals (£69.10s) and for the first time they received talent money for fielding (often excellent) as well as batting and bowling. At the season's end AGM, Dr Bencraft handed the Presidency to Mr JC Moberley – he would be the last pre-war President. During the winter pace bowler Arthur Jacques was selected for the MCC tour of West Indies although he had yet to play first-class cricket in England. He made his Hampshire debut the following year.

In the English season, the Australians, South Africans and England competed in a triangular tournament and in July, Hampshire beat the Australians for the first time. No county would repeat the feat until Surrey in 1956, while Hampshire managed it again in 2001. In 1912: Hampshire 371 (Mead 160*) & 86-2 (Mead 33*) beat the Australians 197 (Bardsley 60, Kennedy 6-90) & 256 (Gregory 85, Kennedy 5-91) by 8 wickets. In the last match of the season, Hampshire drew with the South Africans with Mead scoring 64* & 77* – an aggregate against the two touring sides of 334 without being dismissed.

Arthur Egerton Knight would play four county cricket matches for Hampshire, in 1913 against Oxford University and then in 1920, 1922 and 1923 he played in one Championship match in each season – the last two as captain. He also captained the Club & Ground and 2nd XI on a number of occasions. He was born in Godalming and moved to Portsmouth where, in 1908, he signed for Portsmouth FC, playing from 1909–1922 as an amateur at full-back. In the Olympic Games of 1912, he represented Great Britain at Association Football, and won a Gold Medal. He represented them again in 1920, when they were less successful. He was subsequently on the Hampshire Committee and a Vice President. He died in 1956 and is buried in Portsmouth.

1913

Champions: Kent.

The weather improved and a number of players produced fine individual performances throughout the season, yet Hampshire slipped to tenth with seven victories. A large part of that decline was because neither Fry nor Barrett played a match while Johnston appeared in only six. Nonetheless, Mead was the first Hampshire player to score 2,000 runs *for the county* in a season (2,146). He had passed the target overall in 1911 but had played nine matches for MCC, Test Trial, Players v Gentlemen and the Rest v Champion County. Cecil H Abercrombie scored 126 on debut for Hampshire v Oxford University, although this was not his first-class debut as he had played previously for the Royal Navy. The aggregate of 1477 runs in that match was a county record that stood for 80 years. Abercrombie and Brown put on 325 in three hours v Essex at Leyton, a Hampshire record for the seventh wicket. They scored centuries, as did Tennyson in a score of 534-7 declared. Abercrombie was a naval officer who scored three centuries in 1913 but never played for Hampshire again and was killed in action at Jutland in 1916, age 30.

In the Championship, Newman took 105 wickets (23.14) and Kennedy 80 (22.70) and they had good support from Brown (83 at 26.38) and Jacques (47 at 28.12). In Hampshire's match v Somerset at Taunton they were dismissed for 123; Somerset took a lead of 26 then Hampshire posted 452 – with no century. They dismissed Somerset, who batted two short, for 77, Newman taking 6-30 and the margin of 349 runs remains their record victory.

Hon Lionel H Tennyson scored a century on first-class debut, for MCC v Oxford University. He followed scores in that first match of 20 & 110 with innings for Hampshire of 28, 38, 116, 111, 4, 96 & 19 and was one of *Wisden's* Cricketers of the Year (1914). HTW Hardinge scored three centuries for Kent v Hampshire in the matches at Portsmouth and Dover. Hampshire played Nottinghamshire for the first time since 1843 but slumped to 28-5 on the first morning of the match against them, with all five wickets to catches by GM Lee. In late August, Hampshire led Yorkshire at Bournemouth by 66 runs (Brown 122) and, declaring for a second time, had Yorkshire in trouble at 92-6 until Rhodes (66*) and Rockley Wilson (30*) rescued them – Wilson was a Winchester schoolmaster.

A dinner at the South Western Hotel, Southampton, celebrated the Jubilee of the County Cricket Club and for the guests Lord Harris made a speech and proposed the main toast to the club. The President, JC Moberly, responded. Membership fell slightly and there was an overall loss of just over £200. The best gates receipts were during the late August Bournemouth week. In the winter, Mead and Tennyson played five Tests in South Africa and Mead scored two Test centuries, averaging 54.00.

1914

Champions: Surrey.

Hampshire's matches against Warwickshire and Lancashire were scheduled for Portsmouth but switched because the naval ground was required for war preparations. Hampshire won 13 of their 28 matches, finishing in their highest ever position of fifth.

In mid-June, Hampshire dismissed Somerset for 83 & 38 at Bath and Jacques (6-33 & 8-21) and Kennedy (4-49 & 2-15) bowled unchanged in the match. A month later they dismissed Gloucestershire for 34 at Bristol (Newman 6-14) – the latter two were successively the lowest scores against Hampshire (until 1952). On 31 August, Hampshire's deputy captain Jacques took 6-55 as Kent were dismissed for 249, with Hubble 99*. Mead (128) and Brown (93) led Hampshire to a lead of 228 and on the third day Hampshire dismissed Kent in the 52nd over to win by an innings. Sadly, it meant very little; all the remaining fixtures in England were cancelled as war had been declared before the end of the season and Jacques, with match figures of 9-86, was one of many cricketers who marched off to war never to return.

Jacques, bowling an early version of leg theory, took 112 wickets in what would be his final season – he was killed in action in France a year later. War was declared on 4 August and two days later Hampshire began their match at Trent Bridge. Because of war duties, Hampshire played without Major Greig, Capt Johnston and Major Hon LH Tennyson. After six overs rain stopped play, Basil Melle, who had opened the bowling, was called up by his Army Regiment and Stone was allowed to take his place and batted. Stone was playing in his final season and wicket-keeper Walter Livsey dismissed nine batsmen (4 ct, 5 st) v Warwickshire at Southampton. Mead scored 2,235 runs and held 41 catches, the highest in the country. Kennedy also took over 100 wickets and had good support from Newman (who passed 1,000 runs) and Brown, leading to Hampshire's record 13 victories. Once again, Fry and Johnston appeared rarely, as did Tennyson, while Naval Officer Abercrombie was already on service overseas and he too would not return.

Bowell was awarded a benefit and received £425. Sadly, this period of Hampshire cricket came to a temporary halt with a loss of £700.

1864: the English XI at Southampton in June. Daniel Day stands far right

1888: (back) Dible, Young, Armstrong, (centre) Forster, Wynyard, Lacey, Powell, Watson, (front) Roberts, Baldwin

1893: v Warwickshire at Southampton, (back) Light, Baldwin, V Barton, Soar, (centre) Wynyard, Bencraft, Hill, (front) Watson, Wood, Steele, Robson

1895: v Somerset at Taunton, the first Championship match, (back) Baldwin, Capt CG Barton, G Lewis (scorer), Heseltine, Soar, (centre) Robson, Wynyard, Bencraft, Hill, Ward, (front) Bacon, V Barton

1899: (back) umpire, Webb, Gravett, Soar, Baldwin, V Barton, (centre) Robson, Poore, Wynyard, Quinton, (front) English, Bencraft, Heseltine

1901: (back) Chignell, Soar, Bencraft, CG Ward, GW Lewis, T Chamberlayne MP, Webb, (centre) Steele, Sprot, Robson, Greig, Lee, (front) Llewellyn, V Barton

1904: (back) Soar, Llewellyn, Webb, Bacon, Bowell, Stone, (front) Chignell, Hill, Sprot, Hesketh-Pritchard, S Brutton

1907: v Sussex at Chichester, (back) A White (umpire), Langford, Bowell, Badcock, Llewellyn, Stone, S Browne (umpire), (centre) Bacon, Hill, Sprot, Captain CAR Hoare, Persse, (front) Mead, Newman

1910: in Ireland, (back) Kennedy, Newman, Brown, Bowell, Llewellyn, Mead, (front) Remnant, Persse, Bacon, Haig-Smith, Stone

1912: v Australians at Southampton, (back) Remnant (12th man), Stone, Newman, Brown, Mead, Bowell, Kennedy, (front) Bignell, Fry, Sprot, Barrett, Jephson

1915–1918

There was no County Championship for four seasons, although the Lancashire League continued with some competitive matches. However, *Cricket Archive* lists quite a number of matches played during the four war seasons – mostly public schools or representative games and some featuring future Hampshire players. CB Llewellyn appeared in the Bradford League.

The most notable games in the county were those involving Winchester College. For example, in 1915 they played Eton, who included future Hampshire captain William GLF Lowndes. There are more matches listed in 1916 and Charles P Brutton, whose father, Septimus, had played once for Hampshire, played for Winchester. Although not a regular player, Brutton would captain Hampshire occasionally. Lowndes appeared again with Eton, while Winchester's other opponents included Bradfield, Charterhouse, Wellington College, Marlborough College and Harrow. On 7 & 8 August 1916, Lowndes played at Lord's for their Schools XI v the Rest.

In 1917, Marlborough included Anthony EL Hill, son of AJL, in their side against Winchester, for whom Brutton was joined by Douglas Jardine. The younger Hill would appear for Hampshire and in one non first-class match with his father. Eton fielded William R Shirley, who would make his county debut in the famous match at Edgbaston in 1922. He followed Lowndes in playing for Lord's Schools v the Rest. In 1918, RC Robertson-Glasgow, future cricket writer and Somerset cricketer, represented Charterhouse v Winchester and, with peace in sight, England met the Dominions at Lord's on 13 July and their side included Fry, Tennyson, who was home from the Front, and Melle.

In August 1918, AEL Hill represented Lord's Schools and then the Public Schools XI (v PF Warner's XI) while Shirley captained the Public Schools against the Artistics. As the summer came to an end Tennyson played at Lord's alongside Hobbs, Woolley, Warner and others for the latter's XI v FS Jackson's XI.

Meanwhile, at the County Ground

1914: By December, 24 Hampshire county cricketers had joined the Armed Forces; most of the current professionals joined the 5th Hampshire Battalion. Private Philip Mead did not take part in hostilities because of his varicose veins.

1915: At the Advisory County Cricket Committee at Lord's in January, Dr Bencraft on behalf of Hampshire proposed that if the hostilities ceased that year "as much cricket should be played as possible". The Royal Garrison Artillery Signalling School was permitted to use the County Ground.

1916: GH Muir began the first of two periods as Secretary. The AGM discussed winter pay for the professionals but Dr Bencraft spoke against it. Army Contractors used the County Ground pavilion as a canteen.

1917: £215 was raised through lettings at the County Ground. The groundsman's wages were increased to £2–5s pw and he was given an extra sum of £10 in recognition of his work "during these difficult times".

1918: EM Sprot indicated that he did not wish to continue as captain when first-class cricket resumed. The summer was fine until the wettest September for over twenty years. Despite the late rain, Major Tennyson led his XI to victory v Captain Poyntz's side at Dean Park: Tennyson's XI 260 (Hardinge 72, Hobbs 55) & 52-5 beat Poyntz's XI:121 & 167 (Mead 45).

Hampshire's Roll of Honour

1914:
Sir ER Bradford (HCCC, 1895–1905) killed in action in France.
Capt AM Byng (1905) killed in action in France.
Rifleman JT Gregory (1913) killed in action in Belgium.
Capt GPR Toynbee (1912) killed in action in France.

1915:
Asst Paymaster FH Bacon RNR (1894–1911, HCCC Secretary 1903–1915) on mined ship.
Capt G Belcher (1905) killed in action, Belgium.
Major BML Brodhurst (1897) killed in action in Belgium.
Capt A Jaques (1913–1914) killed in action in France.
Lieut-Col CH Palmer (1899–1904) killed in action near Gallipoli.
Capt GAC Sandeman (1913) killed in action in Belgium.
Col Sgt JF Sutcliffe (1911) died at Gallipoli.
Lieut-Col MDF Wood (1907) died near Gallipoli.
2nd Lieut KHC Woodroffe (1912–1913), killed in action in France. Woodroffe, only 22, was the youngest Hampshire casualty in the War.

1916:
Lieut CH Abercrombie (1913) killed in naval action at Jutland.
2nd Lieut ACP Arnold (1912–1914), killed in action in France.
Capt AG Cowie (1910) died of wounds in Mesopotamia.
Private CH Yaldren (1912) died in France.

1917:
Capt CH Bodington (1901–1902), killed in action in France.
Major RWF Jesson (1907–1910) died in action at Mesopotamia.

1918:
Major HT Forster (1911) killed in action in France.
Capt JH Gunner (1906–1907) died of wounds in Belgium.
Major HW Persse (1905–1909) died of wounds in France.

HJ Rogers (1912–1914) died during the war but neither the date nor place has been identified.

1919

Champions: Yorkshire.

First-Class cricket resumed in England on 12 May when Oxford University met the Gentlemen of England in the Parks. Two days later, LG Robinson's XI played the Australian Imperial Forces and Kennedy played his first match of the season for the former. There were almost 30 First-Class matches played before he joined his county teammates in Hampshire's first match v Middlesex at Lord's on 9 June. Hampshire's first home match since 1914 came on 20 June v Australian Imperial Forces.

Worcestershire played first-class matches but did not compete in the Championship in 1919, which therefore had only 15 counties. Championship matches were played over two days with extended hours but many games ended in draws. In 1914, 30% of county matches were drawn but in 1919 there were 56 draws in 124 matches (about 45%). In the inter-war period as a whole (1919–1939), the figure was 37.5%.

Hampshire finished seventh with five wins in 16 matches (seven draws). As in the 1940s, the crowds flocked to matches to forget the miseries of the past few years – despite entrance doubling from 6d to 1/-. Tennyson was appointed captain in succession to Sprot but both wicket-keepers Stone and Livsey plus Remnant and Newman were still in the services and unavailable. Brown could deputise as a wicket-keeper, although the amateur Sydney Maartensz contributed usefully during this season.

McDonnell and USA-born Francis Ryan bowled leg-breaks and slow left-arm, respectively but Kennedy lacked an opening partner – he took 86 wickets for the county (24.55) and no one else reached 40. Mead hit three Championship centuries and averaged 64.68 while Brown (946 at 36.38) and Melle were also effective. G Newcombe, who appeared in a number of matches, was in fact Guy Bignell playing under a pseudonym.

Lord Swaythling was the new President. A First World War Roll of Honour was displayed in the pavilion. After four years without cricket it is unsurprising that membership had fallen below 1,000 and subscriptions to £925. 9s 6d. Full membership cost one guinea, while ladies and boys under 18 were half that (10/6d); perhaps girls were not interested – or not welcome? Only full (male) members were entitled to enter the pavilion or vote at meetings and they too could take advantage of net bowlers for practice. Life membership was offered at 25 guineas. A new motor mower (£360) and horse (£35) were purchased but in the following year the horse was sold. Gatemen were paid 7/6d per day with free meals and the Groundsman's wages were raised to £3pw.

1920

Champions: Middlesex.

Hampshire won seven of their 26 matches in this first full post-war season but lost five of the first six matches and slipped to 11th – a disappointing finish especially with the return of Remnant, Newman and Livsey. The latter was now the regular wicket-keeper while James Evans was briefly his deputy. The batting was strong, led as usual by Mead, who averaged 50.65 in the Championship, followed by Brown who outscored him with 1,863 at 44.35. Bowell, Barrett and Tennyson all passed 900 runs and Newman's 641 runs complemented his 111 wickets, although Kennedy was the outstanding bowler with 164 wickets at 17.62 including two hat-tricks. However, they had little support – no other bowler reached 30 wickets.

Against Gloucestershire at Southampton, Brown and Barrett set the county's second wicket partnership record of 321, which stood until 2011, while Kennedy took 9-33 v Lancashire at Liverpool – the best bowling in an innings for the county until 1931. Hampshire, needing 66 to win the match, reached 54-5 but lost by one run. Hampshire scored 616-7 declared against Warwickshire at Portsmouth with three centurions, Brown, Barrett and Mead, and Kennedy returning match figures of 12-147.

Tennyson hit one ball against Kent at Southampton for a distance measured at 139 yards. Mead was awarded his first benefit, but the match was ruined by rain so the club and subscriptions made up to his guarantee of £1,000. In the same Benefit Match, Jack Hobbs scored 24 runs in one over by Newman at Southampton. At Clifton, Mead was dismissed for a 'pair' for the first time.

One of Hampshire's greatest games came in June at Leeds – particularly since it was against the reigning Champions: Hampshire 456-2 declared (Brown 232*, Mead 122*, Bowell 95), beat Yorkshire 159 (Sutcliffe 58, Kennedy 6-69) & 225 (Holmes 78, Rhodes 64, Kennedy 4-66, Newman 4-69) by an innings and 72 runs.

This was a strong Yorkshire side that was beaten mainly by Hampshire's five great professionals – perhaps, in single match terms, the pinnacle of their many fine achievements *together* for Hampshire.

When Yorkshire returned to Portsmouth at the end of August, they had their revenge, scoring 585-3 declared with Holmes 302* – a record on that ground and the highest innings v Hampshire until 1997. They dismissed Hampshire for 131 & 219, winning by an innings and 235 runs.

1921

Champions: Middlesex.

The season was hot and dry and Hampshire won 14 matches – the highest number until 1955 – and finished sixth. Tennyson captained England in the final three Tests v Australia after England had lost the first two. The Ashes Test Matches of 1921 and 1926 lasted just three days. In his first match as England's captain, Tennyson split his hand in the field but, batting one-handed, scored 63 & 36. Mead and Brown also played in the series and Mead's 182* in the 5th Test was the highest score for England v Australia at the time but Mead was never selected for England *in England* again. He made his highest first-class score of 280* v Nottinghamshire, and followed it with two centuries in the match at Horsham. That highest score at Southampton followed 45 in the first innings but Hampshire were defeated by two wickets, following a Nottinghamshire eighth wicket partnership of 119.

This was the first of three consecutive seasons in which Mead scored three centuries in successive innings and at Horsham he scored a double and single century in the same match – only Hayden in 1997 has equalled that for Hampshire. Mead scored over 3,000 runs in all first-class cricket and led the national first-class averages at 67.72. Brown played in the Tests as wicket-keeper but did not 'keep' for Hampshire, and Livsey was the country's leading wicket-keeper and set a new Hampshire record of 80 dismissals. In addition, his innings of 70* v Worcestershire was Hampshire's highest at number 11 until David Balcombe in 2012.

Bowell and Kennedy set the county's 10th wicket partnership record of 192 v Worcestershire at Bournemouth, which still stands. In addition to Mead, Bowell passed 1,000 runs while Kennedy and Newman performed the 'double' – the first Hampshire men since Llewellyn in 1910. Both bowled more than 1,000 overs, yet once again Hampshire lacked supporting bowlers – Remnant with 46 wickets and Brown with 36 were next best. Newman took 177 wickets for Hampshire – a record that would stand for just twelve months. Among the occasional players to appear in 1921 were CP Brutton, Alexander L Hosie, Lionel CR Isherwood and Harry S Altham, who recorded his only century for the county, 141 v Kent at Canterbury.

Hampshire played Glamorgan for the first time when they became the 17th side in the County Championship and before lunch Kennedy took 8-11 at Cardiff, as Glamorgan were dismissed for 37 in the 26th over. Kennedy then opened the batting and took four more second innings wickets as Hampshire won by an innings. The Australians scored 708-7 declared at Southampton, the second highest score against Hampshire, although the county's 370 was the second highest against the tourists in 1921. Receipts from that match helped Hampshire to achieve a "satisfactory" financial statement. Lancashire beat Hampshire at Liverpool, taking the final wicket from the last ball. Yorkshire won the match at Sheffield but Tennyson bowled an extra ball, enabling E Oldroyd to reach his century. In the earlier fixture at Southampton, Tyson, making his first-class debut for Yorkshire, scored 100* & 80* played in the next two matches and then never played for Yorkshire again.

AJL Hill played in one match on the day after his 50th birthday and then retired. Kennedy and Newman bowled unchanged through an innings on five successive occasions. Hampshire won seven consecutive victories in August – their best-ever winning run. In the Bank Holiday match between Hampshire and Kent at Southampton, Oswald W Cornwallis was selected for his Hampshire debut and his brother WS was selected by Kent, who took the field, with WS opening the bowling without success. During the day the two brothers were informed that their older brother, Captain FWM Cornwallis, had been killed by an IRA ambush in Ireland. The two men left the game and while WS played again for Kent, OW, who had never taken the field, did not appear for Hampshire again.

Slow-left-armer Stuart Boyes, who was employed at the Ordnance Survey Office in Southampton, played in two matches in 1921 and in October Hampshire's Committee agreed to take him on to the professional staff from the following season. He had been on the groundstaff just before the war. Alfred J Evans made his England debut v Australia having played twice for Kent and once for MCC in 1921. In 1920 he had played once for Hampshire and seven times between 1908–1920. He scored 14 & 4 in his only Test appearance and played for Kent until 1928. Sir Godfrey Baring was Hampshire's new President.

1922

Champions: Yorkshire.

Hampshire won 13 of their 28 matches and finished sixth but a number of surprising collapses prevented them reaching a higher position. Three men, Harold LV Day, Shirley and Boyes were effectively newcomers while Ronald Aird played more frequently. Boyes at last provided the support that Kennedy and Newman needed, with 94 wickets. HLV Day was another serving Army officer who played as an amateur and represented England at Rugby Union – he scored 56 & 91 on debut for Hampshire in 1922. Shirley came from Eton and Cambridge University; Aird too was at Cambridge, and was later Secretary of MCC.

Hampshire won one of the most remarkable victories ever v Warwickshire at Edgbaston on 14–16 June 1922: Warwickshire: 223 (Santall 84, Hon FS Calthorpe 70, Boyes 4-56, Newman 4-70), Hampshire: 15 (Mead 6*, Howell 6-7, Calthorpe 4-4) & (following on) 521 (Brown 172, Livsey 110*). Warwickshire (needing 314 to win) 158 (Smith 41, Quaife 40, Newman 5-53, Kennedy 4-47).

The Hampshire first innings lasted 8.5 overs or 53 balls, which is the shortest ever *completed* first-class innings. The eight ducks equals the record for a first-class innings and there has been only one other instance in the Championship. In the second Hampshire innings, the wickets fell at 177-6, 262-7, 274-8, 451-9 & 521 all out.

As well as their remarkable victory at Edgbaston, Hampshire also scored 522-6 on the second day of the match v Warwickshire at Southampton. Mead passed 2,000 runs at 63.05 even though he had been dangerously ill the previous winter. Despite his somewhat 'dour' reputation, he scored 235 in 285 minutes v Worcestershire as Hampshire won by an innings. Hampshire also beat Yorkshire on a wet Bradford wicket thanks to Tennyson (51), Kennedy (11-73) and Boyes (9-78). In Swansea, Hampshire were bowled out for 83 but then dismissed Glamorgan for 36, which remains their lowest score against Hampshire. Newman took 4-3 and Boyes 4-19 & 6-33 as Hampshire won by 178 runs. Mead scored 37 & 39, the two highest scores on either side.

Hampshire's captain ordered Newman from the field at Trent Bridge but Newman was successful again with 122 wickets and over 500 runs. In the same match, Nottinghamshire's TL Richmond took 9-21, the best innings figures ever against Hampshire in a *Championship* match until 2007. Kennedy took 190 wickets (15.61) which remains a record for Hampshire and also performed the 'double'. In the following winter, he played in five Tests in South Africa, as did Mead, while Brown played in four. Day was also selected for the tour but withdrew due to service commitments, while Livsey travelled but had to return home with an injured hand without playing. This is the only official MCC/England tour for which four Hampshire players were selected. Kennedy took 31 wickets in the series but was never selected again for England.

Lt-Col JG Grieg became Hampshire's new Secretary. Groundsman Jesse Hopkins, who had played a few games, received £400 from his Testimonial, while F Doran replaced A Brent as groundsman at Bournemouth. Membership went beyond 2,000 with receipts reaching £2,300, although wages and salaries were also up, to £1619. Hampshire County Cricket Club held 1100 of the 1545 shares in Southampton's Ground Company but with no tour, the bank balance fell and some members made a voluntary extra contribution. Remnant retired at the end of the season in his late 30s, having played 121 matches in a career interrupted by the war.

1923

Champions: Yorkshire.

Hampshire won ten matches and finished seventh. They were still one of the better teams, without ever challenging for the title. They had a particularly disappointing end to the season, winning only one of their last ten matches, v Somerset at Portsmouth, when Kennedy had match figures of 12-72 as he and Newman (7-62) bowled unchanged in the match. The Earl of Northbrook was the new President.

Mead again exceeded 2,000 runs and averaged over 60. He passed 50 in six consecutive innings, including one double century and three centuries. Otherwise, Kennedy and Newman passed 1,000 runs and both completed the double, while Brown and Tennyson scored over 900 runs each but Boyes had a disappointing season, with no other bowler reaching 40 wickets. Four Middlesex batsmen scored centuries in an innings of 642-3 declared at Southampton.

Twenty-eight men played for Hampshire during the season and while two of the amateurs, Percy E Lawrie and Brutton, scored centuries, these were isolated successes. AEL Hill played but with little success, while Herbert D Hake managed one half century in his county career. Day could play in only three matches in 1923.

Hampshire played their first first-class match v West Indians, winning by 144 runs (Mead 54 & 87, Kennedy 11-101). Hampshire beat Nottinghamshire by four wickets after scoring 323 runs in 180 minutes and they made Warwickshire suffer again with a record ninth wicket partnership of 197 between Mead and Shirley. This was the third consecutive season that a new record was set for this wicket, which then stood until 1962. However, they conceded 50 runs in extras at Canterbury, while the first four Middlesex batsmen scored centuries in an innings of 642-3 declared. In the match v Nottinghamshire at Southampton, Newman conceded 255 runs, which until 2009 was a record in an innings for Hampshire, passing 236 by Llewellyn in 1910.

Notices were posted in the pavilions requesting members to refrain from joining the public in "barracking" opposing teams. Membership increased to 2,613 but the weather was poor so overall receipts were down. Ground turnstiles were erected (£120). A new agreement was drawn up with the professionals, although less than they requested. The basic pay was £200; there was winter pay of £70, with groundstaff wages of £4 pw in the season. Home matches paid £8, away matches £10 but when ill or injured, those groundstaff and match figures were halved.

1924

Champions: Yorkshire.

This was a frequently wet summer and not particularly happy for Hampshire on the field as they won only one of their first 11 matches and only five of 28 throughout the season, slipping to 12th place, their lowest since 1907. As a result, the Committee asked AJL Hill, PM Hall and GH Muir to investigate the problems and re-establish the club's nursery; from the first group of young players taken on, Lewis Harfield would play 133 matches for the county.

Mead's 1591 runs at 44.19 was a decline on recent seasons but still far ahead of anyone else, although the amateurs Day and Aird both passed 1,000 while averaging below 25. Kennedy took 118 wickets, but in his benefit season, Newman's 81 were expensive – he received £1,000. Until Leo Harrison received £3,188 in 1957 no Hampshire benefit would reach £2,000, yet even before the Great War, Yorkshiremen Hirst (£3,700), Haigh (£2,071) and Rhodes (£2,002) had been more fortunate.

The supporting bowlers were Boyes and Brown, although the 21-year-old leg-spinner Frederick Gross showed promise. It is indicative of the cricket of that period that Livsey's 42 dismissals were split evenly between catches and stumpings.

At Southampton, Hampshire dismissed Gloucestershire for 92, of which FG Rogers scored 69*. Kennedy took 8-24, including a hat-trick, and Hampshire required 95 to win but could score only 72-5 in 26 overs. Newman took his benefit in the match against Surrey at Southampton when Hampshire, needing 235 to win, were 192-9, but Livsey and Boyes took them to victory. At the end of season AGM, Hampshire's former player Lieut-Col C Heseltine was elected President.

1925

Champions: Yorkshire.

The summer was drier but Hampshire again disappointed, winning six of 28 matches and finishing ninth. Mead topped the averages again but only he and Tennyson passed 1,000 runs and only those two and Tom O Jameson averaged over 25. Jameson was also an amateur squash champion. Kennedy took 132 wickets and Boyes 90 (including a hat-trick v Surrey) but Newman's 62 were again expensive (33.24). Tennyson scored 184 in 165 minutes v Middlesex at Southampton. Mead and Brutton set county's eight wicket record of 178 v Worcestershire at Bournemouth, which stood until 1985. H Howell took 9-32 for Warwickshire v Hampshire at Edgbaston, the best figures of the season.

Groundsman Jesse Hopkins supervised the nursery 'boys' A Hayward, N Bowell (son of Alec), L Harfield and HG Gibbons until a new coach, R Relf, arrived in July. Membership subscriptions exceeded £3,000. Tennyson and Jameson were selected for the MCC's winter tour of West Indies.

1926

Champions: Lancashire.

Hampshire won only one match in May but recovered to win 10 of their 28 matches, although they also ended poorly with no victories in August. Nonetheless, they rose to seventh, although at the end of July they had been third.

Tennyson missed some matches early in the season because he was acting as a Special Constable during the General Strike. The professionals made a significant contribution to Hampshire's improvement. Newman returned to his best form, performing the 'double', including 145 wickets, and against Gloucestershire at Bournemouth, he scored 66 & 42* and took 14-148. Mead increased his aggregate to 2,326 (62.86), Brown was only just short of 2,000 runs at 41.84 and Bowell made 1,000 runs again. Boyes passed 100 wickets (22.87) and while Kennedy was not at his best, he passed 700 runs and 80 wickets. Kennedy's benefit match v Surrey was badly rain-affected but subscriptions raised the sum over £1,000. Among the newcomers were the amateur batsman John P Parker from Havant who scored 156 at Canterbury and Walter N McBride, a strong fast-medium bowler who would go on to win a 'Blue' at Oxford (and one for 'soccer'). George Geary took 14-86 for Leicestershire at Southampton.

At a special committee meeting in July, the captain Tennyson charged two professionals with disciplinary offences. The players had complained about mistakes by the captain; they were censured by the committee. The financial position was stronger and R Relf was engaged as coach during the summer months for the next five years – subscriptions approached £3,500 and the Test matches v

Australia provided £1,111. Norman Bowell and Hayward left the Nursery, replaced by AE ('Sam') Pothecary and the South African Len Creese – both would make good contributions to Hampshire cricket in the 1930s.

HS Altham's brief Hampshire career was over but the Winchester schoolmaster published his first edition of *A History of Cricket*. The English Women's Cricket Association was formed.

1927

Champions: Lancashire.

Hampshire won just five of their 28 matches but 14 were drawn or no result and they finished 13th.

Pothecary was the first of the new Nursery graduates to hold a regular place – he was known as 'Sam' after his uncle, who had played 12 matches between 1912–1920. Newman, who performed the double again, was the only bowler to reach 100 wickets – he took 8-23 & 8-65 (16-88) v Somerset at Weston, the best match figures ever by a Hampshire bowler. Against Surrey at the Oval, Newman scored 102 & 102* and took 5-123, while Jack Hobbs scored 112 & 104 for Surrey. In the County Championship, there are only eight instances of batsmen on both sides scoring centuries in both innings and with Hampshire it occurred again in 1997.

Apart from Newman, Kennedy took 94 wickets but otherwise only Boyes, with a disappointing 34, took more than 20. Brown scored 1674 runs while Mead passed 2,000 at an average of 75.19 and he and Brown set the county's third wicket record of 344 v Yorkshire at Portsmouth, which stood until 2011.

Mead scored his 100th century at Northampton and was rewarded with a collection of £382. Kennedy had second innings figures of 10-7-8-7 v Warwickshire at Portsmouth and for the Players v Gentlemen (Oval) took 10-37, the only instance of ten wickets in an innings in an English first-class match by a Hampshire bowler. Maurice Tate scored 101 in 68 minutes and took 6-52 & 4-43 for Sussex at Portsmouth. Tennyson completed his century in 55 minutes v Gloucestershire at Southampton. Wally Hammond, educated at Portsmouth Grammar School, reached 1,000 runs in May in the same match and Mead scored 187 – the match was drawn. Kent beat Hampshire at Canterbury when Mead was dismissed off the last ball of the match but in the match against the same opponents at Southampton, Hampshire set a county record, scoring 375-6 to win in the fourth innings.

Hampshire scored 521-8 declared v Yorkshire at Portsmouth in late June, thanks mainly to Brown 204 and Mead 183 but there was only time for Yorkshire to reply with 156-3, as this was one of a number of matches ruined by bad weather in 1927. Hampshire's match at Worcester was one of five across the country abandoned without a ball being bowled and many others featured less than the equivalent of one day's play – in Hampshire's case, four such matches.

Livsey played in the Test Trial so Brown kept wicket v Northamptonshire at Southampton. The visitors followed-on but when Hampshire struggled to take wickets, Brown bowled and then resumed keeping wicket. He took 18 first-class wickets during the season. Bowell received £338 from a Testimonial after 26 years at the club (he had a benefit in 1914) but at the age of 47, was not offered another contract. He had scored 18,446 runs in 473 matches with 25 centuries.

Sir Francis Lacey was Hampshire's new President. A proposed car entrance at the County Ground would cost £200. A company was formed to take over the lease of Dean Park, the overdraft was increased to £1,500 and groundstaff players had neither work nor wages out-of-season. In addition to Pothecary, the younger uncapped players included Creese, Jim Bailey, OW ('Lofty') Herman and Harfield.

1928

Champions: Lancashire.

Once again, Hampshire won five of their 28 matches although they went up one place to 12th. Mead, at the age of 41, scored 2,854 runs, including 12 centuries, both records for the county. His season's total beat his own records set previously in 1921 and 1913 and his centuries total set in 1926 (10). During the winter, he toured Australia and played in the first Test Match – his final one. England won by 675 runs, Mead scored 8 & 73 and his Test career ended with an average of 49.37 – just 15 more runs and it would have been 50.

Newman and Kennedy performed the 'double' in all matches but neither did so in the Championship although both passed 1,000 runs, as did Hosie. Newman's double was his third in consecutive seasons and his fifth overall – both Hampshire records. Only Jim Bailey in 1948 would achieve the feat after 1928. Of the Colts, Lew Harfield played regularly but ill health spoiled his career – he played his last match at just 26 in 1931. Pace bowler RPH (Richard) Utley took 59 wickets but his too was a brief career; he entered the Benedictine Order and taught at Ampleforth School. HG Gibbons left the groundstaff and was replaced by batsman John Arnold, who had followed Bowell and Herman from Oxfordshire. In the match against Leicestershire at Bournemouth, all eleven batsmen on both sides scored at least one run in both innings – the only instance in a Hampshire match.

Individual members could hire tents during matches at £3 pd. Bournemouth hosted a match between Gentlemen and Players and another between North and South. Five Hampshire players helped the South win their match while Mead scored a century for the Players and Kennedy took 6-91.

The club had financial problems and raised the members' subscription to £1.10s; a number resigned and the subscriptions came to £3,342. New members were required to pay a 10/- entrance fee. Brown struggled with injury during the season but received £1,000 from his benefit.

1929

Champions: Nottinghamshire.

Tennyson was still officially the club's captain but suffered from a broken finger in a season of injury problems. Hampshire won eight matches and finished 11th. Mead, Brown and Harfield passed 1,000 runs although Mead missed 10 matches with a broken thumb and Brown had a motorcycle accident. Boyes strained his bowling arm but was 'capped' – the first of the professionals whose career began since the war. He took 70 wickets at 21.65 but Newman's form declined. Fortunately, young Herman took 53 wickets and Kennedy was in his best form with 140 wickets at 17.57 as well as nearly 800 runs. He took 9-46 & 4-54 v Derbyshire at Portsmouth but in a low scoring match, Derbyshire won by five wickets.

Walter Livsey fell ill during the winter and never played again after this season – he caught 45 and stumped 29 and in his final match at Cheltenham his was the last wicket to fall as Hampshire lost by just 14 runs. 1929 was his benefit year and he chose the match v Surrey at Southampton; he will have enjoyed the result but not that Hampshire won in two days. Herman took 6-73 and Boyes 5-20 while Mead with 56 was the only man to pass 30 on either side. Livsey received £750.

AJL Hill replaced FE Lacey as the third successive former player to be elected President. Part of the upper floor of the ladies pavilion was allocated for use by non-members. Financial problems continued, with winter wages for the professionals being split over the period and the club reported the loss of nearly 150 members.

1930

Champions: Lancashire.

Hampshire lost a number of close matches but with just five wins they finished 13th. They had not finished in the top half since 1926 and would do so only once more until 1955. This season marked a transitional moment, with Bowell and Livsey recently departed, Newman playing his final season, brought on by illness in the following winter, Mead and Brown over 40 and Kennedy 39. Brown deputised as wicket-keeper for this one year but Relf recommended the signing of a young wicket-keeper from Portsmouth, Neil McCorkell. Harfield missed the whole season with illness.

There was a surprise in the batting averages as Mead was displaced at the top. He was awarded a second benefit (£681) but scored just one century with 1,305 runs at only 31.07. Brown had 1,341 at 28.53 but the highlight of the season was John Arnold. He had played once in 1929 but now scored 1,186 at 32.05. He was a fine cover fielder and played 'soccer' for Southampton and Fulham. He would represent England (once) in both cricket and football.

Boyes led the bowling averages although Kennedy was the only man to pass 100. Newman's final season brought him 77 at 23.89 (plus 578 runs). He played 506 matches for the county with almost 14,000 runs and in all first-class cricket over 2,000 wickets, one of only three men to pass that figure without playing a Test Match. Giles Baring from Cambridge University impressed as a pace bowler but his career was blighted by an arm injury in a road accident. In the match v Australians at Southampton on 31 May, DG Bradman completed 1,000 runs for the season. CG (Charles) Fynn made his debut v Lancashire at Bournemouth and took two wickets in his first over. An amateur, Fynn played infrequently – nine matches in two seasons – but received his county cap.

Somerset scored 545-9 declared against Hampshire at Taunton with all eleven batsmen and extras reaching double figures but no one reaching a century. Hampshire beat reigning champions Nottinghamshire in strange circumstances at Southampton. They took the extra half-hour on day two, at the end of which they still needed one run to win. The game resumed on the third morning with the visitors fielding in their day clothes and Hampshire won from the second ball.

Finances continued to trouble, with the overdraft over £3,000. During the winter the ground was used for hockey. (Frank) Jesse Hopkins, the groundsman at Northlands Road, died in January aged 54. He had played for Warwickshire and three first-class matches for Hampshire.

1931

Champions: Yorkshire.

Hampshire won five matches, finishing 12th. Baring took 9-26 v Essex at Colchester, Hampshire's best bowling in an innings until 'Bob' Cottam in 1965. Hampshire played the New Zealanders for the first time and Arnold played against New Zealand in his only Test Match, the first of the season, at Lord's. He was the youngest Hampshire player to represent England in a Test Match and scored 0 & 34 but was never selected again. Arnold and Bailey, both under 25, shared five century opening partnerships during the season and Bailey scored 899 runs and took 26 wickets. Mead improved on 1930 with 1,463 runs and led the averages while Arnold and Brown also passed 1,000. There was a fairly well balanced attack, Kennedy with 115 wickets leading the way with Baring, Herman and Boyes all passing 50 and sharing 192 wickets.

Tennyson was not always available to captain Hampshire and three other amateurs Aird, Baring and Stephen H Fry, son of CB and father of CA, deputised, as did Mead, who led Hampshire's first-ever side of 11 professionals against Yorkshire at Hull. Sadly, the match was wrecked by rain with only 51.5 overs possible, but that was sufficient time for Yorkshire to be bowled out for 135 (Kennedy 7-45). Yorkshire fielded one amateur, FE Greenwood, who was bowled by Kennedy for 5.

The results were disappointing, albeit in a wet summer, and this was largely due to a lack of support for the leading batsmen. Neither was there a regular wicket-keeper, as the ageing Brown stood on occasions, so too Fry and Lieut-Cdr Edward LD Bartley from the Royal Navy. There was controversy at the Oval when Fry, captaining the side in a rain-affected match, declared behind on the third day. Surrey too declared and Hampshire chased 222 in less than three hours. The match was drawn but the authorities did not approve. EJ ('Ted') Drake who would find greater fortune in 'soccer' and Richard H ('Dick') Moore both played their first matches in first-class cricket.

Major-General the Rt Hon JEB Seely was the new President, while GH Muir had taken over as secretary. In another anticipation of future developments the Committee considered selling advertising space on the ground as the overdraft hovered around £3,000 – roughly the equivalent of the income from members subscriptions – the number of members just exceeding 2,000.

1932

Champions: Yorkshire.

Hampshire won eight matches and finished eighth – a brief improvement in a twenty season period of being in the bottom half of the table. Harfield was so seriously ill that his contract was paid up and terminated. Baring was injured in a car accident in the winter and was unable to play a match in this season. He was just 22 years old and had taken 79 wickets at 23.83 in the previous season. He did continue to play until 1946 in a total of 91 first-class matches with 176 wickets. Bailey had figures of 7-3-7-7 v Nottinghamshire at Southampton. Arnold (227) shared three successive century partnerships v Glamorgan at Cardiff and topped the averages with 1506 runs at 33.46. Mead and Brown also passed 1,000 runs. While Tennyson and Pothecary scored over 800 runs, they averaged only around 20.

Kennedy was one of *Wisden's* Five Cricketers of the Year and took 134 wickets at 18.45. Herman, Boyes and Bailey bowled regularly and finished with averages below 25 per wicket. Mead scored 104* v Derbyshire at Southampton, thereby completing a century against every other county. He also scored centuries against Australia, South Africa, West Indians, Lord Hawke's XI, Cambridge University, Jamaica, Gentlemen, Tasmania and Transvaal and he scored 15 centuries v Kent. Hampshire played the Indians for the first time and beat them by an innings. They beat the Champions Yorkshire in a low-scoring match at Leeds – their first victory over them for ten years and despite Sutcliffe carrying his bat for 104.

The *Guide* reported that Hampshire had "faced financial difficulties with a stout heart" in 1932, noting the "drop in membership", which was normally the "surest means of financial security".

1933

Champions: Yorkshire.

This was Tennyson's final season as official captain but he led in only four matches and had no fewer than six deputies including three professionals, Brown, Kennedy and Mead, plus AK (Arthur) Judd, JP Parker and GLO (Gilbert) Jessop, son of the England cricketer GL Jessop.

It was a dry summer, favouring batsmen but Hampshire were poor, winning just two of their 28 matches and finishing 14th (of 17). The season opened with a match v Surrey at Southampton. Sandham (169*) and Brown (150*) both carried their bats for their respective teams. Despite the disappointments, Mead, at 46, was just 22 runs short of 2,500 (68.83) with 10 centuries. Creese, Pothecary, Brown and Arnold passed 1,000 runs with Bailey 923 and Kennedy 889. Kennedy also took 89 wickets and Boyes passed 100, but Herman's 76 were expensive and the other bowlers ineffective. Nineteen-year-old Moore scored 159 at Bournemouth in the last match of the season but Essex replied with 564-8 declared, only McCorkell did not bowl and the match was drawn. It was typical of the season. At lunch time on the third day Essex declared but the umpires incorrectly added 15 minutes to the interval for the pitch to be rolled.

John Arnold played football for England v Scotland at Hampden Park, becoming the only Hampshire player to represent his country in cricket and football, although in 1901, CB Fry had done so in football before joining Hampshire. Other Hampshire cricketers who played football for England were E Haggarth (1875), L Bury (1877–1879), LV Lodge (1894–1895), GB Raikes (1895–1896), AE Knight (1920) and E Drake (1935–1938).

Sir George Meyrick was the new President. The pavilions were repaired and painted (£253). At the end of the season, the Committee announced that 1,000 members had been lost since 1926 – presumably a combination of the difficult financial times and the poor results by a team that had reached its peak immediately before that. Membership receipts were £2,662. 12s. 6d.

1934

Champions: Lancashire.

Tennyson indicated that he would not be available throughout the season as he was to report on the Ashes series, so WGF Lowndes was appointed captain. Lowndes (140) and Mead (139) added 247 for the fourth wicket v the Australians. Hampshire had the Australians 10-3 with Woodfull, Brown and Bradman (c Mead b Baring 0) dismissed. Nonetheless, the Australians led on first innings and the match was drawn. Arnold scored 109* in the second innings and Baring took 5-121. The crowd was reported as 10,000.

Hampshire won just three of their 28 matches, drawing half of the games and finishing 14th again. Bailey joined the Lord's groundstaff, hoping to qualify by residence for Middlesex. In the event he moved on to be a professional at Accrington in the Lancashire League and eventually returned to Hampshire. Brown retired prior to the season and received a Testimonial of £292, while 1934 was Kennedy's final full-time season, leaving only Mead from the great players of the immediate pre-post-war period. He led the county's averages, although Arnold was top-scorer with 2,000 runs – Moore also passed 1,000. Kennedy scored over 900 runs and took 87 wickets but at 28.40, while Herman, Creese and Boyes all passed 50 wickets but they were more expensive in a weak bowling attack.

Boyes bowled 480 balls v Nottinghamshire at Southampton, a record for Hampshire; his final figures were 80-28-138-3. Five players, Arnold, Kennedy, McCorkell, Mead and Moore played in every match. Drake joined the professional staff, which was ten-strong, including Gerry Hill from the New Forest and Lloyd Budd from Southampton. Membership subscriptions remained below £3,000 but Hampshire did declare a surplus of income over expenditure for the year of £2,083.

1935

Champions: Yorkshire.

Lowndes, in his second year as captain, did not play regularly, while his eventual successor, Moore, was unwell and missed most matches. Hampshire won five matches, two more than in 1934 but they dropped to 16th place with only Northamptonshire below them. At Bournemouth, Hampshire scored 458-3 and beat Northamptonshire by an innings & 213 runs, a club record innings victory. C Smart of Glamorgan scored 32 (6, 6, 4, 6, 6, 4) from one over bowled by Hill at Cardiff – then a world record for a six-ball over. Lowndes scored a century before lunch v Kent at Portsmouth, the two sides scoring 552 runs on the first day and 433 on the second. Kent won by seven wickets. In the match at Worcester the weather was so cold the players and umpires were served coffee on the field.

Hampshire batted in both innings at Trent Bridge without three players and lost by an innings – they were 37 'all out' in the second innings having lost just seven wickets. Boyes and Hill added over 50 for the 10th wicket in both innings v Middlesex at Lord's. McCorkell became a regular opening batsman; he scored his maiden century v Lancashire at Southampton and another against the same opponents in the next match at Liverpool. With Arnold, he shared five century opening partnerships during the season and both passed 1,000 runs, as did Creese and Mead – at 48, again topping the averages. WL (Lloyd) Budd, later a Test umpire, scored 67* v Glamorgan at Bournemouth batting at number 11.

Hill took 93 wickets at 24.49 and Boyes 79 at 25.10 but the pace bowling was weak until Kennedy returned in August from his new coaching post to head the averages. Twenty-seven players appeared in the County Championship – 13 of them amateurs and one newcomer was batsman Arthur Holt, who would enjoy a career as player and coach of more than 30 years. Howard Lawson, whose father had played briefly for Hampshire, appeared in a few matches. Two older men who had played for other counties, Stanley Fenley (Surrey) and Thomas Collins (Nottinghamshire) also appeared briefly. EH Bowley (ex-Sussex) coached the Nursery players and A Solly was taken on to the staff.

Sir Russell Bencraft was elected President. Hampshire played at Basingstoke for the first time since the Great War. Public seating was installed at the stadium end of the County Ground (30/- per yd).

1936

Champions: Derbyshire.

At Southampton in the first match of the season against the eventual champions, the new captain RH Moore and Cecil GA Paris, his vice captain, came together in the second innings at 8-1, added 183, and both scored centuries. Hampshire was undefeated in their first 15 matches – their best record at that time – but faded late in the season and finished in 10th place with seven victories. Naval officer John E Manners topped the averages in four innings – of the regular players Creese led Mead while Arnold, Moore, McCorkell and Pothecary made six men who exceeded 1,000 runs. Herman took 107 wickets and Boyes and Creese both exceeded 90. Hill and Donald 'Hooky' Walker added 235 v Sussex at Portsmouth. It remains the county's fifth wicket record partnership.

At the Oval, Surrey scored 592-9 declared but Hampshire held on to draw (Creese 94*). Herman 5-23 and Boyes 4-3 dismissed Somerset for 39 at Southampton and Hampshire won by 10 wickets. Boyes received £764 from his benefit. All India came to Bournemouth in late August and won a thrilling match by just two runs. Hampshire led by 46 on first innings and Herman's five wickets reduced them to 99-9 before Banerjee and Nayudu added exactly 100. Hampshire, requiring 154 to win, reached 140-7 with Mead scoring 53* in each innings.

Solly left through ill health but younger groundstaff players included Ernie Hayter, Dick Court, George Heath and PA ('Alec') Mackenzie. Jim Bailey began three seasons with Accrington in the Lancashire League and became the first English professional to score 1,000 runs in a season. In April, Hampshire cricketer Ted Drake scored the winning goal for Arsenal in the FA Cup Final v Sheffield United.

Mead retired having scored 48,892 runs for Hampshire – more runs than any other player ever scored for any single first-class side. He also passed 1,000 runs in 27 consecutive seasons, scored 138 centuries, a Hampshire record, held 627 catches in 701 matches and took 266 wickets. He played one tourist match while qualifying in 1905 then from 1906–1936 missed only 39 of 739 county matches – mostly due to selection in representative games. He scored his last century, 104 v Essex at Southend, at the age of 49 years and 161 days, the oldest man ever to score a century for Hampshire. Kennedy returned again in August to play a few matches but then retired completely, having taken 2,549 wickets for Hampshire – a county record beaten only by Derek Shackleton some 30 years later. Kennedy also scored almost 15,000 runs.

Colonel Heseltine succeeded Sir Russell Bencraft as President and Alastair McLeod, who played 18 matches for the county from 1914–1938, was appointed Secretary.

1937

Champions: Yorkshire.

Hampshire won seven of their 28 matches, finishing 14th – but they played some enterprising and entertaining cricket even though the defeats rose from five to 16. For the first time since 1904, not one of Hampshire's 'big five' (Tennyson, Mead, Newman, Kennedy, Brown) appeared in the side but four men, Arnold, Moore, McCorkell and Pothecary, passed 1,000 runs and Walker scored 847. Among the bowlers, Herman enjoyed an excellent season with 133 wickets at 21.58, Hill took 80 at 23.57 and another newcomer, George Heath, took 67 wickets. Heath, born in Hong Kong, played his school and club cricket in Bournemouth and for the Club & Ground in the previous two seasons. Walker was a squash rackets professional in Bournemouth in the winter and had been a pilot officer in the RAF as well as playing occasionally for Surrey 2nd XI. The *Guide* suggested that he "has many years in the cricket field ahead of him". Sadly, events on a greater field destroyed that hope.

In the match v Warwickshire at Bournemouth on 28 and 29 July, Hampshire's captain, RH Moore, scored 316, which remains the highest innings ever for Hampshire. It lasted 380 minutes and he was last man out, lbw from the penultimate ball of the final over of the first day. Hampshire won by an innings on the second day.

The county declared a loss for the season of just over £1,000 and appealed again for more members to adjust that deficit.

1938

Champions: Yorkshire.

CGA Paris was appointed captain. He was one of five different 'official' captains during the decade and there were also a number of deputies, both amateur and professional.

Hampshire played 30 matches this year, two more than in previous seasons. They won nine but remained 14th. Moore was unable to play regularly but topped the averages, scoring 637 runs, including three centuries. The captain and three professionals, McCorkell, Creese and Pothecary, passed 1,000 runs and Walker reached 925. Boyes took 103 wickets (21.57) and Heath 97 at 23.21. Herman took a hat-trick v Glamorgan at Portsmouth but his 101 wickets were rather expensive, and the Rev John WJ Steele, an Army Chaplain, bowled quickly in a number of matches. Hill's spin bowling was much less effective but the Southampton amateur, CJ 'Charlie' Knott, made his debut and Bailey was called into the side for midweek matches in the north. He would leave Accrington at the end of the season and return to the county. Arnold had a very poor season and at one point was not sure of a contract for 1939, although he and McCorkell passed 100 for the first wicket in both innings v Kent at Southampton and Hampshire won. This was the only county season from 1930–1950 inclusive that Arnold failed to reach 1,000 runs. At Leicester, the home side scored 535-8 declared while McCorkell did not concede a bye.

In the match v Australians at Southampton, DG Bradman completed 1,000 runs in May, as he had in 1930 also at Southampton. Roland B Proud made his debut v Derbyshire at Chesterfield, scoring 28, which included four sixes from the bowling of TB Mitchell. Hampshire were dismissed twice in 89.4 overs, and although scoring at more than three runs per over, they lost by 10 wickets on the second day.

At Bournemouth, Hampshire led Nottinghamshire by 107 runs on first innings but, set 243 to win in 56 overs, collapsed to 57-8. Mackenzie and Knott took them to 75-8 with two balls left, whereupon RJ Giles took two wickets and Nottinghamshire won. In late August, Hampshire played first-class cricket on the Isle of Wight for the first time when they beat Northamptonshire by seven wickets at Newport – despite a rain-ruined second day. Boyes scored a century and took 6-40, and when they returned in 1939 he took 5-45, although Hampshire lost to Middlesex by an innings. Hampshire did not return to Newport after the war but played at Cowes from 1956–1962.

This Australian summer was Hampshire's best ever financially. Two thousand, six hundred and thrity-two members paid £3,419 and 76,738 spectators paid £4,486 at the gate. Gross income was £11,020, with a profit of £1,907, although that included just over £2,000 from the Board of Control.

1939

Champions: Yorkshire.

Local solicitor George R Taylor was the latest captain; appointed because he was an amateur, he had played once in 1935 and would play 23 more times this year, with a top score of 41, an average of 9.21 (and one wicket). Hampshire reverted to 26 matches, winning just three and dropping one place to 15th.

Leo Harrison celebrated his 17th birthday during this season but would not play again until 1946. He was highly rated as a young batsman – Essex cricketer and journalist Charles Bray suggested he might be the "new Bradman". Harrison was elected a Life Vice President of Hampshire in 2011 and so has been associated with the club for exactly half its 150 years. Herman had followed Bailey's lead and moved to the Lancashire Leagues, playing for Rochdale but with no matches for Hampshire. This decision allowed the Committee to reconsider Arnold's position and he recovered his form with 1441 runs at 35.14. 'Hooky' Walker passed 1,000 runs, as did Bailey, Creese and McCorkell, but the bowling was not strong – Boyes with 67 was the leading wicket taker, followed by Heath (54) and Bailey (42).

Hampshire gave matches to two leg-spinners – PA (Percy) Mackenzie, who played briefly in 1938, and Tom Dean, who made his debut aged 18. Dean played at the end of the season in the three matches of the Bournemouth 'Festival' (all defeats) and Arlott suggested that as a forward short-leg he was good enough "to challenge comparison with any player the game has known". As a bowler he took four wickets in five balls, including the hat-trick v Worcestershire and 5-58 v Yorkshire in what would be Hampshire's last Championship match until 1946. For Hampshire's 'Hooky' Walker and Yorkshire's Hedley Verity (6-22), 1946 never came.

Membership rose to its highest of the decade, 2,285, and the club were sufficiently secure to engage Sam Staples of Nottinghamshire as Coach. None of this would mean much over the next six years and John Arlott (1957) wrote of the penultimate match v Worcestershire "The impending war weighed heavily on the cricket. The game already seemed unreal against the background of darkening and towering clouds".

1914: (back) Livsey, Down, Kennedy, Brown, Bowell, Newman, (front) Stone, Haig-Smith, Jaques, Greig, Mead

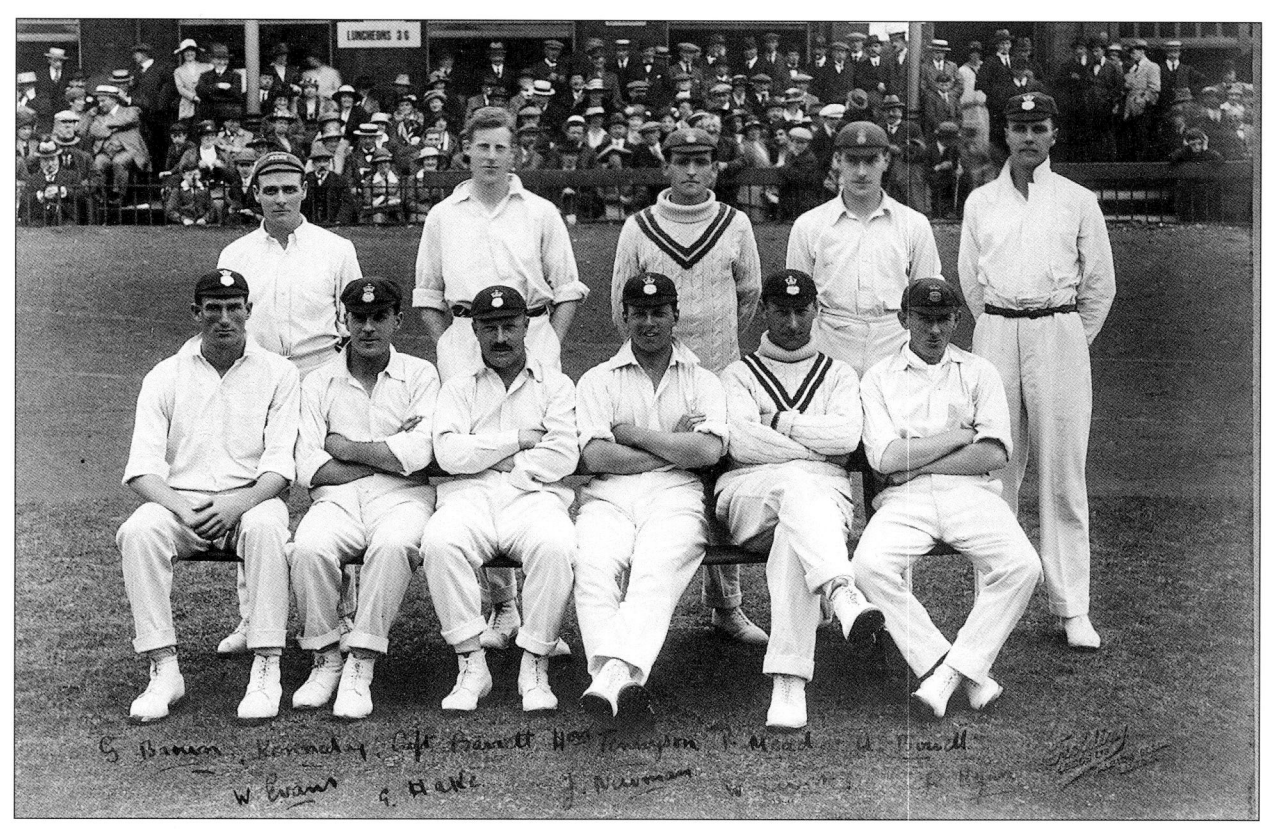

1920: v Yorkshire at Leeds, (back) Evans, Hake, Newman, Livsey, Ryan, (front) Brown, Kennedy, Barrett, Tennyson, Mead, Bowell

1922: v Warwickshire at Edgbaston, (back) Brown, umpire, Livsey, Boyes, Shirley, Kennedy, umpire, Newman, (front) Bowell, McIntyre, Tennyson, Day, Mead

1927: v Yorkshire at Portsmouth, (back) umpire, Livsey, Brown, Boyes, Kennedy, (centre) Bowell, Parker, Tennyson, Mead, Newman, (front) Gross, Utley

1931: (back) Bailey, Creese, Herman, Brown, Harfield, Arnold, (front) Mead, Pothecary, S Fry, Kennedy, Boyes

1934: Hampshire & Australians at Southampton, (back) WL Sprankling (scorer), Creese, Kennedy, Chipperfield, Boyes, Barnett, Baring, McCabe, (centre) D Hendren (umpire), GH Muir (HCCC secretary), Bromley, Bradman, WA Brown, O'Reilly, Darling, Kippax, Fleetwood-Smith, W Reeves (umpire), H Bushby (manager Australians), (front) Moore, Mead, Arnold, Woodfull, Sir R Bencraft, Lowndes, Tennyson, Oldfield, (ground) Pothecary, McCorkell

1934: (back) McCorkell, Arnold, Herman, Sprankling (scorer), Boyes, Creese, Pothecary, (front) Mead, Moore, Lowndes, Paris, Kennedy

1935: (back) Creese, Pothecary, Herman, Budd, Hill, McCorkell, (front) Arnold, Moore, Lowndes, Mead, Boyes

1938: (back) Arnold, Bailey, Walker, Heath, Hill, McCorkell, (front) Creese, Pothecary, Paris, Boyes, Herman

1939: (back) Hill, Bailey, Holt, G Heath, L Harrison, DF Walker, (front) Pothecary, Boyes, Taylor, Arnold, Creese

1940–1945 *Not first-class*

1940

With the outbreak of war, first-class cricket ceased in England until 1946.

In March, Hampshire's AGM agreed that Boyes would supervise junior coaching classes and the County Ground would be available for club matches. WL Sprankling took over as Acting Hon Secretary. By December 1940, over 1,000 members had renewed their subscriptions but conditions for any cricket were difficult on the south coast – especially in the port cities, which were subject to regular bombing raids.

Midwinter has recorded that Paris, Hill, Court and Heath joined the Army – Rogers, who spent 1939 on the groundstaff, was an additional name, as was Harrison, joining the RAF alongside Taylor, Mackenzie and McLeod. Arnold joined the Auxillary Fire Service and McCorkell has been identified with a number of roles: in the Royal Navy, building spitfires or fire-watching. Captain Frederick AV Parker, who would play briefly in 1946, was a member of the British Expeditionary Force captured that year.

A number of clubs were able to play during the season, with competitions in Southampton, Bournemouth and Winchester. At the Southampton Sports Centre, an Australian XI scored 152-7 to beat Southampton Touring Club (110). At the County Ground, Arthur Holt and Stan Broomfield shared a century opening partnership for H Eggerton's XI and Charlie Knott took 8-40 to beat John Kemp's XI. Future Kent cricketer Tony Pawson starred for Winchester College v Eton with 100* and 5-45. On 31 August, Aldershot Services met the New Zealand Expeditionary Force at Aldershot.

German bombing damaged the pavilions at the County Ground. Dean Park was used by the Army and there was also a display there of a captured German bomber.

1941

DF 'Hooky' Walker was killed in action on a bombing raid over Holland.

The London Counties Cricket XI played Southampton & District at the Sports Ground, Hythe on Sunday 11 July. The match was all-day and entrance was 9d. Hampshire clubs often played matches against teams from the services but there was nothing from the county side in a quiet season. Matches on Cricket Archive include:

Various games played by Winchester College v other public schools

Aldershot & District (home) v Cambridge University on 20 June: John R Bridger played for the University and Howard Lawson (plus Alf Gover and Dicky Dodds) for the home team

Aldershot & District (home) v RAF on 26 July: AC Johnston and DCS Compton played for the home team. On the following day at the County Ground, Southampton, Southampton Touring Club selected Holt, Reg Haskell, Pothecary and Jack Treherne v London Counties, who included Lloyd Budd, Ted Drake, Leslie Compton and Arthur Fagg. Bowler Jack Treherne played regularly for Hampshire Club & Ground and 2nd XI after the war and his son Roger, a former Hampshire Colt, has been on the Committee for many years, including a spell as Chairman.

1942

On 1 July, Lieut-Col. Francis G B Arkwright MC, DSO was shot and killed in North Africa. He was laid to rest at the El Alamein Commonwealth War Cemetery. He was right-hand batsman who played three matches for Hampshire in 1923, scoring 44 runs in five innings and taking two catches. In addition to the death of Arkwright, Captain Alan NE Waldron, who would play twice in 1948, was captured in 1942 as a member of the Royal Hampshire Regiment and spent the rest of the war imprisoned in Germany.

1943

Norman Bowell, who played twice for Hampshire and was the son of their batsman, Alec Bowell, was reported killed while a Japanese prisoner-of-war. Second Lieutenant Alistair K Campbell, who served in the Royal Artillery, died of pneumonia in Queen Alexandra Hospital, Portsmouth. He played for Hampshire in 1908–1909 and also in 199 matches for Southampton FC. Major Ronnie Aird was awarded the Military Cross for bravery in the Middle East.

As early as 16 March (in warm weather) two visiting Air Force sides met at Bournemouth and an Australian XI (including Keith Miller) defeated New Zealand. On Saturday 7 August a Hampshire XI met an Empire XI (although not the more regular *British* Empire XI) on the County Ground. Hampshire included Mackenzie, Holt, Arnold, Paris, CJ (Jack) Andrews, Budd, Boyes, Knott, Herman plus CCP Heseltine (son of) and Arthur Robinson, an 18-year-old who had played at Sherborne School. The Empire XI scored 138 (Herman 5-35) and Hampshire won by nine wickets after an opening partnership of 107 between Mackenzie (68) and Holt (56). They batted on to 232-7 (Paris 52, Chadda 5-61).

Southampton Police played matches v Civil Service and London Counties. Cricket Archive lists a number of matches played by Southampton Police from 1943 onwards. There are often interesting names on both sides – in the first match listed, for example, the Police include Lloyd Budd and Jack Andrews.

1944

Captain John P Blake MC, a Royal Marine Commando, was killed on active service in Yugoslavia. He was born in Portsmouth and was just 26 when he died. He played 29 first-class matches for Cambridge University and Hampshire, including the University Match in July 1939 when he played alongside HS Altham's son-in-law 'Podge' Brodhurst and future Hampshire cricketer AC (Alan) Shirreff. In the opposition were RB (Roland) Proud and EDR (Desmond) Eagar. John Blake's younger brother David played 50 matches for Hampshire as an amateur from 1949–1959 – he was a batsman and wicket-keeper and a dentist in Portsmouth. David Blake still lives in Hampshire and celebrated his 88th birthday in April 2013.

Southampton Touring Club enjoyed a members' evening, entertained by Major Lord Tennyson. Basingstoke's RC Smith returned figures of 10-8 v Farnborough. The south coast of England had other priorities in this D-Day summer but Southampton Police played matches against Civil Defence, British Empire XI and London Counties. Membership stood at 527.

1945

Hampshire CCC held their AGM at the Dolphin Hotel in High Street, Southampton on 20 April. The meeting noted the deaths of their Patron Princess Beatrice and their President and former player Lieut-Col C Heseltine. There was an announcement of "seven one-day fixtures". Germany surrendered early in May 1945, too late to organise a County Championship but sufficiently early for a resumption of regular cricket, much of it involving top players. The AGM Agenda promised seven Hampshire fixtures, five at Northlands Road against Southampton Police, Sussex, Northamptonshire, Southampton & District and Aldershot Services, a return v Sussex at Hove and v RAF at Bournemouth.

In addition to their Hampshire match, Southampton Police played against the British Empire XI and London Police. After the Police match in May, Hampshire beat Sussex at home but lost at Hove. In the match against the RAF at Bournemouth on 25 August, Sid Buller and George Cox were in the RAF side while Hampshire fielded Boyes, McCorkell, Mackenzie, Holt, Parker, Pothecary, Rodney Exton, Geoffrey GL Hebden, Herman, Knott and Charrett – the latter did not play first-class cricket for Hampshire.

Gannaway records that in addition to Southampton, police cricket "flourished" on the Isle of Wight, while Jack Andrews, Lloyd Budd and LC Watkins were selected for the National Police XI v the Club Cricket Conference at Lord's. Youngsters JR ('Jimmy') Gray and Ralph Prouton played for Southampton Touring Club, as did Don Roper. Learie Constantine gave a talk to Southampton Rotary Club praising village green cricket in England and the country's cricketers prepared themselves for the resumption of normal service.

In October 1945 Desmond Eagar was interviewed at the County Ground for the post of captain and Joint-Secretary with WL Sprankling. Eagar had played for Oxford University and Gloucestershire as an amateur before the war. He had not yet been demobbed and was interviewed in uniform, while the Committee offered the post to the Surrey and England cricketer FR ('Freddie') Brown. In the event Brown preferred Northamptonshire and the appointment of Eagar was made which, in 1957, he revealed had brought him "much happiness". He took over as captain from the start of the 1946 season.

During the war, the Chairman Lieut-Col WK Pearce, Hon Secretary WL Sprankling and Hon Treasurer WF Hodges had ensured that Hampshire County Cricket Club continued to function while over 500 members maintained their subscriptions.

In addition to the award to Major R Aird MC, Squadron Leader PA Mackenzie was awarded the DSO and DFC.

Boyes, Mackenzie and Moore appeared in Hampshire sides in 1945 for the last time while Creese had taken up a coaching appointment. 'Sam' Pothecary was appointed groundsman and Sam Staples returned as coach.

The accounts at the AGM showed a surplus of £22.6s.9d and members' subscriptions produced just over £650 – a very similar amount to 1943. In the spring of 1946 an appeal was launched to mark Hampshire's fifty years as a 'first-class' county. We know now that some years pre-1895 are considered first-class, so that fifty years marked their admission to the official County Championship.

Second World War – Decorated Hampshire Cricketers

R Aird MC 1942
*FGB Arkwright MC 1940, DSO 1942
*JP Blake MC 1944
J P Gornall DSO 1945
GAFW Jewell MC 1945 also Czech Military Cross
AM Lee DSC 1941
PA Mackenzie DFC 1942, DSO 1943
JE Manners DSC 1945
RH Palmer MC 1943
I N R Shield MBE 1946
ANE Waldron MC 1945

*Killed in action/died of wounds.

1946

Champions: Yorkshire.

Hampshire's first post-war President was JG Grieg but, at the AGM in late 1946, HS Altham took over the post, which he held for twenty years, until his death. Desmond Eagar and WL Sprankling were joint Secretaries but not until April could Hampshire confirm that their new captain would be available to play under the Special Registration Rule.

On Wednesday 8 May the English County Championship resumed after six blank seasons with a single match at Lord's. On the following Saturday (11 May) a round of county matches started, including Hampshire v Worcestershire at Southampton. Bailey scored 133 and Neville Rogers, who had been on the staff in 1939, scored 90 on first-class debut, the highest score for Hampshire in a debut *innings*, although three men have scored higher in the second innings of their debut match. Hampshire scored 346 but Worcestershire declared with a lead of one run (Heath 5-74). Bailey led the way with 76 in a total of 214 and Herman (5-39) and Heath (4-47) dismissed Worcestershire for 120 to win the match.

It was a good start to a season in which Hampshire won eight of their 28 matches and finished 10th. However, *Wisden* noted their "inconsistency", in particular through the "lack of stability in batting" and the fielding was often poor. At Guildford Alec Bedser and Gover of Surrey dismissed them for 48, although Hill made a century in the second innings. Nonetheless, Arnold and Bailey both passed 1,000 runs. From early July to mid-August, Hampshire lost nine consecutive matches, equalling their record of 1904. The run included a thrilling finish at Portsmouth against Nottinghamshire when Hampshire led by 62 (Heath 6-80) but were put out for 148. Nottinghamshire lost wickets regularly to Herman and Hill but had levelled the scores when the ninth wicket fell. Nottinghamshire's last pair scrambled leg-byes to win the game.

Herman and Knott took over 100 wickets. Knott played his first full season and appeared for the Gentlemen v Players and in the Test Trial. Hill's 49 wickets came at less than 20 apiece. The match against Northamptonshire at Portsmouth was badly rain-affected and Northamptonshire declared late on the second day. The two teams walked out to begin the Hampshire innings when the umpires realised the declaration contravened a rule about timings of declarations. The players returned to the pavilion and Northamptonshire resumed their first innings, closing day two on 108-4. The match was drawn. Play was delayed at Swansea when a heat haze covered the ground. Yorkshire came to Bournemouth having just won the title and Hampshire beat them for the first time since 1932, by ten wickets. Knott took 8-111 in the match and no batsman made 50.

In 1946, Pothecary was the only Hampshire player over 40, but by 1948 Bailey, Herman and Arnold had reached that landmark in an ageing side – as did Hill in 1953 and Cannings in 1959. Hampshire played a first-class (but not Championship) match against Surrey at Kingston in September to raise funds for the renovation of the Oval but the third day was rained off. Fifty schoolboys attended Easter Coaching, including ACD (Colin) Ingleby-Mackenzie. Hampshire enjoyed a record summer with 3,694 members and 91,619 paying spectators. The Jubilee Appeal realised £5,590 and additional gross income was £14,457, with a profit of £1,116. Portsmouth organised the first of the local sub-committees and theirs is one of three still active in 2013 (with North & Borders and Southampton).

1947

Champions: Middlesex.

Batsmen Gilbert and Howard Dawson (not related) arrived from the north following a scouting trip and three bowlers, local youngsters Macey and Mervyn Burden and another northerner, Derek Shackleton, joined the staff. John Taylor and Leo Harrison had been 'demobbed' and were available.

This was one of the 'great' English cricket seasons as crowds flocked in on sunny days after a dreadful winter and Compton and Edrich dominated the sports pages. MCC reported that three million spectators watched English first-class cricket during the season. However, the season was less happy for Hampshire, who won four of 26 matches (three at Portsmouth) and finished next-to-bottom, although history was made when the match between Hampshire and Lancashire at Bournemouth ended in a tie, the first in the county's history. Lancashire batted one man short in the second innings and the final wicket was a run out from the fourth ball of the last possible over.

Cliff Walker made his debut for Yorkshire v Hampshire at Bradford, scoring 91 & 21* – he later joined Hampshire, playing for them from 1949–1954. In the return match at Bournemouth, Len Hutton's 270* was the season's highest Championship score, while MM Walford's 264 for Somerset v Hampshire at Weston-Super-Mare was third highest. Clearly the bowlers struggled – Heath's 74 wickets were the highest, while between then, Knott and Herman managed only a third of their previous season's total. Hampshire turned to the 30-year-old amateur Vic Ransom, whose 54 wickets at 27.22 topped the averages.

McCorkell, Arnold and for the first time, Rogers, passed 1,000 runs, all averaging above 35. Rogers was dismissed four times in the nineties before reaching his first century. Eagar scored his first century and fielded superbly. JE Manners had played four first-class matches for the county in 1936; 11 years later, in August 1947, he played his next first-class match for the Combined Services v Gloucestershire, from where he went straight to Canterbury and scored 121 for Hampshire. He would play only two more Championship matches for the county, both in 1948. In the same Kent match, schoolmaster Rev. JR (John) Bridger scored 65 & 43 but Hampshire lost by an innings. Dean set a Hampshire record in holding seven catches in the match at Colchester.

Basil Bowyer captained the 2nd XI and Club & Ground sides. The Club & Ground won 23 of their 32 matches and lost none. At the season's end, the county side visited the Isle of Wight. An open day of coaching in April attracted more than 2,000 schoolboys. The target of 5,000 members was achieved, and 113,078 spectators paid to watch matches in Hampshire, an all-time record for the county. The annual turnover had reached £20,000 with a surplus of £564. A library of 500 cricket books was established at the County Ground. Ernie Knights, who had been on the staff from the 1930s, was appointed Head Groundsman. Mr WL Sprankling retired after 28 years with the club and was presented with a cheque for £873. RCL ('Dick') Court became joint Secretary with Eagar. Following Portsmouth's lead, more local sub-committees were set up around the county – in total, 14 had now been established, although the AGM reported "the lack of petrol makes their work difficult".

1948

Champions: Glamorgan.

Hampshire won nine matches, rising to ninth place and it might have been better but they won just one of their last ten games. The outstanding player, Jim Bailey, at the age of 40, completed the 'double' for the first time, scoring 1,399 runs (31.79) with 121 wickets (18.13). He was the last Hampshire player to do this. In the match against Leicestershire at Southampton, he had match figures of 150 runs and 11-91, while at Lord's he took 5-26 in 22 overs against Middlesex.

Other than England in one Test, Hampshire were the only side to lead the Australians on first innings, although they lost by eight wickets. They won a thrilling match against Kent at Southampton by two wickets, reaching 127-8 in the 21st over. On 19 June a hailstorm halted play in the match at Bath. Glamorgan clinched their first Championship title at Bournemouth, taking 14 wickets on the final day after the first day was almost entirely washed out. Glamorgan won by an innings, Clay taking 9-79 in the match.

The most important moment of the season came neither on the field nor in Committee but in the nets, after the Chairman gave instructions that every player should bowl with pace and Hampshire discovered that their young leg-spinner, Derek Shackleton, had opened the bowling in club cricket and had an aptitude for it. In that first season he took just 17 wickets at 30.52 but thereafter over 100 every year until he retired in 1968. In addition to Bailey, Arnold, Gilbert Dawson, Rogers and Eagar passed 1,000 runs while Knott took 89 wickets. With McCorkell injured, the amateur Jack Andrews kept briefly, after which Harrison showed promise as McCorkell's deputy.

Recruitment of players was limited by regulations to boys under 18, men leaving the forces or men already playing professional cricket, while at 18, most boys went to National Service for two years. Hampshire approached AF Rae but he won his place in the West Indies Test side. A number of amateurs came and went; Hebden played occasionally for Hampshire although AC Shirreff, who had played in 1946–1947, did not play again. He played at Portsmouth for the Combined Services against Hampshire in 1949 and from 1950 for Kent. Exton, who played in 1946, had suffered a serious illness and did not play again, while Guard returned in 1949 but not thereafter. Ransom continued to appear but with less success in 1948 and 1949 and the only regular amateurs were Eagar and Knott.

From 1 January, the club had taken direct control of the Dean Park, Bournemouth ground, with Col RAW Binny as manager and Frank Doran as Groundsman. Five cricketers, J Arnold, J Bailey, OW Herman, G Hill and N McCorkell, were granted a three-year joint benefit. Hampshire adopted a new sweater with blue and gold V and waistband – plus a capped players' tie and a 2nd XI cap. Membership rose to 5,875 with 107,849 paying spectators, while the receipts for the tourist match were a record at £2,147.

1949

Champions (joint): Middlesex & Yorkshire.

Hampshire won six of their 26 matches (three in August) but dropped back to next-to-bottom – a disappointing season despite the fact that seven batsmen scored 1,000 runs for Hampshire, a record for the county.

In the Spring Annual of The *Cricketer*, Hampshire confirmed that their "long term policy" was to develop their own players but admitted that "the great need at the moment is the ready-made player" as Cliff Walker arrived from Yorkshire together with Alan Rayment, a young batsman who had played some 2nd XI matches in his native Middlesex. Local pace bowler RA ('Dick") Carty joined the staff and made his debut.

McCorkell led the batsmen with 1,871 runs at just under 40. Shackleton, for the first time, and Knott both took 100 wickets. Ransom and Heath played rarely and Herman not at all as some of the senior players approached the point of retirement. Bailey had another effective year but this was his last full season.

Hampshire entered the Minor Counties Championship, captained by BGW Bowyer and finished third with Gray as their leading run-scorer. The New Zealanders required 109 runs to win the match at Southampton in just 35 minutes and won with five minutes to spare in 11.5 overs. Middlesex scored 640 runs in their two innings v Hampshire at Bournemouth, during which Blake, in his second match (and first Championship match) for the county, did not concede one bye. McCorkell played as a batsman but retired ill in the second innings.

On 6 June, the President, HS Altham unveiled a War Memorial. Gates totalled £8,539 with 11,000 fewer paying customers through the gates and membership stood at 5,635, a slight fall. There was a deficit of nearly £2,000.

When Sam Staples left Hampshire as coach to join the list of first-class umpires, the county made an important decision, replacing him with Arthur Holt. Staples was unwell and resigned as an umpire after one year. He died in his native Nottinghamshire in June 1950, aged just 57, and was buried in a war grave with his son Roy, who had been killed in action in the Second World War.

On 19 September, Hampshire played a one-day, single innings match against the Duke of Edinburgh's XI at Bournemouth – 10,000 spectators attended the match, held to raise funds for the

National Playing Fields XI, and the Duke's XI won by one wicket when the captain dropped RWV Robins. The Duke of Edinburgh dismissed Gilbert Dawson (c Brown 31) and was bowled by Gerry Hill after scoring 12: Hampshire 254-8 declared (61.3 overs, Rogers 93), Duke's XI 255-9 (48.4 overs, Squires 80).

1950

Champions: (joint) Lancashire & Surrey.

Hampshire won just one more match than in 1949 but those seven victories took them up to 12th place. This were a number of significant changes – not least that Hampshire-born Vic Cannings joined Shackleton as an opening bowler; in his second match he took 7-52 v Oxford University. Herman, Dean, Heath, Gilbert Dawson, Bailey and Taylor left Hampshire, Shirreff joined Kent and Ralph O Prouton joined the MCC staff. Mid-way through the season Arnold's ill health ended his career. As a consequence, Hampshire fielded the youngest side in the Championship.

Arnold, Rogers, Walker and McCorkell passed 1,000 runs, while Shackleton and Knott took over 100 wickets and Cannings 83. Writing about the team's prospects for the next season, Eagar admitted that this "inexperienced" side suffered particularly from inconsistent batting. He identified five young players as being the brightest prospects for the future, Shackleton, Harrison, Gray, Rayment and Alexander Debnam. Some of these young players appeared in the Minor Counties Championship where Blake topped the batting averages and run scorers, while Debnam and Jewell were leading wicket takers.

Hampshire's match v Kent at Southampton was tied, with both sides batting for exactly 137 overs in the match and close scores in the four innings: Kent 162 & 170, Hampshire 180 & 152. Hampshire reached 152 after being 131-9, thanks to Knott and Cannings. Shackleton was the first Hampshire player to be selected for England since Arnold in 1931. He played against the West Indies at Trent Bridge, top-scoring in the first innings. Rogers was selected as 12th man for both sides in the Test Trial at Bradford, where Jim Laker took 8-2. At Leicester, Shackleton took five wickets in nine balls.

In the match against the West Indians at Southampton the tourists scored 539-4 in 142 overs on the first day, Weekes 246* and Roy E Marshall, on his first match in the county, 135. There was no play on the second day and on the third Rogers hit the first ball for six and completed his century before lunch – the match was drawn. At Eastbourne Sussex needed 98 runs to win but were dismissed for 38, with Knott's figures 7-4-5-5. Knott also achieved the 'hat-trick' for the Gentlemen v Players at Lord's and took over 100 wickets.

Mr WJ Arnold replaced Mr W Pearce as Chairman. The joint benefit for five players realised £7,352. Membership again dropped slightly to 5,496 while gates brought £8,439. The accounts showed a significant improvement on the previous year although partly as a consequence of £1,493 from Test receipts, which exceeded expectations, and a slightly lower amount from the winter Whist Drives. Despite a wet second day, the tourist match at Southampton realised £1,574 – otherwise, only the Sussex match at Portsmouth (£795) reached 50% of that amount.

1951

Champions: Warwickshire.

The AGM was informed of the death of Hampshire-born AJL Hill, who played in Hampshire's first Championship match, was their first England Test cricketer and had also been Chairman and President of the Club. Hampshire won just five matches but finished ninth. Rogers was just short of 2,000 runs with five centuries and Gray and Harrison passed 1,000 for the first time alongside McCorkell and Walker. Shackleton and Cannings each passed 100 wickets and Knott took 69.

RCL Court, who had played before the war and subsequently joined the administrative staff, left the county and Col Binny replaced him as Joint Secretary. Mervyn Burden, Malcolm Heath and Peter Sainsbury joined as full professionals. Ray Pitman and Dennis McCorkell left for National Service and John Newman and Ray Flood joined the groundstaff.

Hampshire made a very good start to the season and after three consecutive victories Hampshire were briefly top of the Championship and they were not beaten until the eleventh match of the season, at Worthing. Poor weather did not help the side in the closing weeks.

During the match at Chesterfield, the two sides stood in silence to mark the death of Lord Tennyson. When Knott bowled to Sir Derrick Bailey (Gloucestershire) at Portsmouth, the ball struck and killed a butterfly, which was later mounted and presented to the bowler. In his final match for the county v Sussex at Bournemouth, McCorkell was allowed to captain the side. When he retired, his total of 685 dismissals was a Hampshire record. Debnam played a few matches but did not return. Young batsman Colin Ingleby-Mackenzie was dismissed without scoring in his single and debut innings. He played alongside HM ('Mike') Barnard, Burden, Sainsbury and Heath in the 2nd XI.

MG Melle, who toured with the South Africans, was the son of the former Hampshire player BG Melle. Shackleton played in the fifth Test Match, taking Melle's wicket. Shackleton also toured India with MCC in the winter and played in another Test Match. Rogers was nominated 12th man for England at the Oval.

The 2nd XI played ten matches in the Minor Counties Championship, including Sussex at Newport, Isle of Wight. There was also a full programme of Club & Ground fixtures with matches against a variety of sides including Old Tauntonians, Portsmouth & Southsea, Sydenhurst Ramblers, Trojans, Petersfield, Havant, Hayling Island, Deanery, Romsey, Aldershot, Fareham, Southampton, Stoats and Hampshire Hogs.

There was a slight fall in membership and paying spectators and an overall loss of £800, not least because of the poor weather. Funds were boosted by £1,400 from the Whist Drives held during the winter.

1952

Champions: Surrey.

Hampshire won seven of their 28 matches but in a generally fine summer, finished 12th. A number of younger players showed promise for the future following recent departures of many senior men. Rogers was the first Hampshire batsman to pass 2,000 runs for the county since the war and reached 10,000 career runs in his seventh season. Gray opened the batting and enjoyed his best season with 1,634 runs plus 48 wickets, Harrison, Rayment and Eagar all passed 1,000 runs while Shackleton and Cannings took over 100 wickets and bowled over 2,000 overs between them. Prouton was the regular wicket-keeper following McCorkell's retirement. Off-spinner Reg Dare from Dorset scored 627 runs with 56 wickets but Knott played infrequently. Ingleby-Mackenzie played in six games and finished third in the batting averages.

Shackleton, 12-67 and Cannings, 8-55 bowled unchanged through the match against Kent at Southampton – the first occasion in first-class cricket since 1935. Hampshire won as Kent were dismissed for 32 & 91, the first innings being then the lowest-ever v Hampshire. Against Worcestershire at Bournemouth, Hampshire scored 475-9 in 127 overs (Dare 109) and the following match v India came to a thrilling conclusion. Ingleby-Mackenzie scored 91 but the tourists led by 101. Eagar declared at 206-8 and, chasing 106 in a maximum of 20 overs, India lost wickets regularly (Shackleton 6-41) and finished six runs short with eight wickets lost.

Hampshire competed in the Minor Counties Championship for the last time – withdrawing for economic reasons. The Hampshire & Isle of Wight Cricket Council was established. Former Hampshire cricketer R Aird was appointed Secretary of the MCC. Membership fees were raised and resulted in the loss of about 1,000 members – the total falling to 4,112 – although membership income increased, as did daily revenue from paying spectators. There was a small profit of just under £200, helped by a sum over £1,500 from the third annual Whist Drive. George Heath received £606 from his Testimonial. He had retired having taken 404 wickets at below 30 and with a batting average of 5.58, the lowest by any Hampshire player playing more than 50 matches. Don Roper, who had played one match for Hampshire in 1947, appeared for Arsenal's losing side in the FA Cup Final v Newcastle.

1953

Champions: Surrey.

Hampshire started quite strongly but declined in July and August and, winning one match fewer, slipped to 14th, although they continued to give opportunities to the next generation who would bring the greatest success to the county.

Southampton footballer Henry Horton, who had played for Worcestershire, joined the staff and played in half the matches – with modest success. Roy Marshall also arrived and while qualifying for the Championship, made his first-class debut for Hampshire v MCC. In his third match he hit five sixes in an innings of 71 v Australians, and took 4-68 in the first innings. In that match, Cannings dismissed WA Johnston for the only time on the tour; the first-day crowd was estimated at 15,000 with the boundaries shortened to accommodate them. In a non first-class match Marshall scored 122 and took 7-50 v the Army.

Walker, Gray and Rogers passed 1,000 runs although the latter lost form after injuring a finger, while Knott averaged 13.71 with the ball but also suffered injury and appeared in just seven matches. Shackleton and Cannings again passed 100 wickets and Gray took 64. Barnard made his debut and Harrison replaced Prouton as wicket-keeper during the season although the amateur David Blake also 'kept' in seven games.

Hampshire played two intriguing matches in a week v Leicestershire. At Leicester they lost Knott and Harrison through injury and ten wickets fell for 47 as they trailed the home side by 111. Shackleton (6-49) and Cannings (4-23) then dismissed them for 84 and Rogers and Gray took Hampshire to 134-0 at the close, winning the next day by nine wickets. In the return at Portsmouth, Shackleton took 6-48 and Leicestershire 91 all out trailed Hampshire 370-7 declared (Walker 101*). Leicestershire slumped to 125-8 on the third day with Walsh unable to bat. Then the rain delayed play for 75 minutes after which captain Charlie Palmer (101*) and number 11, Goodwin (23*) resisted for over two hours and earned a draw.

On Coronation Day, 2 June, Hampshire and Gloucestershire played their third and final day v Gloucestershire at Bristol. Gloucestershire resumed their first innings and took the lead – Jack Crapp 103, wicket-keeper Wilson 94, Jimmy Gray 3-46. The game meandered to a draw (Hampshire 62-2) after Rogers retired hurt without scoring –Tom Graveney took both wickets (2-16).

Derek Shackleton dismissed JD Clay of Nottinghamshire with the 1,000,000th ball bowled for the county. Against Glamorgan he took 9-77. In the match at Portsmouth, Gloucestershire's wicket-keeper AE Wilson held 10 catches, then a World Record in first-class cricket. It was equalled *against* Hampshire by Derbyshire's Bob Taylor in 1963 and for Hampshire by Parks (1981) and Aymes (1989).

The Australian tour and England's success created considerable interest in cricket and Hampshire made a profit of £1,930 – the best financial results in their history to that point. Membership stood at 4,644 and over 100,000 spectators paid at the gate. Mr WK Pearce was the first man to be appointed Life Vice President.

1954

Champions: Surrey.

In a season of dreadful weather, Hampshire won just four matches and finished 14th. In eight innings they were dismissed for less than 100, and in another 10, for less than 175.

Shackleton bowled 54 overs unchanged v Sussex at Worthing (54-29-60-4). Rogers carried his bat four times in the season; only CJB Wood of Leicestershire has done so more often in one season. Rogers, Gray and Eagar passed 1,000 runs and Cannings took 100 wickets. Shackleton took 94 for the county but passed 100 in all first-class matches. Hampshire were the slowest scoring side in the country, averaging 2.29 runs per over although their bowlers conceded runs at 2.28 per over.

When Eagar broke his thumb in August, the amateur Rev JR Bridger led Hampshire in his absence – he was awarded his cap but did not play again after this year. Hampshire played the Pakistanis for the first time and Portsmouth-born Barnard, just 20, scored his maiden century on his home city ground. 'Nightwatchman' JM Allan scored a century for Oxford University at Oxford. Fifteen thousand, five hundred and ninety-eight watched the Yorkshire match at Bournemouth but this was the wettest season since the war and the total of 73,741 paying spectators was also the lowest in those nine seasons – although only just ahead of the pre-war lowest. The membership was 4,488.

For family reasons Walker was released during the season to return home to Yorkshire, Carty and Prouton left and three capped spin bowlers, Knott, Dare and Hill, all made their final appearances as Hampshire turned increasingly to their new generation of mainly local players. Gerry Hill played 371 first-class matches for Hampshire, more than anyone else who played no other first-class matches for any other side. The departure of Dare was unusual. For a spinner he was young at 32 and in late May he was awarded his cap against Derbyshire after taking 5-49 and scoring 41* & 74 (in 55 minutes) as Hampshire won against the clock. He played regularly until mid-August but then he was gone. Towards the end of the season, young spinners Burden and Sainsbury (the latter having completed his National Service) played with promise, while another local youngster, pace bowler Malcolm Heath (not related to George) headed the bowling averages.

On 11 September, Hampshire, for the second time, played against Duke of Edinburgh's XI, this time at Southampton, and won by three runs. Although they no longer ran a regular 2nd XI side, Hampshire played 36 Club & Ground games. Arthur Holt received around £1,700 from his Testimonial.

1955

Champions: Surrey.

The Runners-Up were Yorkshire but Hampshire finished third for the first time in their history and their 16 victories was a record for the county. The weather was good throughout the season, Hampshire beat 14 of the 16 other counties and their total of 210 points would have won the title in four of the previous six seasons. They won eight of their last nine Championship matches, including a 10-wicket victory over Leicestershire at Bournemouth when Marshall (47*) and Gray scored 71-0 in 52 balls. Hampshire defeated Yorkshire in two days at Bradford where, on his 21st birthday, Sainsbury dismissed Len Hutton twice and Marshall had match figures of 9-50. Hampshire also beat the Champions Surrey at Bournemouth at the end of August; Horton scored 109 in an innings of 368-7 declared and Heath (5-69) and Sainsbury (5-40) bowled them to victory by 129 runs.

Ingleby-Mackenzie kept wicket in one match, deputising for Leo Harrison, who was representing Players v Gentlemen, otherwise Hampshire used just 13 players throughout the season, including Marshall in his first full season. He scored 1,890 runs and led the averages, followed by Horton, Rogers and Gray all past 1,000 and Barnard with 908. Shackleton took 157 wickets at 13.41 and Sainsbury 102 at 18.53 – seven bowlers finished with averages lower than 22 per wicket and Shackleton's total of wickets was the highest since Kennedy in 1923.

The match at Eastbourne v Sussex ended in a tie and Hampshire's captain, Desmond Eagar, became the first man to play in three tied matches in the County Championship. On the third day Hampshire, needing 140 to win, were 84-8, but Sainsbury and Cannings brought the scores level before Sussex took the last two wickets without addition.

Shackleton had innings figures of 8-4 and match figures of 14-29 v Somerset at Weston-Super-Mare, the best match figures for Hampshire since 1927. Somerset scored 135 in their two innings combined, while Rayment scored 104 in one innings for Hampshire. Shackleton also took 10-75 in the match at Lord's. When Fred Titmus scored a century for Middlesex at Bournemouth, it was a year and 10 days since the previous century scored against Hampshire (by George Dawkes for Derbyshire at Burton-on-Trent) – nonetheless, Hampshire won by an innings. Don Kenyon scored the only other century against Hampshire on the last day of the season – and Hampshire won again. Hampshire beat Kent at Canterbury with a wicket from the final ball.

Writing in 1957, Eagar suggested Hampshire's success two years earlier was because they "scored quickly and did not make too many runs … fielded brilliantly and … had the best-balanced attack we have ever possessed".

The gates were closed on a capacity crowd for the first day of the match v South Africans. Membership increased to 4,573 and paying spectators numbered 111,330, second only to the 1947 figure. The good financial results enabled seating improvements at the two grounds and a new office block at Southampton. A Diamond Jubilee appeal was launched. During the season Hampshire scored their 500,000th run and held their 10,000th catch. With Eagar injured, Rogers captained the side in the last five Championship matches of the season, winning them all, but, disappointed by the offer of a short contract, accepted employment in the winter and retired. He was awarded a Testimonial in 1956 and received £1,696. Desmond Eagar was now sole Secretary, a position he held until his death in late 1977.

1956

Champions: Surrey.

Hampshire won nine matches and finished sixth. Ingleby-Mackenzie missed matches through injury but led the averages, while Gray, Horton, Marshall and Rayment all passed 1,000 runs. Shackleton took 134 wickets and he and Cannings averaged less than 20 per wicket, but Rogers had retired and neither Sainsbury's bowling nor Marshall's batting was as effective as in 1955. The weather was poor with nearly 100 hours lost and the side suffered more injuries but while they had declined from third in 1955, only twice had Hampshire finished higher than sixth.

Hampshire beat the Champions Surrey once more, this time at Portsmouth despite being bowled out for 191 & 71 (having been 17-6). They dismissed them for 126 (Burden 6-23) & 108 (Marshall 6-36), while only Gray, who opened on the Saturday morning, passed 50. Hampshire played their first match at Cowes IOW v Worcestershire. They scored 370-7 declared with an undefeated century from Ingleby-Mackenzie and enforced the follow-on but dropped catches and could not conclude with victory. Hampshire defeated Oxford University by one run when Cannings took two wickets with the last two balls.

Guy Jewell had played one match for Hampshire in 1952. This year playing for Basingstoke & North Hants CC against twelve of Bedford CC, he took every wicket, 11-52, possibly a record in Hampshire club cricket.

Two hundred and fifty boys attended Easter Coaching. Early in the season the new Office Block was opened in a ceremony with HS Altham and Phil Mead. Membership had risen above 5,000 as a result of the success of 1955 and an Australian summer in 1956. Income from Members' Subscriptions was nearly £9,000, gate receipts from 85,000 paying spectators was about £1,000 more and the surplus was £2,652.

1957

Champions: Surrey

In seven seasons from 1955–1961 Hampshire had a run of unprecedented success, although 1960 and 1957 were exceptions. In 1957, Hampshire won seven matches, finishing 13th. Desmond Eagar retired after his 12th and final season as the senior county captain, handing over to Ingleby-Mackenzie.

Fourteen men played regularly, with brief opportunities for David ('Butch') White, Bernard Harrison, Derek Tulk and Colin Roper. Marshall, Gray, Horton and Ingleby-Mackenzie passed 1,000 runs but Barnard was still splitting his time between county cricket and First Division football with Portsmouth FC and in his absence the close catching suffered. Nonetheless, Sainsbury held 56 catches – a county record for one season. Except for Shackleton, the bowlers were more expensive than in recent seasons. Marshall hit the season's fastest century in 66 minutes v Kent at Southampton and in an innings defeat against the Champions at Portsmouth he scored 56 & 111 – excluding extras, 49.8% of Hampshire's runs in the match.

In May, Hampshire lost to Essex in a low-scoring match dominated by Trevor Bailey who scored 59 & 71* and had match figures of 14-81. In June, Middlesex beat Hampshire by 116 runs. In the first innings Cannings dismissed Denis Compton, as he frequently did – Compton was Vic's 'bunny' to the extent that Vic played in Compton's Benefit Match, on his side. This was revenge for Middlesex as, in early May, Hampshire won a thrilling victory when the two sides met at Portsmouth. In a low-scoring game, Middlesex required 244 to win; Robertson opened with 49 and three men passed 50 but none achieved more than Compton's 52. At 207-5 Middlesex were favourites to win, but the last pair needed 12 and could manage only eight. Shackleton took 5-31 & 6-41. Overall he took 144 first-class wickets and enjoyed match figures of 14-111 at Old Trafford, yet Lancashire won with some ease, recovering from 16-4 thanks to a century from Geoff Pullar. In mid-July not a ball was bowled in the match at Swansea.

Leo Harrison took his benefit in 1957 and received a Hampshire record of £3,188. Although not competitive, the 2nd XI played a fairly full fixture list against the other southern counties. Membership remained above 5,000 and Hampshire County Cricket Supporters Club was formed. The club's official history, *Hampshire County Cricket*, by EDR Eagar, J Arlott, HS Altham and R Webber, was published. After 12 post-war seasons Hampshire were 11th in the aggregate Championship, with Surrey first and Somerset last.

1958

Champions: Surrey.

Colin Ingleby-Mackenzie's first season as captain was a very wet one, especially in August, and Hampshire lost over 100 scheduled hours. Nonetheless, they led the Championship table for long periods and finished second for the first time in their history.

Marshall, Gray, Horton and Ingleby-Mackenzie all passed 1,000 runs in a bowler-friendly season – indicated by the records of Shackleton with 163 wickets at 15.31 and Heath (126 at 16.42). In his benefit season, Shackleton's figure was a record for Hampshire in a post-war season – and he was awarded £5,000. Only Kennedy and Newman ever took more, five times in total and all between

1920–1923. In 1958, six bowlers averaged less than 22.5 and Sainsbury, with 715 runs, 46 wickets (20.76) and 43 catches, made an excellent all-round contribution. The captain hit the fastest century of the season and was elected Young Player of the Year by the Cricket Writers Club.

From 21 May to 12 August only one match was lost and it seemed that Hampshire might win their first title. They beat Kent in the traditional early August Bank Holiday match at Canterbury, drew the next two and then went to Burton, where Shackleton and Heath bowled unchanged in the match, dismissed them twice for 74 & 107, yet Hampshire lost by 103 runs, having been bowled out for 23, their second lowest Championship innings. This was the last instance of two Hampshire bowlers bowling unchanged through a match. Barnard top-scored in both innings with five and 16, which may be a county record, and the match aggregate of 259 runs is the lowest in a Hampshire match in which all 40 wickets fell.

Hampshire won the next match at Clacton, lost at Eastbourne and failed to win their last three matches. Derbyshire beat them again in the final game, and in four innings against Derbyshire they managed just 435 runs, while Jackson took 20 wickets for 91 runs. Despite that, this was a fine season under a new captain and John Arlott suggested, "no other county team enjoyed the cricket of 1958 so hugely as Hampshire" *(Playfair Cricket Annual)*.

Alan Rayment retired – he would later take a coaching position at Lord's – while a younger batsman, Hampshire-born BL (Barry) Reed, made his debut. He would return more regularly in the late 1960s. Shackleton took his benefit and was awarded £5,000, at the time a club record. Phil Mead died during the winter preceding the season and Desmond Eagar published a tribute in the *Handbook*. Eagar was Assistant Manager of the MCC tour of Australia and New Zealand 1958–1959 but England lost the series 4-0 and with that, the Ashes.

The *Cricketer* Spring Annual reported from the Special Committee set up by the MCC to Examine the Amateur Status in English Cricket. The Committee was chaired by the Duke of Norfolk and from Hampshire included Desmond Eagar, Harry Altham and the Secretary, Ronnie Aird. They emphasised the "wish to preserve in first-class cricket the leadership and general approach to the game traditionally associated with the Amateur player" but recognised that in the modern world most amateurs can no longer afford to play "entirely at their own expense". The Committee rejected the idea of abolishing the amateur/professional distinction but expressed concern at the "over liberal interpretation of the word expenses".

1959

Champions: Yorkshire.

At the start of the season, *Wisden* selected Shackleton and Marshall as two of their five Cricketers of the Year. By contrast with 1958, this was a glorious summer, yet ironically the first season in which wickets were covered, although this first experiment was retracted after a few seasons. Hampshire won 11 of their 28 matches but slipped to eighth place although they were in contention until mid-August when an exciting drawn match v Surrey at Portsmouth effectively ended the London county's seven year reign as Champions and Hampshire's challenge.

Marshall, Gray and Horton all passed 2,000 runs for the season – the first time three men had achieved this for Hampshire – while Gray was the first Hampshire-born man to do so. Dennis

Baldry joined Hampshire from Middlesex and scored 151 on debut v Glamorgan at Portsmouth, the second man to do so for Hampshire. To date there have been four more, but not one was making his *first-class* debut. Wicket-keeper Leo Harrison dismissed 83 batsmen, a record for the county. During the season Shackleton bowled more overs for the county than any bowler has ever done but his partnership with Vic Cannings ended when the latter accepted a coaching post at Eton College following his Benefit season (£3,787).

Hampshire beat the reigning Champions Yorkshire at Bournemouth by just 28 runs when Heath bowled Wood in the final over – their first home victory against them since 1946. In the next match they beat Middlesex in the first-ever Championship match at Hornsey, scoring 190-8 in 40 overs.

Hampshire joined the new 2nd XI competition and White took four wickets in four balls against Gloucestershire 2nd XI at Southampton. The leading players included Daintes Abbias ('Danny') Livingstone, BRS (Bernard) Harrison, BSV (Bryan) Timms, AR (Alan) Wassell and White – under the captaincy of Arthur Holt.

The new indoor school opened at the County Ground during the winter of 1959–1960. HS Altham was elected as President of the MCC.

1960

Champions: Yorkshire.

The weather was very poor throughout the summer; Desmond Eagar described it as the "worst summer weather in living memory". For the third consecutive season, the Test series (v South Africa) was one-sided and poorly attended. The series was blighted by the regular no-balling of South Africa's Geoff Griffin and this led to a degree of anxiety around the subject. At Hove, umpire Paul Gibb no-balled White for the only time in his career.

Hampshire made a good start, winning five of the first nine matches, and in mid-June they were third in the table. After this they won only three of the remaining 23 matches and they finished 12th.

Despite this disappointing finish, Marshall and Horton both passed 2,000 runs, Gray came close again and Sainsbury passed 1,000, to which he added 71 wickets. Shackleton took 130 wickets and for the first time White passed 100 wickets (124 at 19.10). On the final afternoon v Warwickshire at Portsmouth, Shackleton had a spell of 6-0 in five overs and finished with his career best figures of 9-30. Gray was awarded his benefit and chose the match v Middlesex at Portsmouth when he and Marshall put on 249 for the first wicket – a county record. Hampshire lost only two wickets and won the match by an innings, which was a record margin of victory for the county. Gray received £4,350.

In the match v Oxford University, White scored 28 runs from an over by off-spinner JD ('Dan') Piachaud, who later in the summer played for Hampshire with his University colleague CA (Charles) Fry, son of S Fry and grandson of CB Fry – the first occasion that three generations of one family represented the same county. Leo Harrison struggled with injury and he and BSV (Bryan) Timms each played 17 matches.

Hampshire's match v Derbyshire in August was their 1,500th in first-class cricket – estimated then only since 1895. Middlesex won by one wicket at Lord's, the third occasion on which that result had occurred for Hampshire. Hampshire scored 82 & 180, Middlesex 182 & 82-9, Shackleton 11-81.

H Wildeman replaced F Doran as groundsman at Bournemouth. There were 5,382 members and record receipts of over £10,000. However, at the end of the year and despite around £5,000 from the Board of Control, Hampshire reported a loss of £5,835 and over the previous three years in excess of £10,000. Desmond Eagar called it "disastrous" and the Hon Treasurer JP Burnett suggested to the AGM (March 1961), "another year like this and the county club will be pretty well out of play".

Yet, in the six years before the war, spectators averaged 71,420 *per annum* with 2,234 members. By contrast, while figures had declared from the immediate post-war period, the six years to the end of 1960 showed an average of 82,811 spectators and 5,073 members. Cricket had grown in popularity post-war but costs had risen more. Other counties were in a similar position and English cricket hoped for good weather in the next 'Ashes' season and considered again the possibility of a knock-out competition. Eagar, in a article in *Playfair Cricket Monthly* (March 1961), wondered whether cricket was "too cheap" and stressed that "membership is our life's blood … one third of our total income comes from this source".

1961

Champions: Hampshire.

For the first time in their history, Hampshire won the County Championship when, at 4.08pm on 1 September 1961, they beat Derbyshire at Bournemouth. John Arlott wrote in the *Hampshire Handbook* (1962) that "it was not only the peak season of most of the players but also the fruition of a studied team-building programme which the Committee – particularly Harry Altham and Cecil Paris – and Desmond Eagar carried out on a meagre budget … The result was a team deep in run-making power, soundly equipped at all points of attack and in which every man was worth his place – a true Championship side".

In the same publication, Desmond Eagar wrote that after his 16 years at the club "we can rejoice that all the hopes and dreams of these post-war years have come true at last". In the decisive match, there were important innings from Gray, Marshall, Sainsbury and Barnard, while Wassell took five first innings wickets but the key was Shackleton. On the last afternoon, on a largely unresponsive pitch, his figures were 24-10-39-6.

Hampshire won 19 matches, the highest number in their history and despite the myths about the captain's declarations, 15 were won by taking 20 wickets, one more with 19 (a first innings declaration) and only three against declarations: at the Oval, when because of an experimental rule, Surrey could not enforce the follow-on, at Cowes, when Essex set a target, not least because Marshall was injured, and at Portsmouth, when Hampshire won a thrilling finish against Gloucestershire after rain cost the whole of the second day. Overall Hampshire lost just under 40 hours to rain in 32 matches. In the match at Cowes, Ingleby-Mackenzie's century and highest first-class score was key to victory after Hampshire, set 241 to win, slumped to 35-4 & 121-5. Wassell, promoted in the order, helped his captain add 50 and then Marshall batting at eight and Ingleby-Mackenzie (132*) took Hampshire to victory.

Marshall, Gray and Horton all passed 2,000 runs, while Livingstone, Sainsbury, Barnard, Baldry and the captain brought a new stability to the middle order. Marshall received £5,865 from his benefit and his 212 v Somerset at Bournemouth was Hampshire's first double century for a decade. Against the same opponents at Frome, Burden took 8-38 and 12 wickets in the match.

Shackleton passed 150 wickets, White 100 and Burden, Wassell, Heath and Sainsbury over 50 each. Fourteen men formed the essential Championship-winning side, with Baldry and Barnard competing for one batting slot and Burden, Heath and Wassell offering bowling options. Leo Harrison suffered an injury, which gave opportunities to Timms before the captain had a few matches keeping wicket. Bernard Harrison deputised when Marshall was injured and scored his first century in first-class cricket v Oxford University at Portsmouth. White contributed significantly to two important victories at Portsmouth, first in that match v Gloucestershire with big hitting in the final overs and then v Sussex in the second match of the August Portsmouth week. Very late on the second evening Sussex, who had trailed by 38, were 179-4 in their second innings. In gloomy weather White took a hat-trick and four in the over (plus a dropped catch denying him a county record four in four). Sussex added just one leg bye on Friday morning and Hampshire won easily.

In the winter of 1961–1962, White played for England on tour of India and Pakistan.

1962

Champions: Yorkshire.

Hampshire's Championship-winning team represented the Duke of Norfolk's XI in the first match of Pakistan's tour at Arundel and raised the Champions flag for the first time. The match was drawn: Norfolk's XI 204-6 declared (Marshall 61, Horton 55, Farooq 4-42) Pakistanis 173-6 (Intikhab 45).

The same 14 men represented Hampshire for most of the season and this first draw was to indicate the pattern for a season in which the Champions failed to challenge again. They won seven matches but drew 19 and ended in 10th place. Ingelby-Mackenzie's eight years as captain split neatly into two halves; four successful years leading to the title and four years when they slipped to the bottom half.

The batting remained strong. Gray, in his benefit year, scored 2,224 runs with a highest score of 213*, Marshall also passed 2,000 runs, while Horton and Livingstone were close and Sainsbury and Barnard passed 1,000 with the captain just three short. Shackleton took 160 wickets in 1596.1 overs – a Hampshire record in one season – but White, after problems with injury on the winter tour, could manage only 71 at 30.67 each. The three spinners passed 50 wickets but, apart from Shackleton, the bowlers all averaged in the high twenties or beyond. Victories were elusive.

Livingstone and leg-spinner Alan Castell shared a ninth wicket partnership of 230 v Surrey at Southampton, a county record, after Livingstone was dropped on Lock's hat-trick ball. In May, Hampshire played their final match at Cowes, IOW, which ended in a frustrating draw. Worcestershire, set 291 to win, were 99 short with two wickets and 10 minutes remaining when rain drove the players from the field.

A number of players suffered from injuries and at the season's end Baldry and Heath retired, the first of the Champions to depart. Among the promising 2nd XI players were GL ('Geoff') Keith (Hampshire born but from Somerset), RG ('Bob') Caple (from Middlesex), Castell, RMH ('Bob') Cottam and Peter J Haslop – the latter made his first-class debut v Pakistan in a televised match at Bournemouth.

1963

Champions: Yorkshire. Knock-out Cup: Sussex.

1963 was a remarkable year in Britain, including diabolical winter weather that savaged most sporting fixtures for the first two months of the year, the scandal and resignation of Minister John Profumo, the Beatles' first British number one hit records, the sporting end of British 'New Wave' cinema with *This Sporting Life* and the first episode of *Doctor Who* on British television – in the last year before two domestic channels became three.

In cricket, *Wisden* reached its 100th edition, the distinction between amateur and professional cricketers was abolished (and with it went Gentlemen v Players matches) and the English counties' knock-out cup was launched, sponsored by Gillette (65 overs, won by Sussex). The West Indies enjoyed a tremendous tour of England, including one of the great Test matches (at Lord's), and Derek Shackleton was brought back by England for that match and the series, after a gap of 103 matches – the longest ever by an England player. The front-foot no ball law was introduced in English domestic cricket – largely to eliminate dragging. It has now been adopted worldwide.

Hampshire won seven matches and again finished 10th although they lost more games than in 1962. For Hampshire, the knock-out cup began and ended at Bournemouth on Wednesday 22 May with a defeat to Derbyshire. The five-man attack (permitted 15 overs each) was White, Gray, Baldry, Sainsbury and Wassell; chasing 251 to win, they fell seven runs short when Barnard (98) was dismissed from the third ball of the final over. He did not win 'Man-of-the-Match' but received a silver medal as best player on the losing side.

While 10 of the main 12 players had been regulars in 1961, Timms replaced Harrison behind the stumps and Cottam completed Hampshire's finest pace attack. Meanwhile, Caple, Castell and Keith were given opportunities. Marshall (1,800) led the run scorers, Horton, Livingstone, Sainsbury and Gray passed 1,000, and Shackleton took 124 wickets for the county and was recalled by England to play in the last four Test Matches of the summer. On the second morning at Lord's he took three West Indian wickets in four balls. White (94) and Wassell (70) gave main support in the bowling and Castell's leg-spin gathered 28 wickets at 18.85.

Livingstone scored 151 v his fellow-countrymen in the tourist match and at the season's end, in celebration of their Centenary, Hampshire played a three-day first-class match v MCC All England: MCC 264-3 declared (Bolus 73, Watson 62, Parfitt 61*) & 262-5 declared (Parfitt 101) beat Hampshire 194 (Titmus 5-71, Lock 4-36) & 303 (Ingleby-Mackenzie 77, Horton 55, Titmus 6-149) by 29 runs.

Questions were asked about whether the first day (11 September) was the exact centenary date, celebrating the first General Meeting, which approved rules and committee, or whether it should have been the 'glorious' 12 August when the first meeting to form the club was held. The question becomes relevant again in 2013.

Burden and Heath received £1,000 each from a joint Testimonial. Membership stood at just over 6,000 with an income of almost £15,000, while those who paid at the gate contributed £5,705 and there was a tiny profit of just under £200.

1964

Champions: Worcestershire. Knock-out Cup: Sussex.

In many respects even this 'Ashes' season was overshadowed by the previous West Indian 'knockout' summer. Hampshire won just five (of 28) matches and slipped to 12th, equal with Derbyshire. Livingstone, with 1,671 runs at 35.55 led the batting and again Shackleton (142 at 20.40) headed the bowling, but Sainsbury with 57 wickets was the only other to average less than 30, although White had 98 wickets at 30.19. The young spinners Castell and Wassell were less successful and while batsmen Marshall, Horton and Sainsbury passed four figures, Gray took up a teaching post and played fewer matches. Keith, Caple and the captain averaged only around 21.

Shackleton took 8-27 as Gloucestershire were dismissed for 50 at Bristol and White 6-33 as Glamorgan fell for the same total at Portsmouth. Timms equalled Ubsdell's 1865 record, dismissing six batsmen in the first Leicestershire innings at Portsmouth, but the match was lost; only Worcestershire's Roy Booth had more dismissals than Timms over the season. The match v Australia featured another century by Barnard against a touring team and Hampshire, 279-8 at the close, were 30 short of victory. In the next match, at Bournemouth, Hampshire chased 269 to win, Barnard led the way again with 65 but wickets fell regularly until Titmus bowled the last over to the last pair, who needed seven to win. Wassell and Shackleton scored a single from each ball but the sides finished with the scores level. Livingstone scored centuries in both innings in the Bank Holiday draw at Canterbury, while Colin Cowdrey replied with 99 & 100*.

Hampshire won their first 'cup' match against Wiltshire at Chippenham (Cottam 4-9, Sainsbury 3-1) but lost by 178 runs in the next round to Warwickshire. They had their revenge when Warwickshire came to Southampton in late August in pursuit of the title. Hampshire declared twice, losing just eight wickets (Horton 96* & 60*) and, chasing 314 to win, Warwickshire lost by 17 runs. Worcestershire took the title for the first time. Horton, who had first played for Worcestershire received almost £6,000 from his benefit.

On 1 January, Hampshire's former amateur batsman EA English reached his 100th birthday. He was the first Hampshire centurion since the club entered the County Championship, although George Deane, who played once v All England in 1848, had reached his personal century in December 1928.

1965

Champions: Worcestershire. Knock-out Cup: Yorkshire.

Hampshire won five matches and finished 12th, exactly as the previous season – despite some outstanding bowling performances. Shackleton (144 wickets), Cottam, Sainsbury, White and Wassell all averaged under 25 but only Marshall and Horton passed 1,000 runs. Gray had virtually retired, Livingstone lost form, averaging less than 20, and Marshall and Horton, with one each, were the only Championship centurions. Gray had passed 1,000 runs in a season every year from 1951–1962. The *Handbook* suggested that Reed, Keith and Caple showed promise, although the 2nd XI failed to win any matches.

Hampshire dismissed Yorkshire for 23 at Middlesborough – Yorkshire's record lowest score and the lowest by any county against Hants. White took 6-10, then Cottam took 9-25 v Lancashire at Old

Trafford, Hampshire's best-ever first-class figures. In Sainsbury's Benefit Match in July at Bournemouth v Warwickshire, Shackleton had match figures of 58.3-28-99-14, although the match was drawn. On the same ground, there was a controversial end to the match v the eventual Champions Worcestershire at Bournemouth in late August after day two was badly rain-affected. Hampshire, 217-6 declared, replied to Worcestershire's 363-9 declared and after one ball from the captain, Worcestershire set Hampshire 148 to win in good time. On an uncovered wicket, Worcestershire then dismissed Hampshire for 31 in just 16.3 overs with no one reaching double figures.

Sainsbury's benefit realised £6,250. In a Gillette Cup match, he scored 76 and took 7-30 v Norfolk at Southampton, while Henry Bloefeld opened the batting for Norfolk and top-scored with 60. Hampshire won the next round v Kent at Portsmouth but fell again to Warwickshire. The match at Portsmouth was the first limited-overs game there and a rare appearance by Kent on the ground, as they always played Hampshire at Southampton over the Whitsun Bank Holiday. Hampshire played Ireland for the first time.

At Northlands Road, the two pavilions were joined together and completely re-decorated with a new Refreshment Room for lady members. Hampshire's President, historian and former player, HS Altham, died before the start of the season and the new Committee room was named in his honour. In the following year, he was succeeded as President by Lord Porchester.

New dressing rooms were constructed. ACD Ingleby-Mackenzie retired at the end of the season although he appeared subsequently in a few Gillette Cup matches. Arthur Holt, Hampshire's coach and former player, retired. The full membership subscription was three guineas, ladies two guineas and junior members £1. Membership stood just below 6,000. The club made a slight loss of £415.

1966

Champions: Yorkshire. Knock-out Cup: Warwickshire.

Once more Hampshire won just five matches although they moved up one place to 11th. The record included victory over Middlesex at Bournemouth, where they had failed to win any of their previous 24 matches.

Marshall was appointed captain and Leo Harrison coach. The first innings in some County Championship matches was closed compulsorily after 65 overs but the experiment was not a success and was not repeated. At Cardiff, Hampshire dismissed Glamorgan for 167 but at 191-5 their first innings was closed. Glamorgan scored 145 and Don Shepherd took 7-7 to win the match for Glamorgan by 45 runs. Young off-spinning all-rounder Keith Wheatley played in 10 of the 12 limitation matches. In the first innings, he batted five times but never bowled.

Southsea-born, former Winchester schoolboy Barry L Reed had first played for Hampshire in 1958 and now eight years later he had his first full season as Marshall's new opening partner. Both passed 1,000 runs, as did Horton, while Shackleton and White took over 100 wickets and those two and Cottam (61 wickets) averaged under 20 per wicket. Castell had struggled with his leg-break bowling after a promising start and turned to seam bowling – he took 6-49 v Derbyshire at Southampton and 6-69 v Worcestershire at Portsmouth. Teenagers David Turner and Trevor Jesty made their debuts in late August in consecutive matches at Bournemouth and Portsmouth.

Hampshire played Oxford University starting on 30 April, the first time they had played a first-class match in April. The University captain was RMC (Richard) Gilliat. At Trent Bridge, Hampshire took points with scores level as they closed on 237-5 (Reed 72, Horton 66*). Hampshire beat Lincolnshire, Kent and Surrey in the cup competition but lost their first semi-final at Worcester by 99 runs. Ingleby-Mackenzie returned as wicket-keeper for the competition and was 'Man-of-the-Match' v Kent (59*).

Union Castle Line made a presentation of the bell from the SS Athlone Castle to be rung from the pavilion; it is now at the Ageas Bowl. Broadcasting to local hospitals began from the county ground and continues today.

1967

Champions: Yorkshire. Knock-out Cup: Kent.

Hampshire started strongly but had a poor finish. They won five matches again but reverted to 12th in a summer of bad weather. Sainsbury and Marshall passed 1,000 runs with an average over 30, while the four figures of Reed and Livingstone were at around 25 per innings. Shackleton and Cottam (for the first time) passed 100 wickets, White took 95 and Shackleton passed Kennedy's record number of wickets for the county. He received £4,966 from his Testimonial. Gilliat joined from Oxford University and was third in the averages but Horton's career came to a conclusion. He scored 21,536 runs for Hampshire (average 33.49), passed 1,000 runs in every season from 1955–1966 and every run for Hampshire came over the age of 30.

Against Kent, Lancashire and Warwickshire, respectively, Hampshire were dismissed for 31, 39 & 44. Tony Lock had been denied a hat-trick by a dropped catch at Southampton in 1962 but he completed one for his new county Leicestershire at Portsmouth. For the first time ever, some Championship matches included play on a Sunday, although none in the county.

Hampshire played two unusual and contrasting matches v Middlesex. In the first, in July, at Lord's Hampshire scored 421-7 declared in 145 overs and Middlesex replied with 371-7 in 176 overs. There was therefore no conclusion to a match in which both captains were criticised for negative play. D Shackleton's figures were 50-23-84-1. By contrast, when the two teams met at Portsmouth in the following month, the match was tied when RS ('Bob') Herman, then with Middlesex, bowled Cottam with the final ball. Herman, the son of Hampshire cricketer OW Herman, later joined Hampshire. This was Hampshire's fourth and final tied Championship match to date. In the Knock-out Cup, Hampshire beat Lincolnshire and Glamorgan but lost at Hove. Marshall's 102 v Lincolnshire was the first limited-overs century for Hampshire.

Hampshire won the 2nd XI competition for the first time, captained by Leo Harrison and with significant contributions from junior players including Keith Wheatley, Richard Lewis, Jesty, John Holder, Turner and Castell. Hampshire Colt CG (Gordon) Greenidge played in one match. Turner won the county's single-wicket tournament (and again in 1968). At the close of the season Hampshire toured Belgium.

Membership stood high at 6,301 but would decline over the next few years.

1968

Champions: Yorkshire. Knock-out Cup: Warwickshire.

Hampshire won eight matches and rose to fifth. The season opened with counties parading their new, instantly registered overseas players. Hampshire hoped initially to sign Clive Lloyd but when he joined Lancashire, the South African Barry Richards arrived. Of the 1961 Champions, Timms and Shackleton were in their final full seasons and otherwise only four men, Marshall, Sainsbury, White and Livingstone, remained.

In his final full Championship season (one match in 1969) Shackleton completed a record 20 consecutive first-class seasons with 100+ wickets, although Cottam took more (128) and headed the averages. The early matches were rain-affected and low scoring – it was not until the sixth match that either side in a Hampshire match passed 200. Then, in the following 60-over Cup match, Marshall (140) and Reed (112) added 227 for the first wicket v Bedfordshire in a total of 321-4. At this point Richards, batting around number four, had scored a modest 194 runs in eight completed innings (at 24.25). At Northampton in warm weather on 29 May, he opened for the first time, scored 130 & 104* and hardly looked back. He scored 206 v Nottinghamshire at Portsmouth and finished this first season with 2,314 runs at 48.21. Next came Marshall with 1,179 at 26.97, with Reed the only other man to pass 1,000. *Wisden* chose Richards as one of their Cricketers of the Year.

The Bank Holiday match v Kent at Southampton attracted good crowds in warm weather but offered very dull cricket. Kent's first innings of 148 took 69 overs, Hampshire led by 82 in 107 overs and with White injured and unable to bowl, Kent simply batted to 342-8 in 135 overs; throughout the match, the two sides averaged just 2.3 runs per over. A few weeks later at Bournemouth, Hampshire and Gloucestershire failed to average two runs per over in another dull draw.

This was an Ashes summer in which the controversial issue of D'Oliveira's selection for the winter tour of South Africa led to the cancellation of that series and subsequently the termination of Test Matches by South Africa for some decades. MCC (England) did tour Pakistan, and Cottam, who had played for the MCC President's XI v the Pakistanis in August, was selected and made his Test Match debut. He took nine wickets in two Tests at 20 apiece, and the third Test was abandoned due to riots with England on 502-7. Cottam did not retain his place.

Hampshire played 32 first-class matches, 28 in the Championship plus both Universities, Australia and the Rest of the World at Bournemouth, where Richards scored 68 and took 7-63. Hampshire won by 68 runs. During those 32 matches they lost 14 minutes under 130 hours to rain, a higher total than in 2012, although a lower average per match.

Sir Reginald Biddle was the new President. Mike Barnard received £4,212 from his Testimonial. Membership fell just below 6,000. Expenditure had risen by more than 50% in five years and there was a loss of over £8,000. English cricket had a new central management body, the Test and County Cricket Board (TCCB) replacing two previous bodies, The Test Match Board of Control (1898) and the Advisory County Cricket Committee (1904). There was now also the Cricket Council and the National Cricket Association, which, together with the TCCB, covered cricket at all levels in England.

1969

Champions: Glamorgan. Knock-out Cup: Yorkshire. Sunday League: Lancashire.

A year after the arrival of the overseas stars, an even bigger change took place as the counties adopted a limited-overs league competition to be played in 40-over innings on Sunday afternoons. In the early years a special membership rather than entrance fee was charged and on the field, bowlers' run-ups were limited. Hampshire began with two defeats in their first three matches but won nine of the next 10 including a thrilling one-run victory over Leicestershire at Basingstoke with a last ball run-out. Hampshire beat Lancashire in mid-August in front of 12,500 spectators at Old Trafford, but at Portsmouth the following week (estimated at 8,500) they lost. Chasing 196, Richards and Reed reached 93 before the first wicket fell but they were all out for 153. Lancashire took the title with Hampshire runners-up.

The Championship was reduced to 24 three-day matches per team. In the match against Glamorgan at Bournemouth, the Hampshire side left the ground after tea on the last day with no result possible and believing rain had caused the match to be abandoned. The umpires then decided play was possible and the match was awarded to Glamorgan, although on appeal that decision was rescinded. Hampshire finished fifth again with Richards and Gilliat passing 1,000 runs and Cottam 100 wickets. Shackleton played in the Sunday league but only once in the Championship, taking 5-58 v Sussex at Portsmouth – he took 2,669 first-class wickets for Hampshire, a record for the county.

Hampshire struggled with injuries throughout the season with Marshall and Richards missing a number of matches and Marshall's average dropped below 23 in the only season from 1955–1972 that he failed to reach 1,000 runs. Twenty-year-old Turner scored 181* v Surrey at the Oval. Among the bowlers, Castell, bowling medium pace, had a better season to support White and Cottam. White received £4,200 from his benefit.

Turner, Jesty, Greenidge and Lewis enjoyed successful seasons for the 2nd XI. This was the first year of the new Southern Cricket League and Trojans (Southampton) were Champions. Gilliat was selected for the MCC tour of Ceylon and the Far East. 'Mike' Barnard, who was due to take over as coach at the start of the season, was badly injured in a road crash on a cricket tour of Germany and was unable to take up his position. Peter Faulkner, who had played for Hampshire 2nd XI, was also badly injured in the same accident.

Membership stood overall at 5,887.

1970

Champions: Kent. Knock-out Cup: Lancashire. Sunday League: Lancashire.

Hampshire slipped to 10th in the Championship with just four wins in 24 matches and 12th in the Sunday League, winning six of 16. They also had a difficult year financially and suffered again with injuries. Gilliat played in only two matches, White missed much of the season and Richards played in the Rest of the World games following the cancellation of the South African tour. He had played four Test Matches for South Africa v Australia and in his fourth Test he scored 81 & 126 at Port Elizabeth but he never played in another Test Match. At Hull he scored 155 in a Sunday League match in which the next highest score was 18*. Unfortunately, he missed the Cup match at Old Trafford, Wheatley was run out first ball and Lancashire won easily.

Richards' fellow opener Reed was not always available for business reasons and at various times he, Richards, Sainsbury, and Lewis opened until, in mid-August at Portsmouth, Hampshire selected Gordon Greenidge against the reigning Champions Glamorgan; he scored 65 and Hampshire's immediate future changed significantly. Marshall and Livingstone added 263 for the fourth wicket v Middlesex at Lord's, which remained a record until 2010. Marshall enjoyed an improved season with 1,590 runs (40.76) although this would be his final season as captain. Richards averaged 58.75 and Turner (for the first time) and Livingstone also passed 1,000 runs. Cottam topped the wicket-takers with 77, while Holder, with 55 wickets at 23.27, headed the bowling averages.

Shackleton played in half the Sunday League games but finally with little success. Jesty made a useful all-round contribution while Richards scored 592 runs in his 12 matches. The 2nd XI finished third with good performances from Greenidge, AJ ('Andy') Murtagh, Lewis and two bowlers, David O'Sullivan and TJ ('Tom') Mottram.

Sir Reginald Biddle, Hampshire's President, died in September and was succeeded by former player and MCC Secretary, R Aird. Membership was 5,879.

1971

Champions: Surrey. Knock-out Cup: Lancashire. Sunday League: Worcestershire.

Richard Gilliat was appointed captain in place of Marshall, who remained as a player for two more seasons and received a Testimonial. Hampshire rose one place to ninth but with the same four wins in 24 matches. It was a golden summer for Sainsbury, the only Hampshire player to come close to Bailey's last 'double' of 1948. In a reduced season, Sainsbury took 107 wickets (17.51) and finished just 41 runs short of 1,000 runs, following the last match against Surrey, in which the Londoners won the Championship at Southampton.

Cottam took 80 wickets at 22.30 but there was little significant support for him and Sainsbury, so unsurprisingly 14 matches were drawn. The batting was strong, led by Richards (1,938 at 47.26) with Marshall, Gilliat, Greenidge and Turner completing 1,000 runs. A few days short of his 20th birthday, Greenidge scored his maiden century v Oxford University. O'Sullivan made his Hampshire debut against the Indians and had match figures of 8-143 in a five-wicket defeat.

Hampshire won nine Sunday League matches and rose to sixth place. They beat Nottinghamshire in the first round of the Cup in a rain-affected match at Portsmouth. Nottinghamshire scored 129-9 in 60 overs (Cottam 12-6-10-2) while Sobers' 12-6-11-4 was not sufficient to stop Hampshire winning by three wickets with five overs to spare. No batsman reached 40. In the next round Warwickshire beat them by 95 runs.

Hampshire won the 2nd XI Championship for the second time under former batsman GL Keith, who was appointed Coach. The outstanding contributions came from Turner, Peter Ryan, Reed, Lewis, O'Sullivan and Mottram. A Hampshire XI also played a Sunday afternoon match v the England Women's Cricket Association which drew over 400 spectators to the County Ground: Hampshire 217-5 (Reed 62, Murtagh 56, Ferdinand 3-48) drew with EWCA 164-8 (Heyhoe 83, Burden 5-76).

Ernie Knights won the award as Best Groundsman of the Year. Membership was falling rapidly – down to 5,138.

1972

Champions: Warwickshire. Knock-out Cup: Lancashire. Sunday League: Kent.
B&H Cup: Leicestershire.

1972 was the first year of the new 55-over B&H Cup, and for the 2nd XI, the Under-25 knock-out competition. Hampshire's first B&H match v Gloucestershire at Moreton-in-the-Marsh was scheduled for Saturday 6 May but rain prevented play and the game had to be played on the following Monday and Tuesday. Hampshire won by 99 runs but lost two of their group matches and did not progress to the knock-out stages. In the original cup competition they beat Wiltshire and Nottinghamshire but lost to Lancashire at Bournemouth, despite a magnificent 129 (of 223) by Richards. Hampshire finished sixth again in the Sunday League.

In the Sunday League, Peter Haslop, who played once v Pakistan in 1962, returned for a single appearance, dismissing Mike Procter in a tied match at Bristol in which Turner finished 99*. Essex dismissed Hampshire for a record low of 43 at Basingstoke, winning by 129 runs (Boyce 4-6). Livingstone who chose the match v Surrey at Southampton for his benefit, was not selected but Hampshire won by five wickets.

In the Championship, there were now just 20 matches and Hampshire, winning four, finished ninth. Richards, Marshall and Greenidge passed 1,000 runs but Gilliat struggled badly and dropped himself, while Turner and Sainsbury were less successful although Turner impressed with 131 v Australians. 'Lofty's' son, Bob Herman, returned to Hampshire and took 81 wickets at 21.66 after Cottam departed for Northamptonshire. No other bowler reached 50 wickets although Jesty continued to show all-round promise and Mottram took 5-45 on his Championship debut in August.

On 12 September the great Roy Marshall ended the season 69* v Yorkshire at Southampton and retired after 20 seasons with Hampshire – their second highest aggregate scorer behind Mead. White, who had taken over 1,000 wickets, and Livingstone, who had a benefit, had also left, so of the 1961 Champions, only Sainsbury remained.

Hampshire announced a small profit of just over £500 although this included £27,000 from the central pool from Test matches and television revenue. In September, Turner received an offer from one of the leading sports equipment manufacturers for free kit for the following season, providing he agreed to use "solely" their equipment. The offer comprised two bats, one pair of pads and batting gloves, three shirts and three pairs of trousers.

1973

Champions: Hampshire. Knock-out Cup: Gloucestershire. Sunday League: Kent. B&H Cup: Kent.

Hampshire won their second Championship title with bonus points in their match v Gloucestershire at Bournemouth. They won 10 of their 20 matches and were the first Hampshire side to avoid defeat in a Championship season – not since Lancashire in 1928 had any team won the title undefeated while winning at least 50% of their matches. They equalled Glamorgan's 1969 record, winning the title with just 13 players. Of the 13, Murtagh was the regular reserve and generally either batsman Lewis or left-arm spinner O'Sullivan took the final place. Mottram played his first full season, MNS ('Mike') Taylor joined from Nottinghamshire and O'Sullivan enjoyed a fine end to the season. When selected for the match v Essex at Portsmouth in August, he had taken only 10 Championship wickets at 35 apiece but he finished the season with 47 wickets at 21.10.

Richards' 240 at Coventry was the season's highest score and he and Greenidge scored around 3,000 runs between them, both averaging about 50, so Hampshire frequently enjoyed a good start. Turner, without a century, was just short of 1,000 runs and Gilliat returned to form but it was their bowling which was particularly effective – six men averaged between Sainsbury at 17.83 and Herman at 25.32, while Herman, Mottram, Taylor and Sainsbury took over 50 wickets. Hampshire took all 20 wickets in their first nine victories and 19 in the last one, Gloucestershire declaring only after the title had been decided.

The bowlers were supported superbly by their catchers and outfielders, including wicket-keeper Bob Stephenson. The key match came in mid-August at Southampton, when Northamptonshire, in second place batted first and a huge crowd saw them reduced to 56-8 by lunch. Bedi led a fightback with bat and ball but Richards twice batted superbly and Hampshire won in two days.

In the cup, Hampshire beat Wiltshire but lost to Kent despite a century from Greenidge, who set a record in the B&H Cup with 173* v Minor Counties South. They reached the quarter-final but lost again to Kent by just 11 runs. In the Sunday League three matches were abandoned, yet Hampshire won nine games and finished third.

In mid-season Hampshire met the West Indians and gave a debut to fast bowler Andy Roberts, who was not yet qualified for the Championship. Despite O'Sullivan's marvellous finish to the season, Hampshire had to choose between them at the season's end and Roberts' 40 wickets for the 2nd XI helped to clinch his contract. O'Sullivan had made his Test debut for New Zealand in the season of 1972–1973 – the first of 11 Test Matches. Off-spinner Larry Worrell played regularly for the 2nd XI but left at the end of the season.

Membership stood at 5,359 and would rise significantly during the 1970s. The club showed a profit of almost £3,000.

1974

Champions: Worcestershire. Knock-out Cup: Kent. Sunday League: Leicestershire.
B&H Cup: Surrey.

Hampshire were runners-up in the Championship, lost a thrilling quarter final in the B&H Cup and finished fifth in the Sunday League. They won nothing in that season, yet 1974 was perhaps *the* year in their history when they were the strongest all-round side in the country.

They lost their first Championship match of the season at Lord's immediately after playing MCC there as the Champion County. Then they drew with the Indian tourists before embarking on a run of four consecutive innings victories. They had no O'Sullivan to finish the season, although Cowley from Dorset played in some matches, but Roberts was outstanding with 119 wickets at less than 14 apiece. He had good support from Taylor and Herman with over 70 wickets each at less than 20, while Richards, Gilliat and Turner led the batters, although Greenidge had a slightly disappointing year. Nine men appeared in every Championship match. Sainsbury was awarded a Testimonial.

Hampshire led the Championship to the conclusion of the penultimate match, although by then the rain had taken a deciding hand. Things seemed very different on 8 August when their nearest challengers, Worcestershire, left Portsmouth on the back of a two-day innings defeat in which they failed to reach 100 in either innings. Worcestershire seemed far behind and remained so as both sides drew their next games in bad weather. There were just four matches left.

Then, in mid-August, Hampshire had their one bad day, as Worcestershire beat Essex at home. In Cardiff, Hampshire led by 144 on first innings but the last wicket stand of 18 just prevented the follow-on and Hampshire, caught on a drying wicket, were dismissed for 137. Glamorgan then batted for 155 overs to reach 284-5 and win the game, although Hampshire still led the table.

They did not play as Worcestershire met Mike Taylor's old teammates at Trent Bridge and in fine weather the challengers won a thrilling match by just five runs. This was perhaps as crucial as any of the other games. Harry Latchman and Bill Taylor needed 23 for the last wicket to win the match and managed 17 but Brian Brain bowled Taylor and Worcestershire sat back while Hampshire welcomed Glamorgan to Southampton. Unfortunately, the weather did not hold, with only 15 minutes possible on the second day after Hampshire had scored 393-8 declared. They dismissed Glamorgan for 156, enforced the follow-on and had them at 81-8 when time ran out.

So came the penultimate matches. At Bournemouth, Hampshire led Somerset by 141 runs on first innings and the visitors were 90-4 at the end of a sunny second day with Parks injured and unable to resume. The forecast was fine – sadly the weather was not and they lost the whole of the final day. Meanwhile, in Worcester, the home side had led Glamorgan by 107 runs and the Welshmen replied with 121-4 so Worcestershire had more to do. But the weather held there, Glamorgan collapsed, losing six wickets for 50 runs, and Worcestershire won easily.

So Hampshire had the slightest lead going into the last round. But the sunshine of Thursday had vanished and although they managed a reduced overs game at Portsmouth in the Sunday League, not a ball was bowled in the Championship against Yorkshire over the next three days. Worcestershire meanwhile managed 82 overs on the first day in Essex before their game drowned too, but in that time they dismissed Essex for 84, took sufficient bonus points and won the title.

The B&H Cup was also frustrating for a side that had never reached Lord's, although here it was a teenage wonder that beat them. At Taunton, Jesty (79) helped Hampshire post 182 and, with 4-28, reduced Somerset to 113-8. A young Ian Botham (2-33) came to the wicket without helmet or cap, was felled by Roberts, got up and hit Somerset to a remarkable victory with 45*. Jesty completed the Sunday League career double but it was scant consolation in such a disappointing season for such a fine side. With an eye to the future, TM ('Tim') Tremlett, John Southern, John Rice and Cowley performed well in the 2nd XI.

1975

Champions: Leicestershire. Knock-out Cup: Lancashire. **Sunday League: Hampshire.**
B&H Cup: Leicestershire.

Hampshire enjoyed another fine all-round season although once again they might have been County Champions, finishing third after a disappointing conclusion. In the Knock-out cup, Greenidge (177) and Richards (129) enjoyed a record-breaking day as Hampshire, 371-4, hammered Glamorgan, which remain their record individual and team limited-overs scores, but they were dismissed for 98 in the next round at Old Trafford. In the B&H they won every group match, gained revenge in the Quarter Final against Somerset and, with Greenidge (111) leading the way, set Leicestershire 217 to win. At 115-4 it was very even, but a century by Chris Balderstone took the Midlands side to Lord's in the last over.

Hampshire lost their first Sunday league match but then won five in a row before another Old Trafford hammering but they lost only once more and, for the last match, went to Darley Dale, Derbyshire for the only match ever played there between two first-class sides, needing victory to clinch their first limited-overs title. Half-centuries from Richards and Greenidge helped them to 222-8 and with Roberts unfit, Mottram 5-21 and Rice 4-14 bowled Hampshire to the title. On Sundays, Rice led the bowlers with 27 wickets at 11.48, while Richards scored 689 runs. Jesty took 6-20 v Glamorgan in Cardiff, the best limited-overs figures by a Hampshire cricketer in an inter-county match. At the Scarborough Festival, Hampshire beat Gloucestershire and Yorkshire to win the four-team Fenner Trophy.

In the Championship, Hampshire won four of the first five matches and with three matches to play were second to Yorkshire, two points behind with a game in hand. If it did not rain, they were favourites. On the first day of the next match, Greenidge scored 259, reaching every 50 and century with a six, Hampshire declared on 501-5 and Sussex followed-on but with Roberts injured while warming-up, Faber made his highest score and the match was drawn. Leicestershire then pulled ahead. In the next match Hampshire led Derbyshire by 175, but JM Ward, not re-engaged and only playing because of injuries, made his only first-class century; again the match was drawn and despite victory by an innings at Worcester, the title had gone.

Greenidge and Roberts missed some matches due to the staging of the first World Cup mid-season. Richards, Gilliat, Greenidge and Turner passed 1,000 runs but none of the bowlers reached 60 wickets. Roberts led the way with 57 at 15.80, but this was not the devastating performance of twelve months earlier. Rice added to the strong all-round centre to the side with 619 runs and 49 wickets.

Full membership now cost £7.56. Groundsman Ernie Knights received a Testimonial of £2,648. Hampshire's coach and former player Geoff Keith fell ill during the season and, at the age of just 38, died on Boxing Day.

1976

Champions: Middlesex. Knock-out Cup: Northamptonshire. Sunday League: Kent. B&H Cup: Kent.

With Greenidge and Roberts touring with the victorious West Indies side, Richards was the sole overseas player and he, Turner, Gilliat and Jesty passed 1,000 runs. Jesty in particular fulfilled his batting promise at last with 1,288 runs and his first (and second) Championship century to add to 42 first-class wickets. Over the next few seasons he was probably as good as any English county player not to win a Test cap – and better than some who did.

Two slow-left-armers, Southern and Sainsbury, led the wicket takers, the latter in his final season before becoming Hampshire's new coach. Sadly, the pace attack faltered with Herman losing form, Mottram through injury playing only occasionally and Taylor's 31 wickets costing 29.29. So Hampshire won just four matches and slipped to twelfth, including a mid-season spell of eight consecutive defeats. They were eighth in the Sunday League and failed to qualify in their B&H Zone, although they did manage a 'double' in the two Yorkshire festival knock-out competitions, winning the Tilcon Trophy at Harrogate in June and the Fenner Trophy at Scarborough in September.

The major excitement of 1976 was in the Knock-out Cup, still sponsored by Gillette. They beat Leicestershire from the final ball by just three runs at Leicester, beat Derbyshire by 47 runs at Southampton and in the home semi-final set Northamptonshire 216 to win in 60 overs (Turner 86). The visitors looked well set throughout their reply but slipped from 202-4 to 211-8 and it went to the penultimate ball from Rice, which Bedi hit to the boundary to win the match.

For many years, Hampshire's illustrious overseas players had joined the county with few if any Test match appearances behind them. Roy Marshall played in just four Tests, Richards the same, all after joining Hampshire, Roberts made his Test debut after his first-class debut for the county in 1973, Malcolm Marshall played three Tests in India in the winter before his Hampshire debut, while Gordon Greenidge was discovered in Reading and came to Hampshire in 1966 to play for the Colts and 2nd XI. He played his first Test in 1974–1975 but in England in 1976 he established himself as a player of top class. He began the series with 22 & 23 at Trent Bridge, 84 & 22 at Lord's and then 134 & 101 at Old Trafford. On the same Saturday as his second century, Richards, Turner and Gilliat passed three figures for Hampshire v Glamorgan at Bournemouth. Greenidge scored 115 in the Fourth Test and 85* in the Fifth, while Roberts took 28 wickets at 19.17 as West Indies won the series 3-0.

1977

Joint Champions: Kent & Middlesex. Knock-out Cup: Middlesex. Sunday League: Leicestershire. B&H Cup: Gloucestershire.

Hampshire won the Fenner Trophy again but lost in the main Knock-out Cup to the eventual winners in the Quarter Final. They finished 11th in the Championship and fifth in the Sunday League, but the main excitement came in the B&H Cup, while the most significant events took place off the field before and after the season ended.

In the B&H Cup, they qualified with three wins, one against Gloucestershire by eight wickets. In the quarter-final at Swansea, Jesty was magnificent, taking 3-20 and then scoring 105 as Hampshire won by six wickets with 13 overs to spare. In the semi-final at Southampton, Gloucestershire's openers put on 106 but they fell away to 180 all out (Mottram 3-21). However, Procter bowled Greenidge at 13, and took a hat-trick to reduce Hampshire to 18-4. Cowley (59) and Turner (49) staged a partial rescue but wickets fell regularly and Hampshire finished eight short of victory with three balls to spare.

Roberts missed a number of matches through injury and Southern, with 53 wickets at over 30, each was leading wicket taker. Greenidge averaged over 60 but Richards, in his benefit season, just failed to reach 1,000 runs – Jesty was the only other man to reach four figures, while Gilliat missed half the matches with injury. Twenty-year-old DJ (David) Rock from Portsmouth scored two centuries. No Hampshire player had previously received more than £7,000 from a benefit until this year, when Richards received £21,255.

By the time the English season started, Tony Greig had captained England in the Centenary Test Match in Melbourne but, more crucially, began recruiting players for Kerry Packer's 'World Cricket' revolution – an initiative that would involve Richards, Greenidge and Roberts. Then, shortly after the season's end, Hampshire's secretary and former captain Desmond Eagar died while on holiday. John Arlott called him "at heart a staunch Edwardian" and suggested that while he was "an anachronism in the modern world of showbiz sport" he was a "happy, healthy, honest, selfless and utterly enthusiastic anachronism". He had served his adopted county wonderfully well for over 30 years.

Membership reached a peak of 8,331, including 1,567 juniors.

1978

Champions: Kent. Knock-out Cup: Sussex. **Sunday League: Hampshire.** B&H Cup: Kent.

Hampshire welcomed a new Secretary, AK 'Jimmy' James (from Somerset). The 'Packer affair' and the future involvement of Hampshire's overseas players hung over the season and halfway through it, Richards and Roberts turned their backs on county cricket although Roberts would return subsequently with Leicestershire. Nonetheless, Hampshire's season was reasonably successful as they rose to eighth in the Championship and clinched the Sunday League on a thrilling final day. On that Sunday, they beat Middlesex at Bournemouth, thanks mainly to Greenidge (122) and Jesty (47 & 5-32). There followed a 25-minute wait for the result from Taunton where a Somerset victory could clinch the title, but they could only score nine of the 11 runs needed from the final over and Hampshire took the title.

In the following week, Gilliat captained Hampshire in a final Championship victory over Leicestershire and, arguably the most successful captain in their history, retired as player and secretary and moved eventually to Charterhouse School. He received £24,637 from his benefit. Greenidge (1,771), Turner and Jesty all passed 1,000 runs, while Southern led the bowlers with 76 at 24.12. Cowley and Keith Stevenson, recently arrived from Derbyshire, gave support with 56 each and there were opportunities for a number of youngsters, including David Rock, NEJ ('Nick') Pocock, Tremlett, MCJ (Mark) Nicholas and VP (Paul) Terry. At Bournemouth, Greenidge hit three successive centuries, a feat last achieved by Mead in 1933.

Membership fell but remained (just) above 8,000 with subscriptions just above £70,000. Gate income was £38,728 but the club announced a loss of £25,000.

In the Southern League Havant won the title, followed by Deanery, Gosport Borough, Waterlooville, Trojans, Old Tauntonians and South Hants Touring Club – all of them sides from in or around Southampton and Portsmouth.

1979

Champions: Essex. Knock-out Cup: Somerset. Sunday League: Somerset. B&H Cup: Essex.

Hampshire appointed their first English professional captain, Bob Stephenson. It was also Stephenson's benefit season, from which he received £24,204. Hampshire signed a relatively unknown fast bowler, Malcolm Marshall from the West Indies, as their new overseas player. Both Greenidge and Marshall missed some matches to participate in the second World Cup and Greenidge was a member of the West Indies side that retained the Trophy.

With so many changes it was not a happy season at the end of a remarkable decade. Hampshire won just three of the 22 scheduled Championship matches, with one game abandoned with no play – one of 10 in the Championship that season. As defending Champions they fell to 10th in the Sunday League, lost all four B&H matches and went out to Middlesex in Round 2 of the Knock-out Cup. Greenidge and Jesty passed 1,000 runs and Stevenson took 69 wickets, while Marshall, with 47 at 22.26 hinted at what was to come.

Paying gates for tourist and championship matches were 7,000, while over 12,000 attended home Sunday League matches. Total membership fell to 6,942. The cost of full membership rose to £14 and the following year to £17. In the *Hampshire Handbook* (1980), editor Peter Marshall wondered whether the new decade would bring "floodlit cricket and coloured cricketing attire" following the influence of the World Series.

1946: (back) Sprankling (scorer), Hill, G Heath, Dean, Godfrey, Court, Rogers, Holt, S Staples (coach), (front) Herman, Bailey, Eagar, Pothecary, Knott, (ground) Arnold, McCorkell

1948: Aldershot week, (back) RCL Court (secretary), Gray, Rogers, Shackleton, G Dawson, H Dawson, L Harrison, (front) Hill, Bailey, Eagar, Field Marshall Montgomery, Waldron, Arnold, G Heath

1950: v Worcestershire at Dudley, (back) Rayment, Gray, Dare, Sprankling (scorer) Carty, L Harrison, Cannings, C Walker, (front) Rimell, McCorkell, Eagar, Hill, Rogers

1952: (back) Prouton, Rayment, L Harrison, Dare, Cannings, Gray, (front) Shackleton, Hill, Eagar, Ingleby-Mackenzie, Rogers

1955: NB Edwards (secretary), Gray, Rayment, Marshall, M Heath, Horton, N Drake (scorer), (centre) Cannings, Rogers, Eagar, L Harrison, Shackleton, (front) Sainsbury, Barnard, Burden

1958: v Worcestershire at Worcester, (back) Horton, White, Pitman, N Drake (scorer), Burden, Barnard, Sainsbury, (front) Gray, Shackleton, Marshall, Ingleby-Mackenzie, L Harrison, Cannings

1961: (back) Baldry, Livingstone, White, Heath, Wassell, Burden, Sainsbury, (front) Horton, Marshall, Ingleby-Mackenzie, Shackleton, Gray

1964: (back) Timms, Livingstone, Cottam, Keith, Caple, Barnard, (front) White, Shackleton, Marshall, Ingleby-Mackenzie, Horton, Sainsbury

1967: (back) Reed, Timms, Caple, Holder, Cottam, Keith, Castell, Wheatley, Jesty, (front) Lewis, White, Horton, Shackleton, Marshall, Sainsbury, L Harrison, Livingstone, Turner

1969: v Surrey at the Oval, (back) Turner, Jesty, Holder, McIlwaine, Wheatley, Lewis, GR Stephenson, (front) Richards, White, Gilliat, Livingstone, Cottam

1971: (back) Turner, Lewis, GR Stephenson, Ryan, Hill, Rice, Keith, Castell, Greenidge, Jesty, Worrell, (front) Livingstone, Richards, Sainsbury, Gilliat, White, Cottam, Marshall

1973: (back) Lewis, Herman, Mottram, Taylor, Greenidge, O'Sullivan, (front) Turner, Richards, Gilliat, Sainsbury, GR Stephenson, Jesty

1975: (back) Murtagh, Taylor, Southern, Mottram, Rice, Jesty, Greenidge, (front) Turner, Sainsbury, Gilliat, Richards, GR Stephenson

1978: (back) Stevenson, Terry, Elms, Edwards, Rock, Pocock, Southern, Tremlett, Nicholas, Murtagh, Cowley, Parks, (front) Sainsbury (coach), Taylor, Richards, Gilliat, GR Stephenson, Turner, Jesty, Rice

1980

Champions: Middlesex. Knock-out Cup: Middlesex. Sunday League: Warwickshire.
B&H Cup: Northamptonshire.

Gate charges rose to £1.20 in the Championship and £1.50 for the Sunday League. For the first (and so far only) time since 1905, Hampshire finished in last place in the Championship, winning just one match. It was a season of transition. After just one season Nick Pocock replaced Stephenson as captain, while Greenidge and Marshall were touring with the West Indies. Australian all-rounder Shaun Graf came for one year and South African batsman CL ('Chris') Smith was also available. Pace bowler SJ ('Steve') Malone came from Essex but Rock announced his retirement in April.

In the absence of Greenidge and Rock, Chris Smith and Rice or Tremlett generally opened the batting, Smith alone passing 1,000 runs, although Tremlett with 717 at 27.57 did well and his top scores of 76 & 67* against Worcestershire at Bournemouth did much to secure Hampshire's only victory, and he 'carried his bat' against Leicestershire. Stevenson and Southern passed 50 wickets but Jesty lost form with bat and ball, and the new captain made five half-centuries but no hundreds. RJ ('Bobby') Parks took over from Stephenson and the latter and Taylor both retired, although Taylor continued to work as Assistant Secretary, then in Marketing until the move to the new ground two decades later.

Hampshire lost all four zonal B&H matches again, beat Derbyshire and lost to Yorkshire in the last year before the Gillette Cup became the Nat West Trophy and finished level with Kent in 11th place in the Sunday League.

Among the promising cricketers playing for Hampshire Schools was TC ('Tony') Middleton. Havant (Champions) and Deanery continued to dominate the Southern League and Longparish reached the Lord's final of the Village Championship – sadly they lost to Marchwiel. Similarly, Gosport reached Lord's in the Club Championship but lost to Moseley, although Jim Stares received Man-of-the-Match.

The club had 5,853 members and the membership fee was rising rapidly – now £20. They announced a loss on the season approaching £6,000.

1981

Champions: Nottinghamshire. Knock-out Cup: Derbyshire. Sunday League: Essex.
B&H Cup: Somerset.

1981 was the year of Botham and Willis at Headingley but there was cheer too in Hampshire. Their two West Indians returned and they improved on the previous season, finishing seventh in the Championship with six wins, beat Cheshire and Glamorgan in the (now) Nat West Knock-out Trophy and finishing sixth in the Sunday League. The B&H Cup was frustrating. They began by beating a strong Middlesex side by one wicket with three balls to spare, their first B&H win since 1978. Then, needing 183 to beat the Minor Counties (with Richard Lewis), they struggled to 179-8 but lost two more wickets without adding to the score. There followed a two-day washout against Surrey, then Sussex beat them with one ball to spare and they went out.

In mid-July, Hampshire beat Derbyshire by an innings at Portsmouth and were challenging at the head of the table. Greenidge scored 109 and there were wickets for Stevenson 5-49 and Tremlett 4-11, plus a county record for Parks, who held six catches in the first innings and 10 in the match. Sadly, they won only one of the last 12 matches. Rice scored his maiden century and against the Sri Lankans, RE (Richard) Hayward scored a century on debut for the county, although like his predecessors Abercrombie and Baldry, he had played a first-class match, albeit only one for the Minor Counties.

Greenidge dominated the first-class averages and was the only man to pass 1,000 runs, while Marshall (68), Jesty (52) and Stevenson (57) led the wicket takers but the spinners were generally ineffective. In the Sunday League, Cowley led the run-scorers and wicket takers. Sainsbury's 'reserves' clinched the 2nd XI title boosted by Chris Smith and his younger brother Robin Smith who were both qualifying by residence. Terry, Kevin Emery, Southern, Simon Massey and MJ ('Mike') Bailey also made significant contributions. Membership stood at 5,191. Turner received £23,011 from his benefit.

The all male Committee was 30 strong, including former players, Leo Harrison and Barry Reed, a father and son, a Brigadier, two Majors, a Squadron Leader and a Southampton City Councillor. The Chairman was Geoffrey Ford and Charlie Knott chaired the cricket Committee, which included former players Jim Bailey, Richard Gilliat, Arthur Holt, Cecil Paris, Bob Stephenson, GR Taylor and the current coach and captain.

1982

Champions: Middlesex. Knock-out Cup: Surrey. Sunday League: Sussex. B&H Cup: Somerset.

Hampshire's progress under Pocock continued and they finished third with three outstanding contributions. Marshall took 134 wickets at 15.73, scored his maiden century and with 633 runs was fifth in the batting averages, Beneficiary Trevor Jesty (£24,000) led the batsmen with eight centuries and 1,645 runs at 58.75 and debutant Emery took 79 wickets at 23.94. Greenidge passed 1,500 runs, Nicholas 1,300 and six bowlers averaged 24 or less.

Hampshire failed in the B&H Cup again and won just one match in the Knock-out Cup, falling in the quarter final for the eighth time in nine attempts since 1970, although they had an excuse, for the match began in a mist at 10am and only Turner (51) resisted the Surrey seamers – Jackman's 6-22 was a record against Hampshire. In the Sunday League they finished fourth equal. They tied two matches, against Surrey and Lancashire, although might have won both. Rice's last match for Hampshire was in the Sunday League, where he had often enjoyed significant success. He took up a coaching post at Eton College and for some years with Hampshire's Under-19 side.

In the Championship at Bristol the first day was washed out for the fourth time in five days for Hampshire. Play began late on the second day, the two sides forfeited an innings each, Gloucestershire dismissed Hampshire for 99 and scored 101-6 to win. This was the lowest aggregate in a completed Hampshire match although because of the forfeits it is not usually included in records. The single day match v Yorkshire in 1898 heads that list.

On 14 October, Peter May opened the new Squash and Social Centre at Northlands Road. Deanery, Gosport and Tauntonians led the Southern League, Hursley Park won the Hampshire League.

Membership fell to 4,858 – it had been 8,331 in 1977. One notable change was the decline in subscribing clubs, from 217 to 121 in the same period. Full membership was now £23 with life membership £350. The accounts showed a deficit of almost £80,000. Ground advertising revenue was hit when the firm responsible went into liquidation.

1983

Champions: Essex. Knock-out Cup: Somerset. Sunday League: Yorkshire. B&H Cup: Middlesex.

Hampshire finished third again in the Championship with rather more limited-overs success but no trophies.

Jesty played for England v Australia at Sydney in January, the first Hampshire player to represent England in a limited-overs international. Chris Smith was available full time now as an English qualified player and made his Test debut for England v New Zealand at Lord's (Third Test). Like Arnold in 1931 against the same opponents on the same ground, his first innings was a 'duck' – then he scored 43. Unlike Arnold, he played in further Tests. Hampshire staged their first international match, Australia defeating Zimbabwe at Southampton in the World Cup.

In the match at Southend in July, the eventual Champions dismissed Hampshire for 136 and set them a fourth innings target of 410; Chris Smith scored 163 and Hampshire won in the penultimate over. At the time this was Hampshire's highest fourth innings total to win a match, although they passed that in 1990. At Bournemouth, Marshall took 7-29 as Hampshire dismissed Somerset for 76, winning by 10 wickets. One week later against the same opponents at Taunton, he took 6-46 and they were all out for 86 but rain had the final say. The latter performance included a hat-trick and four wickets in five balls. Chris Smith and Jesty with 321 for the third wicket at Derby were within 23 of the Hampshire record held by Brown and Mead in 1927.

Greenidge received £28,648 from his benefit. Marshall and Greenidge missed part of the season on World Cup duty as their West Indian side was surprisingly beaten by India in the Final. Jesty was in the England squad but did not play. Greenidge, Chris Smith, Jesty, Terry and Nicholas all passed 1,000 runs and, as an overseas batsman when Greenidge was absent, 19-year-old Robin Smith scored three Championship centuries.

The bowling was consistent but less incisive than twelve months earlier as Emery lost form and fitness. Marshall led the way with 80 wickets at 16.58, and Tremlett gave excellent support with 63 at 21.36. Neither Jesty nor Southern found bowling form and the latter retired.

Hampshire enjoyed success in the B&H Cup and progressed to the quarter-finals where they held Kent to 198-9, reached 131 without loss and then collapsed to lose by five runs. In the Nat West Trophy they beat Hertfordshire, Gloucestershire and Glamorgan but had to return to Canterbury for the semi-final. They collapsed again but this time they lost by the rather wider margin of 71 runs and remained the only side never to reach a Lord's Final – of which there had now been 33 in the two competitions. In the Sunday League they finished fifth and Greenidge (108*) and Jesty (166*) shared an unbroken 2nd wicket partnership of 269 v Surrey at Portsmouth, as Hampshire won by 104 runs.

Spin bowler Mel Hussain, older brother of future England captain Nasser, took 21 wickets for the 2nd XI, Robin Smith dominated the batting and Middleton, Hardy, Richard Scott and Stephen Andrew showed promise. Lymington won the Southern League and US Portsmouth the Hampshire League.

In October, Hampshire's former batsman Peter Barrett was killed in a road accident at the age of just 28. The cost of full membership rose again to £25 but from the peak of 8,331 six years earlier, numbers had fallen to 4,860 and the club declared a loss of £41,545. Over the previous 20 years, the club's net losses came to £110,074.

1984

Champions: Essex. Knock-out Cup: Middlesex. Sunday League: Essex. B&H Cup: Lancashire.

Cecil Paris succeeded Ronnie Aird as Hampshire's sixth post-war President. Hampshire slipped to 15th in the Championship, failed to qualify in the B&H, beat only Norfolk in the 60-over Knock-out Cup and shared ninth place in the Sunday League.

At the start of the season, Chris Smith was one of *Wisden's* Five Cricketers of the Year. His main success came in the Sunday League and as he struggled in the Championship, it was briefly Terry's turn to be selected by England. With Greenidge and Marshall absent on tour, Hampshire signed Milton Small before he was also selected to tour and then withdrew injured. Instead they recruited the unknown left-arm pace bowler, Elvis Reifer from Barbados. He was a willing trier but, with Emery's brief contribution over, Hampshire lacked a cutting edge. They discovered another West Indian, Cardigan Connor, playing in league cricket in the London area and signed slow-left-armer Rajesh ('Raj') Maru from Middlesex.

At Canterbury in May, Kent reached 144-2 at the close of a truncated first day, there was no play on the second and after a late start they declared on 179-4, after which two forefeited innings left Hampshire 180 to win. On a drying wicket, Underwood then took 7-21, Pocock top-scored with 17 and Hampshire were dismissed for 56 in the 27th over.

Teenage pace bowler Andrew won the Gold Award on his B&H debut at the Oval and took 4-30 on his Championship debut at Hove. Connor took 4-31 on his Championship debut and 7-37 v Kent at Bournemouth. Six men passed 1,000 runs, led by Jesty with 1,625 and, at Southampton, he scored 32 runs from one over by Robin Boyd-Moss of Northamptonshire – five sixes and the fifth ball for two. Tremlett, with 71 wickets at 20.33, was the only bowler to average below 30. Hampshire's batsmen made 22 centuries but the bowlers conceded 16.

With a Gooch century, Essex set a 40-over Sunday target of 255 to win but Turner replied with 114. Three men were run out near the end and, needing eight from the final over, Hampshire lost by just two runs.

Nick Pocock relinquished the captaincy in August and was replaced by Mark Nicholas. Trevor Jesty, upset by the decision, moved to Surrey and then Lancashire. Hampshire took advantage of a relaxation of rules about sponsorship and displayed the TNT logo on their sweaters.

The West Indies won the first Test at Edgbaston by an innings – Marshall and Greenidge contributed but not significantly. At Lord's Marshall took 6-85 but England looked comfortable when they challenged West Indies to score 342 in about 70 overs. Greenidge scored 214* and they won by nine wickets. England picked Terry at Headingley but he scored 8 & 1. Then Marshall, despite suffering a broken arm in the field, battled to allow 'Larry' Gomes to reach his century and then, with one good arm, took 7-53 as West Indies won by eight wickets. At Old Trafford, Greenidge scored 223. Terry was retained but this time Winston Davis, who had replaced Marshall, hit Terry and broke his arm. Terry also returned to support Lamb (100*) but was dismissed for seven and his Test career was over as West Indies won by an innings. Marshall took 5-35 as West Indies won at the Oval by 172 runs. In the series, Greenidge scored 572 runs at 81.71, Marshall took 24 wickets at 18.20 and both headed their respective averages.

Hursley Park reached but lost the Village Final at Lord's, although 20-year-old 'Adi' Aymes impressed with a half century.

1985

Champions: Middlesex. Knock-out Cup: Essex. Sunday League: Essex. B&H Cup: Leicestershire.

Chairman Geoffrey Ford retired and was replaced by Donald Rich. Geoffrey Ford's father, Percy, had been Vice Chairman and his son, Brian, would be Chairman in the 1990s. At the end of the season, Secretary 'Jimmy' James retired and was replaced by Tony Baker, who had bowled for the 2nd XI and in the local leagues. He had been Hon Treasurer and would now be Chief Executive.

On the field there was a new captain too, and while Mark Nicholas's permanent appointment led to the departure of Trevor Jesty, Robin Smith was now English-qualified and available full time. Marshall and Greenidge returned and Hampshire enjoyed an exciting season, finishing third in the Sunday League and reaching another semi-final where, at Southampton, they were unlucky to go out to Essex, with scores level, on wickets lost. Put in by Fletcher, no Hampshire batsman reached 40 but they posted 224-8 and Essex reached 125-3 with Gooch 53* when all the television and photographic evidence suggested a direct throw ran him out. It was not given, Gooch added another 40, and Hampshire were frustrated again.

They lost their quarter-final to Leicestershire by just four runs in the B&H Cup but the real excitement came in the Championship, where they pressed Middlesex to the end before settling for the third time for the runners-up place. Failure to win any of their last three matches cost them, most particularly the penultimate match v Northamptonshire at Southampton, where the visitors, chasing 241 in 60 overs, won with a Harper six from the last ball with one wicket standing.

Chris Smith scored 2,000 runs, brother Robin passed 1,500, and Greenidge, Terry and Nicholas 1,000. Marshall took 95 wickets and Tremlett and Maru over 70. Parks claimed 62 dismissals and Terry 34 catches and the only weakness was in the support for Marshall as an opening bowler, duties shared by Andrew, Connor and KD (Kevan) James, who had followed Maru from Middlesex. James brought all-round abilities and he and Tremlett posted a new county record for the eight wicket of 227 at Taunton. Against the Australian tourists at Southampton, James took 6-22 as Border's side were dismissed for 76.

Lymington won the Southern League again, followed by Trojans and Bournemouth, Hursley Park won the Hampshire League. JA ('Jon') Ayling showed promise in the Colts side, while Middleton, Andrew and JJE ('Jon') Hardy played well for the 2nd XI. Dutch pace bowler PJ Bakker came on trial.

1986

Champions: Essex. Knock-out Cup: Sussex. **Sunday League: Hampshire.** B&H Cup: Middlesex.

In the last year of its sponsorship by John Player, Hampshire won the Sunday League for the third time with a victory over Surrey at the Oval in their penultimate match.

In the Championship, Hampshire slipped to sixth. Greenidge and Marshall were dominant, heading their respective national averages but neither Terry nor Nicholas were in the best form, Chris Smith suffered injuries and the bowling support was not there – Cowley, Maru, Tremlett and Connor reached 40 wickets but none passed 50. Greenidge scored 2,035 runs, the best for Hampshire since Richards in 1968, and posted a county record of four successive Championship centuries. With 125* v Yorkshire he became the first batsman to score ten Sunday League centuries. Greenidge and Terry set a new first wicket partnership record of 250 v Northamptonshire at Northampton, although it would last only until the following season, and Terry participated in four higher first wicket partnerships from 1987–1991. Parks, with 81, dismissals was just two short of Leo Harrison's 1959 record, in fewer matches.

Hampshire made no progress in either of the main knock-out cups but once again went to Scarborough and won a trophy, sponsored by Asda. In the Sunday League, they went to the Oval for the penultimate match, knowing that victory could clinch the title. They batted first and struggled, reaching 149-8 thanks to Greenidge (51) and James (54*). They took wickets regularly but Surrey needed just seven runs to win from the final over bowled by Connor. Two wickets fell and Surrey fell three runs short as Hampshire clinched the title.

Chris Smith played in the last of his eight Test Matches. For England, he scored 392 runs at an average of 30.15 and took three wickets. South Hants Touring Club (Portsmouth) won the Southern League and Bashley (Rydal) the Hampshire League. Julian Wood, Rupert Cox, Ian Turner and Shaun Udal showed promise for the Colts. Middleton, Scott, Bakker and new wicket-keeper, Adrian ('Adi') Aymes performed well for the 2nd XI.

1987

Champions: Nottinghamshire. Knock-out Cup: Nottinghamshire. Sunday League: Worcestershire. B&H Cup: Yorkshire.

Individually the Hampshire players returned impressive performances in 1987 with a very strong batting line-up and good support bowling for Marshall from Andrew and Tremlett. Despite this, the side were fifth in the Championship, and after starting brightly in the Sunday League, lost four of the last six and finished seventh, equal with Surrey. They qualified in the B&H Cup but Yorkshire hammered them by nine wickets in the quarter-final and they made no progress in the Nat West Trophy. Even at Scarborough, for the first time, they failed to reach the final of the four-team knock-out. The sum was very much less than the parts in 1987.

David Turner, who had not always been selected in 1986, scored 1,328 runs at an average just below 50 and was Hampshire's 'Player of the Year', while seven players averaged over 40. Tremlett and Marshall both took 72 wickets at an average around 20 apiece. Marshall received £61,006 from his benefit – more than twice Hampshire's previous record. Chris Smith and Terry set a new first wicket partnership record of 347 against Warwickshire at Edgbaston, which still stands.

Longparish reached their Lord's Final for village sides and became the first Hampshire side to win one. The 2nd XI were beaten in the Final of their limited-overs competition.

At the end of the season, Hampshire knew that Greenidge and Marshall would miss the following season on tour. What was not known was that Gordon Greenidge played his last match for the county in a Sunday League match at Nottingham on 16 August. It was an anonymous and rather unhappy end for one of Hampshire's greatest players – certainly one of the greatest 'home grown' players, since he began as a Colt and 2nd XI player from Reading. For Hampshire he scored 19,840 runs at 45.40, with 48 centuries, held 315 catches as one of the few to average better than one per match and even took 16 wickets. At various times he held a number of limited-overs batting records, was a member of the 1973 Champions and played crucial innings in 1978 and 1986 in the matches when Hampshire won their first two Sunday League titles.

Just over 25,000 spectators paid at the gate for the various competitions while membership stood at 4,499, just 37 fewer than the previous year but 131 up on 1985. The accounts showed a "marginal profit". The elections for Committee were aimed eventually at reducing the number from 27 to 21.

1988

Champions: Worcestershire. Knock-out Cup: Middlesex. Sunday League: Worcestershire.
B&H Cup: Hampshire.

At last, after 25 years, Hampshire became the 17th county to reach a Lord's Final and after winning a tense, rain-affected semi-final at Chelmsford, Hampshire hammered Derbyshire to win their first Lord's trophy with ease. In the semi-final, Essex posted 238-6 (Cowley 2-31) and Terry, Chris Smith and Turner took Hampshire to 192-1 off 46 overs when the rain arrived – at which point Hampshire were behind the required rate. It was not until late in the next afternoon that they could resume but Terry's century took them home.

SJ ('Steve') Jefferies, who replaced Marshall, had only two really good days during the season. In the Championship he took 8-97 at Bristol and then in the Lord's Final he returned what were then record Cup Final figures of 10-3-13-5. At Lord's, all the bowlers were effective as Derbyshire collapsed from 27-0 to 117 – thanks also to some inspired field placing by Nicholas and an excellent run out effected by the Beneficiary, Nigel Cowley (£88,274). Terry went early but Robin Smith hit a dynamic 38, stopped only by a marvellous catch and it was fitting that the captain Nicholas (35*) and 'Senior Pro' Turner (7*) saw Hampshire to their first knock-out trophy.

Ayling made an important all-round contribution to Hampshire's success in his debut season. Against Oxford University he took a wicket with his first ball in first-class cricket and his first nine scoring shots were all boundaries (including one six). He seemed destined for a long and successful career, but that was not to be. Turner passed Greenidge's Sunday League aggregate record for

Hampshire and led the Sunday catchers. He scored 573 runs, a record for Hampshire in the Sunday League. Maru equalled the Hampshire record with seven catches v Northamptonshire at Bournemouth.

Some Championship matches were played over four days for the first time. Hampshire's first scheduled four-day match ended in defeat in two days and the next in victory on the third morning. In the Championship, Hampshire fell to the lower reaches as they generally did without Marshall – in 1988 they finished 15th. James finished top of the bowling averages in 1988, having topped the batting averages the previous season – the only instance of one man heading both season's averages for Hampshire. In the Sunday League they finished halfway but in addition to the B&H Cup they reached the semi-final of the Nat West Trophy as a second Lord's Final beckoned. But in bad light and drizzle at Worcester they fell 30 runs short of the target of 269 to win, despite Terry's 80.

West Indies came to the County Ground for a limited-overs match in early May and Gordon Greenidge scored 103 as they won easily. The West Indies dominated the Test series again but Robin Smith made his England debut at the start of a career that would see him win more England caps than any previous Hampshire cricketer. On 17 December, Malcolm Marshall dismissed David Boon, his 300th Test Match wicket. He was the ninth man to reach that figure and the second West Indian after Lance Gibbs. He achieved this in 61 matches and only Dennis Lillee reached that figure in fewer Tests (56). Pre-season, Hampshire had visited Marshall's native Barbados, winning and losing against the full island side. Hampshire played two limited-overs matches in Holland in May and again won one and lost one.

At the start of the year, Hampshire signed a three-year sponsorship deal with local accountants BKL, worth £100,000. They also embarked on a feasibility study to consider moving from their Northlands Road headquarters. The key issues were the age of the ground and buildings, the playing area, which was the smallest of all the counties' main grounds, and the lack of parking.

Hampshire announced the deaths of two major players, Jim Bailey and Danny Livingstone. Winchester won the Southern League for the first time and Paultons won the Hampshire League. The Southern League's representative XI won the Famous Grouse Trophy, beating the Three Counties League at Southampton. Scott, Middleton, Mark O'Connor, Cox and AD (Alan) Mullally enjoyed some success with the 2nd XI. Mullally then moved to Leicestershire before returning many years later.

1989

Champions: Worcestershire. Knock-out Cup: Warwickshire. Sunday League: Lancashire.
B&H Cup; Nottinghamshire.

By the start of the season Hampshire had competed in eight semi-finals, five in the longer, Gillette/Nat West sponsored competition since 1963 and three in the B&H Cup since 1972. Of those eight, they had won just one, in 1988. In 1989, they beat Cheshire, Glamorgan and Surrey before their home semi-final with Middlesex, who began with an opening stand of 165 and posted 267-7. Hampshire lost early wickets but Chris Smith played superbly for 114 until a full toss from Fraser broke his thumb and Hampshire lost from the last ball by just three runs. In the B&H Cup they won only once, failing to defend their trophy. They rose to equal sixth in the Sunday League, with a tied match at Lord's. Many Sunday games were rain affected and when they scored 254-4 at Trent Bridge in their last match it was only the second time they had passed 200 – Robin Smith (131) and Wood adding a record 152 for the third wicket. Connor, with 23, led the Sunday wicket takers.

Aymes played only against Oxford University, where he equalled Parks' Hampshire record of 10 catches in the match. In the Championship, Marshall returned and they rose nine places to sixth; he took 64 wickets at 16.67, Bakker 77 at 22.49 and Connor 59 at 21.27. Robin Smith, one of *Wisden's* Cricketers of the Year, missed games playing for England and scored 143 v Australia at Old Trafford but he led Hampshire's averages with 968 runs at 56.94. Chris Smith, Nicholas and Terry all passed 1,000 runs and James was only 18 short, as well as taking 37 wickets. Twenty-year-old left-hander Julian Wood made a promising start, hitting his first ball for four and scoring 58, 1, 45, 96 & 65 in his first five first-class innings. Nicholas was bowling more regularly and took 6-37 v Somerset and Maru 8-41 (12-105 in the match) v Kent, both at Southampton

Jefferies was retained as cover for Marshall but the two could not play together. He was awarded his county cap but left at the end of the season. David Turner, who had made his debut in 1966, retired at the end of his 24th consecutive season – the longest unbroken run at Hampshire since the Second World War. He is the only man to have won Championship, Sunday League and Cup Final trophies at Hampshire and shares with Sean Ervine the current record of five 'medals'. On retirement, he stood ninth in the list of runs for Hampshire in first-class cricket, scored many more in limited-overs matches and was a superb outfielder. Cowley left after a good all-round career and had a brief spell with Glamorgan. He is now a first-class umpire. Londoner Andrew, still only 23, moved to Essex.

Pre-season, Hampshire visited Dubai, playing five matches including two v Surrey. Calmore Sports won the Hampshire League for the first time, Darren Flint and Jason Laney showed promise for the Colts and Sean Morris and Kevin Shine were among promising players in the 2nd XI. Hampshire announced the death of their oldest living player, Bill Scott from the Isle of Wight.

Mike Taylor who was still working at the club in a marketing capacity, was awarded a Testimonial. The club had 4,448 members, a reduction of just 33 on the previous year. The net profit announced for the year had risen from £37,280 in 1988 to £63,972. Membership subscriptions, including new life members, reached £130,000. The Australians brought a total attendance of nearly 18,000 including over 4,000 paying over the three days. Almost 28,000 paid at the gate throughout the season.

1990

Champions: Middlesex. Knock-out Cup: Lancashire. Sunday League: Derbyshire.
B&H Cup: Lancashire.

Cecil Paris stepped down as President and Wilfrid Weld was Hampshire's new President – he is now their Patron. In April, Gordon Greenidge scored 149 in his 100th Test match. When Hampshire entertained Middlesex at Bournemouth in August, they needed to win to sustain a challenge for the title but Middlesex posted 430-7 declared and for Middlesex, Neil Taylor, from New Milton, took 3-44 to restrict his home county. Hampshire failed to win the next four matches and had to be content with third place – in the event, the last time Nicholas's side would challenge for the title. In mid-September Hampshire set a county record, scoring 446-8 (in 104 overs) to beat Gloucestershire at Southampton. Robin Smith led the way with 124, Middleton 82, Nicholas 54*, while Terry, Marshall and Maru all passed 40 – against an attack that opened with Walsh and Lawrence.

They began the season with an illustrious new signing, David Gower, although his arrival restricted opportunities for younger batsmen like Scott, Wood and Cox. Chris Smith and Terry led the run scorers although Middleton impressed with 1,238 runs at 47.61. Marshall was only 38 short of 1,000 runs and took 72 wickets at 19.18 but next in the bowling averages came Maru with 66 wickets at 36.66 each.

Hampshire were fifth in the Sunday League, failed to qualify for the B&H knock-out stages and reached their 10th semi-final and their ninth defeat, one so bitter that Man-of-the-Match Marshall could not bear to collect his award. They beat Leicestershire (Maru 3-46), Essex (CL Smith 106), Yorkshire (Marshall 4-17) and met Northamptonshire at Southampton in the semi-final. Their opponents were all out from the final ball for 284 and Hampshire lost three wickets until Gower (86) and Marshall (77) took them towards their target. Bakker faced the last ball needing two to win, completed one but was run out returning for the second. It was little consolation when they went to Scarborough and won the four-team trophy for the seventh time in nine visits.

Chris Smith's benefit realised £181,679 – almost £100,000 more than Hampshire's previous highest. Initial discussions were under way to find a possible site and design for a new ground – probably outside Southampton's city limits. Tremlett played in eight first-class matches but was now working increasingly as a coach alongside Peter Sainsbury. Scott moved to Gloucestershire and West Indian fast bowler Linden Joseph departed, having made little impression except with a batting average of 152.0 – courtesy of one dismissal. Hungerford won the Hampshire Cricket League for the first time.

1991

Champions: Essex. **Knock-out Cup: Hampshire.** Sunday League: Nottinghamshire. B&H Cup: Worcestershire.

With Marshall touring, Hampshire signed Pakistani pace bowler Aqib Javed. They finished ninth in the Championship with five wins in 22 three and four-day matches. Aymes replaced Parks as the regular wicket-keeper, Chris Smith, James, Terry and Gower passed 1,000 runs but the bowling was weak – Aqib with 53 at 31.24 was top wicket taker and only Ayling averaged less than 30. They did not win in the Championship until late July and never took all 20 wickets in a match.

Hampshire lost at Chelmsford in the quarter final of the B&H Cup, and for the first time were bottom of the Sunday League, winning just three of their 16 games. Yet they could play limited-overs cricket, especially when their batters performed. In the Nat West Trophy they were superb; batting second every time they beat Berkshire by 10 wickets, Lancashire by eight, Nottinghamshire by seven and in the semi-final at Edgbaston, only Chris Smith was dismissed as Terry (62*) and Robin Smith (64*) won the match with 10 overs to spare; this was semi-final number 11 and a second victory. At Chesterfield, Chris Smith (114) shared with Kevan James (101) an unusual record when the pair of them scored centuries in an all out total of just 258 – no other batsman reached double figures.

Chris Smith then surprised everyone by departing for a non-playing post in Australia and his replacement, Middleton, opened on Nat West debut at Lord's, scoring 78 as Hampshire chased Surrey's 240-5. Gower captained after Nicholas's arm was broken by Waqar Younis in the previous match, and with Robin Smith also scoring 78, the match came to a thrilling climax in perfect September weather. Ayling hit a huge six in the late evening gloom and then, with two balls and four wickets to spare, a four off Bicknell to win the trophy for the first time. This was Hampshire's first Cup victory in the oldest limited-overs competition, although they shared with Middlesex the record of being the only side never eliminated in the first round.

In December, all Hampshire, probably all cricket, mourned the death of the greatest broadcaster and Hampshire-man, John Arlott. Peter Sainsbury from Southampton, batter, bowler, catcher, coach and double Champion, finally retired. He won three trophies as a player and four more as a coach and his association went back forty years. He scored almost 20,000 first-class runs for the county, took 1,245 wickets, and held 601 catches in 593 matches. Tim Tremlett moved up to coach and was joined by Richard Hayward, who returned to Hampshire to take charge of the 2nd XI.

England shared the Test series with the West Indies. Robin Smith scored 416 runs with two centuries and an average of 83.2. Gordon Greenidge was no longer opening the batting but Marshall took 20 wickets. Mark Nicholas was awarded a benefit in 1991 that realised £175,000. Havant won the Southern League whose representative XI was beaten in the final of the Inter-League Cup by the Essex League.

1992

Champions: Essex. Knock-out Cup: Northamptonshire. Sunday League: Middlesex.
B&H Cup: Hampshire.

Malcolm Marshall returned but Hampshire finished in 15th place in the Championship, the first of six consecutive seasons in the bottom third of the table which had now expanded to 18 sides to include Durham. Hampshire started well, winning four of the first five matches and were undefeated when they met the eventual Champions Essex at Bournemouth in mid-June. Hampshire scored 300-8 declared and forced Essex to follow-on by the narrowest margin. They reduced them to 165-7 but the late order recovered and set Hampshire 160 to win in a minimum of 26 overs. Hampshire went for the runs but were bowled out during the 28th over for just 80. This is the only occasion Hampshire have enforced the follow-on and lost and in 1992 they won only one more match.

Hampshire improved significantly on Sundays and finished third, Middleton top scoring with 592 runs, while Udal took 31 wickets. They beat Dorset in the Nat West Trophy but lost to Kent in the next round, three days before the two sides met at Lord's in the Final of the B&H Cup. In that competition, their first competitive visit to Scotland was abandoned but they won every game against first-class opposition, including a six-wicket victory against Somerset in the semi final. At last, Malcolm Marshall had his Hampshire day at Lord's – or days, as the rain sent play into the Sunday. Robin Smith scored 90 as Hampshire posted 253-5 (Marshall 29*) and Kent wickets fell regularly as they lost by 41 runs – Marshall 3-33. This was the third cup trophy of Nicholas's time – Terry, Smith, Connor and Ayling played in all three and the first three also in the Sunday League title of 1986.

In first-class cricket, Middleton enjoyed a superb season with 1,780 runs at almost 50 per innings. James, Gower and Nicholas also passed 1,000 runs but only Ayling with 48 wickets at 20.6 averaged less than 25, while Udal was leading wicket taker with 58 at 34.69. Middleton, Terry and Smith hit centuries in the innings v Sussex at Southampton to equal the county record. Shine took a hat-trick (and four in five balls) v Lancashire at Old Trafford. His figures were 5-58 & 8-47 in the match but in 15 more matches he took only 27 wickets.

Hampshire met Middlesex in Hampshire's last-ever *home* match at Bournemouth. For the second year, Hampshire 2nd XI finished fourth in their Championship. Hursley Park won the Southern League and Rothmans Village Championship. Parks and Bakker retired at the end of the season – Parks following a benefit that raised £124,642. In the autumn, Hampshire learned of the death of Roy Marshall, age 62 in Taunton. Membership had risen to 5,495.

1993

County Champions: Middlesex. Knock-out Cup: Warwickshire. Sunday League: Glamorgan. B&H Cup: Derbyshire.

The County Championship moved entirely to four-day cricket. Although Hampshire had ceased playing cricket in Bournemouth, they continued to play in Southampton, Portsmouth and Basingstoke while the officers and committee explored options for the new ground.

On the field Marshall returned for his final season but took only 28 wickets in 13 matches at 30.67. Udal led the wicket takers but his 74 wickets also cost over 30 each and while Terry and Gower passed 1,000 runs only those two and Smith (57.05) averaged over 40. Robin Smith scored 167* v Australia, a record for England in a limited-overs match.

Hampshire finished 13th and Gower too retired at the end of the season but the saddest departure was Ayling, the highly talented Portsmouth boy who never recovered from a knee injury caused by a mid-pitch collision in a pre-season friendly. He was only 26. He would return as a coach some years later. Shine, Ian Turner and Wood also left the staff.

The match aggregate of 1,457 runs v Sussex at Portsmouth was a record for a Hampshire match and their fourth innings of 351 their second highest score ever in a match lost. Hampshire beat Gloucestershire by one wicket to equal five other instances of the narrowest possible wickets win.

Hampshire beat Staffordshire but lost their next cup match at Hove by nine wickets with both Sussex openers scoring centuries. They finished 15th in the Sunday League and having progressed to the B&H quarter final lost to Northamptonshire by seven wickets on the second day. There was media excitement for the 2nd XI match v Worcestershire at Southampton when Liam Botham made his debut for Hampshire, taking 4-63.

Tim Tremlett received a benefit of £110,641. Portsmouth, formerly South Hants Touring Club, won the Southern League. Promising 2nd XI players included 'Will' Kendall, Mark Garaway and 'Jim' Bovill from Durham University, whose father had played for Hampshire 2nd XI. Derek Kenway captained Hampshire Schools under-15s and played for England schools. Alan Rowe was appointed Youth Development Officer, working principally with young players from 8-14. Membership fell to at 5,070 with those paying at the gate numbering 22,316. The club declared a "satisfactory operating profit" of £35,000. The gate for the match v Australia realised £31,000 and the sale of the groundsman's cottage at Bournemouth a further £26,000.

1994

Champions: Warwickshire. Knock-out Cup: Worcestershire. Sunday League: Warwickshire. B&H Cup: Warwickshire.

With the exception of a run in the B&H Cup, this was a disappointing year on the field but highly significant in that Hampshire signed the lease for the new ground at West End in the Borough of Eastleigh, which would become the Rose Bowl.

In the winter of 1993–1994 Robin Smith scored 175 v West Indies in Antigua, his highest Test Match score ('Lara's match'). One of Smith's opponents, Winston Benjamin, replaced Marshall as Hampshire's overseas player and former England bowler Norman Cowans joined the staff. Sadly, the new attack was not successful and Hampshire slipped one place to 13th. Sean Morris topped the batting averages, while Smith, Nicholas and Terry passed 1,000 runs but Benjamin played in only nine of the 17 matches and Connor (72) and Udal (69) led the wicket takers. On seven occasions, Udal took five or more wickets in an innings and he was selected by England for his limited-overs international debut v New Zealand at Edgbaston. He took 2-39 as England won. Terry's benefit realised £143,277.

Hampshire scored 603-7 declared v Surrey at Southampton, the third successive year they posted their highest score against that team. At the time, it was the fifth highest total in their history and the first score over 600 since 1920. Paul Whitaker, who had been with Derbyshire without making his debut, joined Hampshire and scored 94 in the second innings of his first-class debut v Leicestershire at Leicester – it remains the highest first-class debut score for Hampshire. Phil de Freitas took a 'hat-trick' for Derbyshire at Southampton.

In the B&H Cup, Hampshire beat Yorkshire and Essex before a rain-affected semi-final at Worcester, which, despite a century from Smith, the home side won with three wickets and three overs to spare on the second day. They beat Cambridgeshire but lost to Kent in the Nat West Trophy and finished 12th in the Sunday League. Cox and Martin Jean-Jacques left Hampshire.

1995

Champions: Warwickshire. Knock-out Cup: Warwickshire. Sunday League: Kent. B&H Cup: Lancashire.

Mark Nicholas's sides won four limited-overs trophies in seven seasons, starting with the Sunday League at the Oval in 1986 and ending in 1992 at Lord's with the B&H Cup. At the end of the 1995 season Mark Nicholas retired and handed the captaincy to John Stephenson, who had arrived from Essex and played under him in that last season.

Nicholas led the run scorers in his last season, only he and Terry passing 1,000 runs as Hampshire finished 13th again. Heath Streak from Zimbabwe replaced Benjamin for one year and he, Udal and Connor all passed 50 wickets but each at an average above 30. Bovill took 12-68 in the match at Durham but could not sustain that promise and injuries curtailed his career. Once again Hampshire finished last in the Sunday League, they lost in the first round of the Nat West and beat only the Combined Universities in the B&H Cup.

At the end of the season, Tony Middleton moved into a coaching role, which he still holds. The greatest cheer came from the good weather and the 2nd XI who won their Championship, winning 10 of their 17 matches. The main players were Middleton, Matthew Keech and Martin Thursfield (both from Middlesex), Glyn Treagus, Morris, Laney, Garaway, Maru, Flint, Whitaker and Kendall

1996

Champions: Leicestershire. Knock-out Cup: Lancashire. Sunday League: Surrey.
B&H Cup: Lancashire

John Stephenson was appointed captain and Benjamin returned as overseas player, while Malcolm Marshall returned as coach. Robin Smith scored 66 & 13 on his final Test match appearance (in South Africa) but there was a strong feeling that he was discarded prematurely. He departed with a Test average of 43.67 – better than his contemporaries, including Gooch, Atherton, Stewart and Thorpe – although he was cheered as Hampshire's first beneficiary to exceed £200,000. At Hampshire, Terry's career came to a similarly unhappy end during the season.

Hampshire struggled in all competitions, dropping one place to 14th in the Championship, 15th in the Sunday League, failing to qualify for the B&H Cup and losing to Essex, after beating Worcestershire in the Nat West Trophy. In the Championship, Smith and Laney passed 1,000 runs and the latter, at 23, showed real promise. Connor took 49 wickets at 21.85 but no one passed 50, although with Hampshire struggling with injuries, two youngsters enjoyed promising debuts. In Portsmouth at the end of August, Liam Botham took 5-67 v Middlesex although the visitors won easily, and in the next match v Glamorgan at Southampton, Dimitri ('Dimi') Mascarenhas had the best debut figures for the county since 1899, with 6-88 (& 3-62). Botham, however, decided not to pursue his cricket career, choosing rugby instead.

Despite the generally gloomy results, two men enjoyed very special days. James began the season unsure of his place but had a reasonable season, including the unique record in the tourist match when he followed four Indian wickets in four balls with a century. Then Connor took 9-36 v Gloucestershire at Southampton – the fifth best figures ever for Hampshire. The new captain tried to lead by example but struggled with the bat, while Benjamin played in just two first-class matches and left the county.

1997

Champions: Glamorgan. Knock-out Cup: Essex. Sunday League: Warwickshire. B&H Cup: Surrey.

For around 45 years Hampshire had favoured West Indian overseas players, but in 1997 Matthew Hayden, the first of a succession of Australians, arrived at Hampshire. He enjoyed a successful season in a weak side. As in 1996, Hampshire finished 14th in the Championship and 15th in the Sunday League and won one match fewer in the Nat West Trophy. They went out to Glamorgan, despite posting 302-6 in their 60 overs.

Hayden, with 1,446 runs at 53.55, was the only man to pass 1,000 first-class runs. He scored 654 in the Sunday League at 43.6, 90 & 20 in the two Nat West Trophy matches and 216 runs at 54.0 in the B&H Cup. He scored 235* & 119 v Warwickshire at Southampton, while David Hemp scored centuries in both innings for the visitors – only the second instance in Hampshire's history (see 1927). Hayden was easily the player of the season but he could not carry a side where no bowler took 40 wickets and only James averaged less than 30. Towards the end of the season Hampshire gave debuts to pace bowlers, Simon Francis and Tom Hansen, against Worcestershire, who posted 538-2 declared. Hick (303*) made the highest score ever v Hampshire and with Moody (180*) added a record 438* for the third wicket.

Cardigan Connor received £147,770 from his benefit. At the end of the season, Hayden departed along with Bovill, who had suffered with injuries, and Stuart Milburn, who had come from Yorkshire with only modest success. Jimmy Gray retired as the Chairman of the Cricket Committee. There was little to cheer on the field but the front cover of the 1997 *Handbook* carried a computer graphic image of the pavilion intended for the new ground at West End and the "Cutting of the First Turf" in the farmer's field took place on Tuesday 25 March 1997.

On 1 January, the England & Wales Cricket Board came into being, bringing together the work of the TCCB, NCA and Cricket Council (see 1968). In August, the ECB Management Board published *Raising the Standard* with proposals for the reorganisation of English cricket at all levels. Not every proposal was implemented but one result was the formation of the Hampshire Cricket Board in partnership with the County Cricket Club. Its responsibility was for cricket outside the first-class, professional game. Membership subscriptions were relatively stable but attendance at the match v Australia boosted income from the gate. The club declared a profit just below £20,000.

1998

Champions: Leicestershire. Knock-out Cup: Lancashire. Sunday League: Lancashire.
B&H Cup: Essex.

After two difficult seasons, Robin Smith replaced John Stephenson as captain, although Stephenson remained as a player. West Indian pace bowler Nixon McLean arrived as the new overseas player.

Hampshire enjoyed a better season, rising to sixth in the Championship, eighth in the Sunday League and reaching the semi-final of the Nat West Trophy. They began with an *away* fixture at Dean Park, Bournemouth v Dorset and, as Julian Shackleton, Derek's son, opened the bowling, were 0-3 before Smith and Aymes rescued them. They beat Essex and then Middlesex at Lord's by 144 runs and met Lancashire in the semi final – rather like the days of the early 1990s. Connor took 3-31 and Hampshire's target was 253 in 60 overs but Lancashire reduced them to 28-5 and despite the efforts of Mascarenhas, James and McLean they lost by 43 runs.

Giles White, with 1,211 first-class runs, was the leading batsman, although Kendall showed promise. McLean took 62 wickets at 25.40 and Alex Morris, who moved from Yorkshire, topped the averages with 50 wickets at 20.24. McLean, White and Mascarenhas received their caps from David Robinson, who had succeeded Jimmy Gray as Cricket Chairman. Richard Dibden and Paul Whitaker were released, while Connor and Maru retired. The latter took up a coaching appointment with Hampshire, while Connor left with a club record of 411 limited-overs wickets.

Australia's Women beat England's Women in their first international at Northlands Road although an earlier England women's XI captained by Rachel Heyhoe(-Flint) had played there against Hampshire 2nd XI in the early 1970s.

Maru's benefit realised £78,220. In April 1998, Hampshire agreed the sale of Northlands Road to Berkeley Homes Ltd for a sum just over £5m. In November 1998, work started at West End on the Nursery Ground and Golf Club and members visited the new site for the first time at the season's end. The timetable planned for Hampshire to leave Northlands Road in 2000 and play 2nd XI matches at the new ground in that same year. The club declared an overall profit of around £6,000, revealing that 65% of income came from the central ECB fund. Membership was "disappointingly" down to 4,124 including around 450 Life Members. Over the next 15 years, the membership rose to around 4,500 while the number of Life Members more than doubled.

GCA (Geoffrey) Adams (1928–1930), Hampshire's oldest living player, died in Australia in February just before his 98th birthday. Cecil Paris, former player, captain, Chairman, President and Patron died in April. He had also been Chairman of the TCCB, President of MCC and Chairman of the ICC.

1999

Champions: Surrey. Knock-out Cup: Gloucestershire. National League: Lancashire.
B&H Cup: Gloucestershire.

This was a period of dramatic changes at Hampshire and across the English game. In 1999, it focused on the World Cup, played during the summer in England. England performed poorly, lost a Test series to New Zealand and then another in the winter tour of South Africa. They won the last Test against an apparently 'generous' declaration by Hanse Cronje. On 24 May at Southampton, West Indies beat New Zealand in the World Cup by seven wickets and six days later Sri Lanka beat Kenya.

In the domestic game there were major changes too. Surrey won the last-ever 18-team County Championship, as from the end of the season the sides were split into two divisions. The old knock-out cup that had started as a 65-over competition was now just 50 overs and included (briefly) all the Minor Counties and County Cricket Board sides.

Hampshire beat a Kent Cricket Board side that included David Masters, then lost a thriller to Lancashire. Laney's 95 helped them post 239 and they had Lancashire 200-8 (McLean 3-27) but Muralitharan won the match with the bat. The Hampshire Cricket Board won against Suffolk and Shropshire before losing an exciting match to the full Glamorgan side at Southampton. For this year, the B&H sponsored competition became a "Super Cup" for the top eight sides in the previous year's Championship. Hampshire played one match, at Headingley, and were knocked out by nine wickets. The new National League was played over 45 overs and in two divisions. Hampshire called themselves 'the Hawks', found a new mascot, Harry, started in Division One but won just five matches and were relegated.

Pre-season, the pitch at Portsmouth was deemed not fit for first-class cricket and the matches switched to Southampton. In the Championship, Hampshire won five matches and finished seventh – in many seasons a perfectly good result but this year crucial in that it ensured them a place in the new First Division in 2000. They did so in controversial circumstances in a match at Derby where the home side clinched their place among the elite with bonus points then 'set up' a finish with 'non-bowlers' on the third day on the basis of forecast rain which did not materialise. On a tense last day, Derbyshire, 279-8 needed six to win, Peter Hartley dropped a catch, had Aldred lbw with three needed and immediately held a catch from his own bowling as Hampshire won by two runs.

Their success condemned Warwickshire to Division Two and the circumstances were not well received in the Midlands. The next day Hampshire played at Edgbaston, where Warwickshire needed to win to avoid relegation in the National League. They seemed in control when the rain came in the 10th over and the match was abandoned, just five balls before a positive result. Warwickshire were down again.

So the season ended in the kind of acrimony that is always possible with promotion and relegation. Hampshire's mood was lightened, however, by the announcement in September that they had secured the services of Shane Warne for the following year. But all these controversies and excitements were put into context with the death of Malcolm Marshall, who had been ill for some time. Hampshire were well-represented at his funeral in Barbados in November with Mark Nicholas reading the eulogy. He described a "universally loved and respected character" and "one of those special people".

Clair Slaney was appointed Women's Cricket Development Officer. Beneficiary Kevan James (£140,000) announced his retirement after 15 seasons and took up an appointment with the BBC. He now commentates on the ball-by-ball Championship service, introduced in 2013 as well as on Hampshire's limited-overs matches. At the new Rose Bowl, the Golf Course opened. Adi Aymes launched his 2000 benefit year and welcomed the new Millennium at midnight on 31 December with a (car) 'floodlit' match at Broadhalfpenny Down, Hambledon, which was halted for 'bad light' after one over and resumed the next morning, 1 January 2000.

Membership increased to 4,409 and the club declared "very satisfactory" financial results, with a pre-tax profit of £40,509.

2000

Champions: Surrey. Knock-out Cup: Gloucestershire. National League: Gloucestershire.
B&H Cup: Gloucestershire.

The new Millennium began with Wilfrid Weld as President and Brian Ford as Chairman of the Committee of Hampshire County Cricket Club but dramatic changes were looming in the constitution and personnel running the 'club'. In February 2000, the membership was asked to approve a proposal that the Club should become an Industrial and Provident Society by the end of the year. By that time, a controversy over new appointments undermined the stability of the Committee, which was struggling to raise the funding necessary to complete the Rose Bowl project – not least through the difficulties of finding a company to fund naming rights. In the autumn, Brian Ford resigned as Chairman and businessman Rod Bransgrove, recently elected to the Committee, took his place.

Nonetheless, cricket was played on the new ground. On 6 June on the Nursery Ground, Jimmy Adams faced the first ball from Hampshire-born Billy Taylor of Sussex 2nd XI and a few weeks later the 2nd XI played Glamorgan 2nd XI on the main ground. Hampshire welcomed Warne and also Alan Mullally, who returned from Leicestershire to the club he had first joined in 1988. These signings clearly strengthened the bowling, although only Udal in support reached 30 wickets while only Kendal with 1,156 runs at 41.28, averaged over 30 with the bat. Twenty-year-old Lawrence Prittipaul scored his first and Northlands Road's last century v Derbyshire. South African Jimmy Cook arrived as Hampshire's new coach.

In the Championship, Hampshire made a poor start, losing four and drawing two of the first six matches, although at the Oval Mascarenhas (59) and Francis (30*) added 90 for the last wicket, taking them within three runs of victory. During the season they played for the last time at Portsmouth, which included an enthralling duel between Warne and Dravid, and Southampton – in the event, their farewell to Basingstoke (with victory) was temporary.

The last match of the season was at Southampton, where Hampshire, already relegated, were beaten by Yorkshire's spinners. As the builders queued up to demolish the historic ground, the ECB's inspectors imposed a points fine for a poor pitch. On the next day, Hampshire lost their final National League game there to Nottinghamshire as they finished next-to-bottom of Division Two. There was farewell dinner in a huge marquee on the ground, attended by over 1,000 guests and presided over by Mark Nicholas, one of a number of Hampshire captains in attendance.

Warne had made his debut at Chelmsford as Hampshire fared better in the B&H Cup, restored to its normal form. They reached a quarter-final at Cardiff but were bowled out for just 69. In the Nat West Trophy they won matches against the Kent Cricket Board, Durham and Middlesex but with Warne away on international duty lost the semi-final at Edgbaston despite 61 from captain Robin Smith.

The structure of local league cricket was altered, with the expansion and renaming of the Southern League (1969–1999), which became the Southern Electric Premier League (Divisions One, Two and Three).

With the arrival of Warne and Mullally and first division cricket, it was not surprising that the membership rose from 4,409 to 4,757 but with the new ground opening, the club declared a significant operating loss and financial results that were "even more disappointing than had been anticipated". Aymes received a benefit cheque for £174,995.

2001

Champions: Yorkshire. Knock-out Cup: Somerset. National League: Kent. B&H Cup: Surrey.

In February 2001, Kate Laven in *Wisden Cricket Monthly* reported, "Hampshire's financial deficit is so bad that … there were rumours that it could become the first cricket club to face bankruptcy".

At an Emergency Committee Meeting that winter, the 18-man Committee acknowledged that they were unable to continue functioning financially. Rod Bransgrove, the new Chairman, underwrote a share issue of £4m, thus converting the club into a private company. He wrote to all members in February urging support for a vote that would establish Hampshire as "the first county cricket club to become privately owned with a full-time professional management team", adding that Hampshire "will be the first club to respond to the changing environment but certainly not the last". This change was approved by the AGM in March and effectively ended the life of Hampshire *County Cricket Club*, although some of the formal management and name changes would follow. The first meeting of the new Members Club was held in May 2001, the Friendly Society ceased trading on 31 October and the new Board of Directors took control of the business. They were, Rod Bransgrove, Graham Walker, Tim Tremlett, Mark Nicholas, Feroze Janmohamed and Nick Pike.

At the AGM, the club reported an operating loss of £193,075. The Rose Bowl opened for cricket in 2001 but the pavilion and dressing rooms were not complete and temporary marquees were erected on the Berm. Graham Walker had arrived from Cardiff's Millennium Stadium to take charge at the Rose Bowl, succeeding Tony Baker, who retired after many years of involvement in Hampshire cricket. Mike Taylor would also retire before the start of the next season.

Pre-season, Hampshire played in South Africa for the first time in the Winelands Tournament. They lost all three matches. The first scheduled fixture at the Rose Bowl, a B&H Match v Essex on 2 May, never started because of rain. Two days later Hampshire lost to Surrey in the same competition but they fared better in the first Championship fixture, beating Worcestershire by 124 runs. Mascarenhas scored the first century and took the first wicket while Alex Morris had match figures of 8-66. Hick scored 120.

Neil Johnson came as the new overseas player and was the only man to pass 1,000 runs, adding 23 wickets. He was also Man-of-the-Match in late July when Hampshire beat the Australians by two wickets. Hayden scored 142 against his old county, Warne took 4-31 and Robin Smith scored 113.

Mullally took 8-90 v Warwickshire, which was the best bowling at the new ground until Balcombe in 2012, and with 62 wickets at 17.50 he led the bowlers. Morris and Udal passed 50 wickets and Tremlett showed promise, as did batsmen Kenway and John Francis but batting was not easy on the new ground – Robin Smith failed to reach 600 runs and averaged below 25. However, he became Hampshire leading 'Sunday' League batsman and set the record for their appearances in the knock-out cup (Nat West/C&G).

Hampshire finished bottom of their B&H group but in the Championship they were runners-up to Sussex and clinched promotion with bonus points at Trent Bridge, where they faced a youthful Kevin Pietersen. Johnson scored a century at Durham but they lost their only 50-overs knock-out match, now sponsored by C&G. They improved in the National League but finished fourth so missed promotion – again Johnson was top scorer and he, Kenway and Morris received their county caps. In that competition, Hampshire played under floodlights at home for the first time, beating Sussex on 5 July in front of a Rose Bowl capacity of 5,000. Alex Morris's brother Zac was released and John Stephenson, Andrew Sexton and Simon Francis also left the staff. Stephenson's benefit had realised £192,097.

Hampshire 2nd XI won their Championship with good performances from Prittipaul, Laney, John Francis, James Hamblin, Iain Brunnschweiler, James Schofield, and Irfan Shah. Spin bowler Charlie van der Gucht was on a summer contract while at Durham University but in July broke both legs in a road accident. Hampshire Academy included 'Chris' Tremlett, Damien Shirazi, 'Chris' Benham, Ian Hilsum and Luke Merry – Tremlett was already playing regularly in the 1st XI.

BAT Sports won the Southern Electric Premier League, with Havant runners-up. Membership rose slightly from 4,757 in 2000 to 4,839. All matches were now played at the Rose Bowl and the Southampton area accounted for around 35% of members.

2002

Champions: Surrey. Knock-out Cup: Yorkshire. National League: Glamorgan.
B&H Cup: Warwickshire.

Neil Johnson returned and John Crawley signed for Hampshire and enjoyed a remarkable start, which won back his England place. His debut score of 272* at Canterbury was a record Hampshire debut and maiden century score and he averaged almost 55 for the county. Johnson was less successful, however, and Hampshire were relegated after one season in Division One. Mullally topped the bowling averages but at 25.13, and only Udal took more than 50 wickets. Udal's benefit realised a record for the county of £241,675. In the new century, changes in the administration and taxation of benefits mean that final amounts are not announced.

At Edgbaston, Warwickshire's Nick Knight and Alan Richardson added a record 214 for the 10th wicket v Hampshire. At the end of the season, Hampshire v Surrey was the second highest aggregate in Hampshire's history (1557 runs for 38 wickets) but the Rose Bowl often caused difficulties for batsmen. A young James Anderson took 9-50 in the match as Lancashire beat Hampshire on a pitch designated "poor" by the inspectors, while the Indians declared to avoid risking Tendulkar and Dravid on the surface. Kendall carried his bat for just 53* v Leicestershire – the first instance at the Rose Bowl. Loughborough University played Hampshire and included Jimmy Adams (53), Chris Benham (54*), John Francis – and Monty Panesar.

After more than 30 seasons, the B&H Cup came to an end. Hampshire won a thrilling last match v Middlesex by three runs although it was not sufficient to take them to the knock-out stages. Crawley scored a century and Angus Fraser played his last match for Middlesex before taking up journalism.

Robin Smith relinquished the captaincy at the end of the season with the expectation that Warne would replace him. Coach Jimmy Cook was sacked in the season and replaced temporarily by Tim Tremlett until Paul Terry returned to Hampshire to take over. At the end of the season, Aymes and White retired and Laney, Schofield and Shah were released.

Wilfrid Weld, who had been President, became Patron, while Colin Ingleby-Mackenzie was welcomed as President. A share issue in March 2002 raised £2.65m and the pavilion was completed and opened for the season. Havant won the Southern Electric Premier League, with BAT Sports runners-up. Hampshire Academy won Division Two and were promoted to the Premier Division.

2003

Champions: Sussex. Knock-out Cup: Gloucestershire. National League: Surrey. T20: Surrey.

Graham Walker stepped down from his position as Chief Executive in November 2002, and was replaced by Nick Pike. In September 2002 Hampshire agreed with Warne that he would return in 2003 and captain Hampshire. Playing for Australia during the winter, he provided samples to the Sports Drug Agency that revealed traces of a prohibited substance and he was banned for 12 months from February 2003. Hampshire needed a new captain and an overseas player to join Simon Katich, so they appointed John Crawley and signed Wasim Akram, who would be 37 in June. They gave another contract to Ed Giddins from Surrey, who had played for Hampshire 2nd XI in his early career.

Katich scored 1,143 runs at 60.15 but Wasim played in only five first-class matches and Giddins three. Neither was really fit for a full county season and both departed in mid-season. Chaminda Vaas came for the last few weeks but had little impact and, as in 2002, Hampshire won just two matches – their worst record since 1980.

Nonetheless, one of those victories was among the most remarkable in their history when they beat Glamorgan at the Rose Bowl after following-on – only the third instance in their history (after 1895 & 1922). It was more remarkable because Wasim and Giddins had just finished, Udal was injured and Kendall was omitted. A very young Hampshire side struggled as Glamorgan scored 437, and no one reached 30 for Hampshire. Two hundred and fifty-two behind, they fell to 194-5 before Pothas (121), Mascarenhas (75) and Havant club cricketer Richard Hindley, with 68 in his only first-class match, helped Hampshire to set a target of 198. Glamorgan were 33-2 overnight and Tremlett (6-51) and Bruce (3-42) bowled them to victory by 93 runs. It was only the third instance in the County Championship that a team with a lead in excess of 250 lost the match.

One of the season's highlights was the first international limited-overs match at the Rose Bowl, South Africa v Zimbabwe on 10 July. There was also the first major concert on the ground, with Darius, Blue and the Royal Philharmonic Orchestra. Aled Jones also performed in concert at the Rose Bowl – a rare opportunity for 'classical' music fans at a venue that mainly promoted 'pop' acts including the Who, Oasis, Neil Diamond, REM and Billy Joel. After a few years, those concerts ceased – at least temporarily.

2003 saw the start of English T20 Competition with the first televised match Hampshire v Sussex at the Rose Bowl plus a crowd of 9,000. Hampshire won that first game but lost all the others and did not qualify. However, amid the disappointments, Hampshire finished third and were promoted in the National League, while the 2nd XI won their knock-out cup.

Robin Smith was awarded a Testimonial following his 1996 benefit and at the season's end he retired. He scored exactly 12,000 runs in limited-overs matches for the county (average 42.70) – the only man to pass 10,000 at Hampshire – while his 19,894 runs in first-class matches (42.09) placed him ninth in Hampshire's records. He had also played more Test Matches for England than any other Hampshire player. John Francis, Alex Morris, Iain Brunnschweiler and Charlie van der Gucht left the staff.

BAT Sports won the Southern Electric Premier League, with Bournemouth runners-up and Hampshire Academy in third place.

2004

Champions: Warwickshire. Knock-out Cup: Gloucestershire. National League: Glamorgan.
T20: Leicestershire.

Shane Warne (captain) and Michael Clarke were the two overseas players although when Clarke returned to Australia, Shane Watson replaced him as the second overseas player and in his one Championship appearance scored a century on county debut, the fifth Hampshire player to do so. Watson also scored 97* v Kent in the T20, helping Hampshire to clinch a quarter-final place. At that time it was Hampshire's highest T20 score. At Hove, Hampshire arrested a run of defeats since their victory v Sussex in the first-ever match in 2003. Mascarenhas took 5-14 including the first ever T20 'hat-trick' as Sussex were dismissed for 67. In the quarter-final, Hampshire lost at home to Lancashire by nine wickets.

In the Championship, Hampshire were promoted, finishing runners-up to Nottinghamshire. Crawley scored 301* and Michael Clarke two centuries in the match at Trent Bridge. Crawley's innings was the first Hampshire triple century since RH Moore's record innings in 1937. Hampshire posted 641-4 declared but Nottinghamshire replied with 612 and the match was drawn. It was only the third time in a Championship match that both sides passed 600 on first innings. At the Rose Bowl, Jacques (Yorkshire) and Jefferson (Essex) both scored double centuries and Essex beat Hampshire by 384 runs, Hampshire's highest-ever runs defeat. No batsman scored 1,000 runs but seven averaged over 30 and Crawley led the way with 938 at 52.11. Mascarenhas took 52 wickets at 18.67 and Warne 51 at 24.13.

Hampshire finished third in Division One of the National League; Nic Pothas was top scorer and Mullally and Warne led the wicket takers, although Mascarenhas was most economical. In the C&G Trophy Hampshire beat Cheshire but at Bristol, Warne elected to bat first on a green pitch and they were dismissed for 154, losing by three wickets.

Clarke and Tremlett received their county caps, while Michael Brown (from Middlesex), Benham, Greg Lamb and Billy Taylor (from Sussex) made debuts alongside Clarke and Watson. At the end of the season, Will Kendall and James Hamblin retired.

Hampshire gained approval to install permanent floodlights from 2006. A scheduled international match between New Zealand and West Indies was abandoned with no play. During September, ICC Trophy matches were played at various English grounds including five at the Rose Bowl (in one of which, England beat Sri Lanka). The tournament was not a success until the exciting final at the Oval and the Rose Bowl encountered difficulties with transport and poor weather.

South Wilts won the Southern Electric Premier League, with Havant runners-up.

2005

Champions: Nottinghamshire. **Knock-out Cup: Hampshire.** National League: Essex.
T20: Somerset.

After 13 barren years, Hampshire won a trophy, defeating Warwickshire in the C&G Trophy Final at Lord's in an exciting match on a fine day. Since they also finished runners-up to County Champions Nottinghamshire, it was a successful season, although the Championship conclusion brought frustration.

During the winter Hampshire signed Sean Ervine, who had played for Zimbabwe in the Rose Bowl's first international match, plus Kevin Pietersen and Richard Logan from Nottinghamshire. Pietersen made an impressive debut for England's limited-overs side in South Africa, scoring three centuries for England in that series. He then participated in England's thrilling recovery of the Ashes in 2005. Chris Tremlett made his limited-overs debut for England and took two wickets in two balls v Bangladesh at Trent Bridge.

Hampshire beat Shropshire, Glamorgan, Surrey and Yorkshire on their way to the Lord's Final. At the Oval, Surrey posted 358-6, a record against the county, but Watson with 132 led the reply, supported by forties from Crawley, New Zealander Craig McMillan and Udal who was deputising as captain for Warne while he participated in the Ashes series. Ervine's century took Hampshire to victory in the semi-final and he repeated the feat in the final, while Australians ('Andy') Bichel and Watson took three wickets each. Despite a fine century from Nick Knight, Hampshire won by 18 runs.

By contrast, Hampshire won just five of their 16 National League matches, finished bottom and were relegated. They won just three of their eight T20 matches so did not qualify for the knock-out stages.

In the Championship, Hampshire won three and drew two of the first five matches before a reverse at Stratford, from where they went to Trent Bridge and, in a rain-affected match, challenged Nottinghamshire to score 276 to win. They reached 250-4 but with 18 needed from four overs, Chris Tremlett's 'hat-trick' reduced them to 261-9 and Warne completed the victory. With Pothas injured, deputy John Crawley effected six dismissals in the second innings – a Hampshire record. They topped the table but two defeats followed.

At Cheltenham, Bichel, who had replaced McMillan, scored 138 on debut, the sixth debut centurion at Hampshire, sharing a record eighth-wicket partnership with Pothas (139), which rescued Hampshire from 81-7 as they added 257. In mid-September Hampshire still had hopes of the title until at Canterbury, Nottinghamshire declared, setting Kent 420 in 70 overs, and bowled them out. The new Champions came to the Rose Bowl for the last match and with Warne still angry about that game, Hampshire posted their record score of 714-5, although he declared on Crawley when, with 311*, he was just five runs short of Moore's record score for Hampshire. Mascarenhas and Udal bowled Hampshire to victory by an innings and 188 runs.

On 13 June, at the Rose Bowl, England beat Australia by 100 runs in the first-ever T20 international, while Oasis appeared in a concert on the ground. The plc announced a significant operating loss. Two local players, Derek Kenway and Lawrence Prittipaul, were released and Alan Mullally, who was the season's beneficiary, retired.

BAT Sports won the Southern Electric Premier League, with South Wilts runners-up.

2006

Champions: Sussex. Knock-out cup: Sussex. Pro40: Essex. T20: Leicestershire.

Glen Delve came to Hampshire as their new Chief Executive; he would later become managing Director, leaving in 2012, at which point Rod Bransgrove took on the role. In the winter of 2006 Shaun Udal was a member of England's touring side and took 4-14 v India in Bombay to help them clinch victory. Udal was the first Hampshire-born, Hampshire cricketer to represent England in a Test Match since AJL Hill in South Africa in 1896. Shane Warne returned as captain and Hampshire finished third in the Championship, although never quite in contention as they had been in 2005.

In the Championship, John Crawley was the outstanding batsman again with 1,737 runs at 66.80 while Jimmy Adams realised his promise and (age 25) scored 1,173 runs at 45.11 – including 262* at Trent Bridge. Pothas averaged 64.86 and he and newcomer Michael Carberry (Surrey and Kent) passed 900. The bowling was less strong; Warne, with 58 wickets at 27.08, led the wicket takers and Tremlett, with 34 wickets at 24.55, topped the averages but missed seven matches with injury. The overseas player, Australian Dominic Thorneley, had an unremarkable season although he was most effective in limited-overs cricket.

Hampshire beat Yorkshire in the Championship twice in season for the first time and were the first side ever to score over 400 in a fourth innings against Yorkshire to win a match – Adams leading the way with 168*. Billy Taylor took a 'hat-trick' v Middlesex – the first by anyone at the Rose Bowl. Crawley scored two hundreds in the same match v Nottinghamshire at the Rose Bowl, the only instance on that ground. Pothas took seven dismissals (all caught) v Lancashire at Old Trafford – a Hampshire record. To induce a declaration, Warne used all eleven bowlers in the match v Middlesex at Lord's – the first instance by Hampshire since 1897 – but the match ended in a draw.

Hampshire enjoyed most success in the revamped National League, now known as the Pro40. They won five of their eight matches, finishing third, which took them into a televised promotion play-off against Glamorgan at the Rose Bowl, which Hampshire won by 151 runs. They posted 265-9 in their 40 overs, led by Chris Benham with 158. Glamorgan collapsed and only a last wicket partnership of 25 took them to three figures. In the C&G Hampshire finished fourth in their group with only the top teams qualifying directly for the final, although again they made Glamorgan suffer, posting 310-7 in their 50 overs, the highest limited-overs total on the ground.

In March, the President, Colin Ingleby-Mackenzie, died and on 29 June many Hampshire players and officials attended his Memorial Service at St Paul's Cathedral. Out of respect, the position of President was not filled. On the evening of the service, Carberry (90), Mitchell Stokes (62) and Thorneley (50) took Hampshire to their T20 record of 225-2 and they beat Middlesex by 59 runs (Thorneley 3-30). Stokes from Basingstoke played a number of T20 matches while on a summer contract but departed at the end of the following season without playing first-class cricket.

'Dimi' Mascarenhas was the beneficiary. David Griffiths was the first Isle of Wight cricketer since the war to play in first-class cricket and Kevin Latouf, who had played in the C&G Final, also made his first-class debut. Liam Dawson took 6-9 for England Under-19 v Malaysia Under-19, the best figures ever for that England age group. James Tomlinson showed promise with 44 wickets for the 2nd XI.

Permanent floodlights were installed and two international matches held at the Rose Bowl, a second T20 in which England beat Sri Lanka and a longer match, England v Pakistan. In November, Hampshire announced £35m plans to develop the ground with new stands, a hotel and enlarged golf course. The ECB awarded the Rose Bowl Provisional 'Category A' status with respect to major matches. Hampshire announced that from 2007, Barry Richards would succeed Colin Ingleby-Mackenzie as President.

BAT Sports won the Southern Electric Premier League, with Bashley (Rydal) runners-up.

2007

Champions: Sussex. Knock-out Cup: Durham. Pro40: Worcestershire. T20: Kent.

Shane Warne continued as captain with the additional overseas players, Stuart Clark (Australia) then Daren Powell (West Indies). Michael Lumb moved to Hampshire from Yorkshire. Chris Tremlett was the first-ever Hampshire-born, Hampshire player to represent England in a Test Match *in England* (v India). England met India in a limited-overs international at the Rose Bowl.

In the Championship, Hampshire finished fifth. Carberry and Brown passed 1,000 runs and Warne took 50 wickets but at almost 30 apiece. Ottis Gibson took 10-47 for Durham v Hampshire at Chester-le-Street – the best bowling ever against Hampshire in the Championship and the only instance of 10 wickets in an innings, for or against Hampshire in the Championship. In the same match Michael Brown carried his bat in the first innings and was not out with Hampshire nine wickets down in the second – no Hampshire player has ever carried his bat in both innings of the same match.

Hampshire featured in two high scoring matches v Surrey. At the Oval in April, Hampshire posted 481-9 declared without a single century and eventually set Surrey 503 to win. Centuries from Batty and Salisbury took them to within 36 of the target – the highest fourth innings ever against Hampshire. In the return match, Surrey's 556 was the highest total by a visiting side at the Rose Bowl and Surrey won by an innings despite a century by Adams. In the next match Hampshire beat Worcestershire at Kidderminster after the game had been switched from a flooded Worcester ground. Seventeen-year-old Liam Dawson made his Championship debut at Headingley in September, shortly after his youngest-ever limited-overs debut for Hampshire.

Hampshire finished fourth in the Pro40 League and with only one victory were bottom of their T20 group. However, they topped their Friends Provident Trophy group and met Warwickshire at the Rose Bowl in the semi final, which they won by 40 runs. They played Durham in the Final and for the first and only time lost a Lord's Final after a poor performance that went into a second day because of rain. Durham posted 312-5 in their 50 overs and reduced Hampshire to 0-2 & 17-3. Crawley (68) and Pothas (47) managed a recovery of sorts but they lost by 125 runs.

For England at the Oval in September, 'Dimi' Mascarenhas hit five sixes in an over by India's Yuvraj Singh – a limited-overs record for England. John Crawley was the season's beneficiary. Shaun Udal retired at the end of the season but subsequently joined Middlesex. During the winter James Bruce retired and then, just before the start of the 2008 season, Shane Warne announced his retirement from all cricket, although he would subsequently play in the Indian Premier League.

Derek Shackleton died. He remains the highest wicket taker in the county's history, with 2669 first-class wickets in 583 matches, and played seven Test Matches. He took 100 first-class wickets in twenty consecutive seasons – a record for any side. None of those records will ever be broken.

Hampshire were awarded their first Test Match, scheduled to take place in 2011. Havant won the Southern Electric Premier League, with Hampshire Academy runners-up.

2008

Champions: Durham. Knock-out Cup: Essex. Pro40 League: Sussex. T20: Middlesex.

'Dimi' Mascarenhas was appointed captain, and in May became the first county cricketer to appear in the T20 Indian Premier League. Hampshire finished third again in the Championship but this was the result of a significant late improvement after they had lost four and drawn six of the first 11 matches. Even their one victory, in Durham, was by just four runs. Then Tomlinson and Imran Tahir induced a second innings collapse by Yorkshire, Hampshire won as they did from three of their last four matches, and they rose rapidly away from threatened relegation. By this time Giles White had replaced Paul Terry as Cricket Manager.

Hampshire's first overseas player of 2008, Shane Bond, took 7-66 v Sussex at the Rose Bowl, the best ever figures for Hampshire on Championship debut. After he departed, Hampshire signed leg spinner Imran Tahir, who equalled that innings record, and his match figures of 12-189 were the best ever on Hampshire debut. Pothas dismissed 10 batsmen in the match v Durham at Chester-le-Street to equal the Hampshire record. On his only Championship appearance for Hampshire over five consecutive seasons, Pietersen scored a century v Somerset at Taunton. Pothas and Brown passed 900 runs but no one reached four figures. Tomlinson's 67 wickets were Hampshire's highest for a first-class season since moving to the Rose Bowl and in seven matches, Imran Tahir took 44 at 16.68.

Hampshire played well in the Pro40, finishing runners-up to Sussex with two of their eight matches ending as No Result. They failed to qualify in the Friends Provident Trophy, while Ian Harvey and M ('Nantie') Hayward played as overseas players in the T20 but Hampshire failed to qualify again and their 85 all out v Sussex, was their lowest T20 score at the Rose Bowl. For the first time, T20 Finals Day was held at the Rose Bowl, and won by Middlesex, including Shaun Udal and with Richard Scott as a coach. Michael Brown moved to Surrey but not before he captained Hampshire 2nd XI to their Trophy success, beating Essex by seven runs. James Vince top-scored with 58 and Danny Briggs showed promise with 2-47.

On Saturday 13 September, a Hambledon XII met 12 men from Broadhalfpenny Down Association to mark the centenary of the only first-class match on the ground when the commemorative stone was unveiled. Hampshire cricketers Nic Pothas, Michael Brown, Derek Kenway, Will Kendall, John Stephenson, James Bruce, Ian Turner and Raj Maru appeared, as did James Fry, the great-grandson of CB Fry and grandson and son of former Hampshire players. JRT Barclay captained the Broadhalfpenny Down side and in the evening there was a supper in the Bat & Ball Inn with musical entertainment arranged by David Rayvern Allen and a group of singers.

Havant won the Southern Electric Premier League, with South Wilts runners-up.

2009

Champions: Durham. **Knock-out Cup: Hampshire.** Pro40 Sussex. T20: Sussex.

Mascarenhas was the captain but Pothas deputised for him until mid-June, as he was playing in the IPL. Dominic Cork joined Hampshire from Lancashire and took 4-10 & 2-27 on debut in an opening match victory. Marcus North was the first overseas player to arrive and scored 15 on the first day v Warwickshire, whereupon Australia called him into their touring side and he left the county.

Hampshire won the Friends Provident Trophy v Sussex at Lord's with Dominic Cork Man-of-the-Match. In the final qualifying match, Hampshire beat Nottinghamshire by 10 wickets and when Worcestershire lost to Ireland, they qualified for a home quarter-final v Middlesex, which they won thanks to 100 by Lumb. In the semi-final at Old Trafford, Lumb and Adams opened with 159 and the latter took two stunning catches to take Hampshire to Lord's. Sussex batted first and Cork struck as Sussex slipped from 30-0 to 43-4. Hampshire's target was 220 and everyone contributed as they won by six wickets with almost 10 overs to spare.

Hampshire's 316-2 v Ireland was their highest limited-overs score at the Rose Bowl and Ervine's 167* was the highest limited-overs innings on the ground. Hampshire finished fifth in the Pro40 and reached a T20 quarter-final at Northampton a few days after their Lord's Final. At 121-6 they needed 14 to win from 10 balls but failed to add a run and were bowled out.

In the Championship, Hampshire won just three matches but finished sixth, avoiding relegation. Imran Tahir returned in mid-season and took 52 wickets, although at an average above 30. Hampshire scored 654-8 declared v Nottinghamshire at Trent Bridge with 219 by Lumb. Adams, Carberry and Lumb passed 1,000 runs and Pothas averaged 74.18. Apart from Tahir, Griffiths with 32 was the highest wicket taker.

Vince made his first-class debut and Briggs became the 500th player to make his first-class debut for the county since entering the Championship in 1895. Briggs appeared in the same side as Griffiths, the first occasion on which two men from the Isle of Wight had played in the same first-class side.

England met Australia in an ODI at the Rose Bowl. Former captain Nick Pocock was elected President to succeed Barry Richards. At the end of the season, John Crawley retired, Chris Tremlett moved to Surrey and Billy Taylor left the staff.

Havant won the Southern Electric Premier League, with South Wilts runners-up.

2010

Champions: Nottinghamshire. CB40: Warwickshire. **T20: Hampshire.**

After more than 30 years, the first-class counties reverted to just three competitions and the two original limited-overs competitions were 'merged' into the CB40 with three leagues, followed by semi-finals and a Lord's Final, held on a Saturday evening – which was generally unpopular.

Michael Carberry made his Test debut v Bangladesh, scoring 30 & 34 and England won by 181 runs. Mascarenhas was appointed captain again but he was injured in the IPL pre-season and replaced variously by Pothas and Cork. There was a selection of players from overseas, including H Herath, P Hughes, N McKenzie, D Christian, and Abdul Razzaq. Cork was captain in the T20, which Hampshire won for first time with Finals Day at the Rose Bowl. The weather was not good but Hampshire beat Essex in the semi-final by six wickets and met Somerset in the Final after Duckworth–Lewis calculations had resolved their match v Nottinghamshire. Somerset posted 173-6 (Cork 2-24) with their big hitter Pollard forced to retire hurt. Hampshire replied well and appeared to be winning until two late wickets, including McKenzie (52). Christian injured himself and required a runner for the last ball with Hampshire needing one to level the scores and take the cup. The runner, the non-striker and Christian all set off, Somerset fielded but failed to spot Christian's indiscretion, he got home and Hampshire had won. Briggs' 31 wickets was a record in one T20 season for Hampshire.

Hampshire struggled in the Championship. Adams and Carberry passed 1,000 runs with McKenzie, Ervine and Vince all performing well, although Lumb was injured for much of the season. Tomlinson (46) and Cork (45) led the bowlers, although with little support – Kabir Ali arrived from Worcestershire but was often unfit and played in only four matches. Another Test bowler, Simon Jones, came on a match contract, seeking fitness. He played in six T20 matches and one each in the CB40 and the Championship.

Batting at number seven, Sean Ervine's 237* v Somerset at the Rose Bowl was the highest ever score by a Hampshire batsman in the lower half of the batting order. Adams set a record of over 2,500 runs in the three competitions for the season. Late in the season, at Scarborough, he and 19-year-old Vince added a new fourth-wicket partnership record of 278, both falling just short of double hundreds. In the following match, Adams scored 194 from 508 balls in 635 minutes – both calculated as county records – in a vain attempt to stave off defeat at Liverpool. No one else reached 50 for Hampshire in either innings.

Hampshire's next and penultimate match was a 'relegation-decider' at Canterbury and they were bowled out for 204, of which Adams made 84. However, Tomlinson's 4-59 helped them take a lead of 22 and four half-centuries allowed Hampshire to declare at 355-9. Kent lost wickets regularly, Cork and Briggs took four each and a fine catch by Adams sealed the victory and another year in Division One.

In May, Michael Lumb and Kevin Pietersen, then both of Hampshire, played for England when they won the T20 World Cup in Barbados. However, Pietersen found travelling from his London home to Hampshire too demanding and he moved to Surrey before the end of the season. In six seasons with Hampshire, he played in seven first-class matches, with three centuries and 17 'List A' matches (HS 98), averaging around 43 in each competition.

The Rose Bowl was voted the Best International Ground in an ECB survey of fans. Bournemouth won the Southern Electric Premier League, with Hampshire Academy runners-up for the second time.

2011

Champions: Lancashire. CB40: Surrey. T20: Leicestershire.

At their AGM, the members elected the surviving members of 1961's Championship-winning side as Life Vice Presidents. Dominic Cork was appointed captain and Imran Tahir returned as overseas player. Hampshire signed three other South Africans, Friedel de Wet, Johannes Myburgh and McKenzie, who returned. As English T20 Champions, Hampshire played in the Caribbean T20 Competition in January, reaching but losing the Final. During that competition they met Canada, Barbados, Leeward Islands, Trinidad & Tobago and the Windward Islands for the first time. They reached a second consecutive Finals Day in the T20 but after a tie in their semi-final with Somerset they lost in the 'super over'.

Hampshire struggled again in the Championship and were relegated. Carberry suffered from a serious illness and played in just nine Championship matches, averaging 56.64. At Taunton, he and Adams added 373 for Hampshire's second wicket, a new county record, and against Yorkshire at the Rose Bowl, Carberry and McKenzie put on 523, a record stand for any wicket for Hampshire, and Carberry scored their fifth triple century. In July, Hampshire had been fined points for a pitch with excessive turn despite a thrilling match v Nottinghamshire. For the next match v Yorkshire, the pitch was flat, the record stand was set and 1,171 runs were scored for the loss of just 13 wickets over four days.

Only McKenzie passed 1,000 runs, although Dawson, with 908 at 36.32, showed promise. The bowling was weak, Kabir Ali again missed more matches than he played and only Briggs, with 38 wickets at 36.65, passed 30 in the season. Hampshire drew seven of their 16 matches, equalled only by Yorkshire who were also relegated. Hampshire failed to qualify in the CB40, although Chris Wood, with 18 wickets, enjoyed a promising season.

The highlight of 2011 at the Rose Bowl was the inaugural Test Match v Sri Lanka in June, although, after a spell of dry weather, it was badly rain-affected and drawn. Chris Tremlett returned to the Rose Bowl and won Man-of-the-Match with 6-48 and Nigel Gray was awarded the *Test Match Special* 'Champagne Moment'. Some of Hampshire's younger players acted as substitutes for England and Adam Rouse held a catch. England beat India in a day–night match in September but that too was badly rain-affected and reduced to 23 overs per side.

Nic Pothas was the beneficiary. At the end of the season Cork, Pothas, Lumb, Jones, Myburgh, de Wet and Tahir all left Hampshire. Imran Tahir would make his Test match debut for South Africa. Former players Jon Ayling and Iain Brunschweiler left the coaching staff. Craig White came from Yorkshire to replace Ayling.

Havant won the Southern Electric Premier League, with Bournemouth runners-up.

2012

Champions: Warwickshire. **CB40: Hampshire. T20: Hampshire.**

Adams was appointed captain – Hampshire's first post-war Hampshire-born captain, with Mascarenhas leading in the T20, Simon Katich returned as overseas player, although Shahid Afridi did not obtain his visa so did not.

Hampshire secured two very important financial deals. Ageas Insurance paid for the naming rights as the ground became known as the Ageas Bowl, while Eastleigh Council took over the lease to the ground and embarked on building the northern end hotel and media centre. These two deals secured Hampshire's immediate financial future and they also chose to focus on the development of their own young players, signing fewer 'star' names from overseas and other counties. At the season's end, Rod Bransgrove handed over as Chief Executive to David Mann, while retaining the position of Chairman.

The investment in their younger players paid immediate dividends as Hampshire won two trophies for the first time, the FPT20 v Yorkshire at Cardiff and the CB40 Final at Lord's v Warwickshire. Both produced thrilling Finals. In the T20, Hampshire posted 150-6 v Yorkshire and seemed to be winning comfortably but after McKenzie claimed a catch that was not confirmed by the umpires, the survivor, Miller, took Yorkshire within 10 runs of victory. Adams (43) and Wood 3-26 made the key contributions, while in earlier rounds, Australian Glenn Maxwell, who had arrived originally to play for South Wilts, was a useful all-round player, not least for his very rapid 60* at Chelmsford. The CB40 Final at Lord's went to the last ball with Carter of Warwickshire needing one run to win. Kabir Ali bowled outside off-stump, Carter missed, Bates gathered and Hampshire had two trophies.

Danny Briggs missed the second Final because he was selected by England in 20- and 50-over competitions. On his T20 international debut just prior to his 21st birthday, he became the youngest Hampshire player ever to represent England and the first England player ever born in the Isle of Wight.

In Division Two of the Championship, Hampshire had the highest run-scorer (Adams), wicket-taker (Balcombe), catcher (Dawson) and wicket-keeper (Bates) but finished fourth and did not win promotion, not least because they lost the last three Championship matches of the season. Balcombe, batting at number 11 v Leicestershire, scored a Hampshire record of 73, sharing a last wicket partnership of 168 with Wood, whose 105* was his maiden century. Dawson held seven catches in the match at Northampton, equalling Hampshire's record set by Dean (1947) and Maru (1988). Balcombe's 8-71 v Gloucestershire at the Ageas Bowl were Hampshire's best-ever figures on their new ground. At the season's end, as T20 Champions, Hampshire competed in the Champions Trophy in South Africa but lost the first two qualifying matches and were eliminated. Their season had lasted six months. It had been one of the wettest English summers, during which Hampshire lost nearly 30% of playing time in the Championship (over 100 hours) and over 25% in all competitions. Only Yorkshire exceeded 30% in both aspects.

Hampshire's former wicket-keeper/batsman Neil McCorkell reached his 100th birthday in March 2012, although sadly he died just short of his next one in early 2013. At the time of his death he had been one of only six pre-war English first-class cricketers still alive and two others, JE Manners and L Harrison, were also from Hampshire. The oldest, and first debutant, is GC Perkins of Northamptonshire (debut 1934). Vic Cannings was abroad before the war so made his debut afterwards but he too is in his nineties and older than Leo Harrison.

England played both tourists, the West Indies and South Africa, in limited-overs internationals at the ground. Groundsman Nigel Gray was awarded a Testimonial. Simon Katich chose to move to Lancashire for 2013 and Kabir Ali, who had played just 17 first-class matches in his three years with Hampshire, followed him. Bilal Shafayat scored 93 on debut v Derbyshire and played in eight matches but was not offered another contract.

Cage Cricket, a new form of the game aimed principally at inner-city youngsters, was developed in Portsmouth by former Hampshire batsman Lawrie Prittipaul and Trevor McArdle. They launched it formally, with the support of Ian Botham and Rod Bransgrove, at the Houses of Parliament, while in 2013 it was featured in *The Times* and on Radio Four. South Wilts won the Southern Electric Premier League, with Bashley (Rydal) runners-up.

2013

Hampshire celebrated 150 years since the formation of the County Cricket Club.

At their AGM, the members elected the 13 members of 1973's Championship-winning side as Life Vice Presidents. A few weeks later the club announced the death of another Life Vice President, Mrs Marjorie Eagar, widow of EDR Eagar. There was no beneficiary. Hampshire's membership figures stood just below 4,500 – around 1,000 were Life Members, a rising proportion of the total.

Adams continued as captain and Mascarenhas captained the T20 side on returning from the IPL. During the winter, Briggs and Vince toured with England's limited-overs and Lions sides, respectively, and Briggs was in England's T20 squad in the summer. Wicket-keeper Adam Wheater joined Hampshire from Essex. Early in the season, county caps were awarded to Balcombe, Dawson and Vince. The first overseas player, George Bailey, joined the Australian Champions League squad in early June and Sohail Tanvir (Pakistan) replaced him.

Immediately prior to a televised, floodlit 40-over home match v Lancashire, Wheater injured his side while warming up. Hampshire called for Bates but he was playing for the 2nd XI in Middlesex so, while he travelled to the match, Academy player Thomas Alsop kept wicket and held an excellent catch, standing up to Mascarenhas. Michel Carberry batted through the Hampshire innings and hit a six to win the match, passing his previous highest limited-overs score and reaching 150 not out. In the home Championship game against Lancashire, Hampshire used nine bowlers as the match drifted to a draw and five bowled left-handed, which may have been a record in a Championship innings by Hampshire. One week later, in similar circumstances, they repeated it against Northamptonshire.

Glenn Querl from Zimbabwe played on trial in a first-class match v Loughborough University but was banned by the ECB shortly afterwards for his action, along with Jack Taylor of Gloucestershire.

England played New Zealand (ODI) and Australia (T20) at the Ageas Bowl while England's Women met Australia's Women in a T20I. In the England v New Zealand match, New Zealand's 359-3 in 50 overs was a record for a limited-overs international match on the ground and Martin Guptil's 189* equalled the record limited-overs international score in England and against England (also IVA Richards).

In Midsummer week, the Met Office held a symposium which reported on the likelihood of a sequence of poor summers, and a few days later England lost a rain-shortened fifth (of five) Limited-Overs Finals since they introduced the shorter form to professional cricket exactly fifty years earlier. Meanwhile, Hampshire reached mid-season in the Championship and YB40 competitions and embarked on another year of T20 cricket. It was not something imagined by those who had formed their club, almost exactly 150 years earlier.

To be continued ...

1981: (back) Savage, Hayward, Bailey, CL Smith, Terry, Nicholas, Tremlett, Hardy, Malone, Curzon, Parks, Sainsbury (coach), (front) RA Smith, Southern, Rice, Jesty, Pocock, Turner, Cowley, Stevenson

1982: (back) Marshall, CL Smith, Malone, Southern, Tremlett, Nicholas, (front) Turner, Greenidge, Pocock, Jesty, Parks

1986: Oval, JPSL Champions (on left) D Rich (Chairman), A Baker (Chief Executive), CJ Knott (Cricket Chairman), P Walker (BBC), the players are Cowley, Terry, CL Smith, Parks, Nicholas, James, (hidden) RA Smith, Connor

1988: Chelmsford B&H Cup semi-final, (back) Nicholas, Andrew, Ayling, Maru, James (centre), Connor, CL Smith, Terry, RA Smith, Cowley, Jefferies, (behind) Turner, (front) Parks

1988: (back) Connor, Cowley, James, RA Smith, Andrew, Tremlett, Jefferies, CL Smith, (front) Parks, Terry, Nicholas, Turner, Maru

1991: Lord's Nat West Trophy Final, Middleton, Connor, James, Terry, Cox (12th man), Nicholas, RA Smith, Maru, Udal, Gower, Aqib Javed, Aymes

1992: Lord's B&H Cup Final, Nicholas, Udal, Maru (hidden), Connor, Middleton, James, Parks, Ayling, Tremlett (coach), Terry

1996: (back) Kendall, Bovill, White, S Francis, Botham, Dibden, Milburn, (centre) Treagus, Whitaker, S Morris, Benjamin, Thursfield, James, Renshaw, Keech, Laney, (front) Thomas, Aymes, Maru, RA Smith, J Stephenson, Terry, Connor, Udal, Garaway

2000: (back) van der Gucht, Kendall, Adams, Prittipaul, Brunschweiler, Hamblin, (centre) Middleton (coach), J Cook (coach), White, S Francis, Renshaw, Savident, A Morris, Mascarenhas, Z Morris, Kenway, (front) Mullally, Aymes, Udal, RA Smith, J Stephenson, Hartley, Laney

2005: (back) Latouf, Ervine, Watson, Bichel, Lamb, (centre) Crawley, Mascarenhas, Pothas, Udal, Tremlett, (front) Pietersen

2007: (back) Stokes, Latouf, Loudon, Griffiths, Burrows, (centre) Bruce, Taylor, Lumb, Benham, Tomlinson, Lamb, Brown, Adams, Ervine, (front) Carberry, Crawley, Udal, Warne, Mascarenhas, Pothas, CT Tremlett

2009: (back) Howell, Riazuddin, Morgan, Vince, Griffiths, Dawson, Burrows, Carberry, (centre) A Nealon (physio), Ayling (coach), Taylor, Parsons, Balcombe, Benham, Ervine, Brunschweiler (coach), Parks (coach), (front) Tomlinson, Crawley, CT Tremlett, White (Cricket Manager), Pothas, Adams, Cork, Lumb

2010: (back) McKenzie, Dawson, Howell, Briggs, Griffiths, Bates, (centre) Parks (coach), AW Weld (scorer), Riazuddin, Vince, Balcombe, Benham, Wood, Ayling (coach), Brunschweiler (coach), Middleton (coach), (front) Carberry, Ervine, Adams, Mascarenhas, White (Cricket Manager), Pothas, Jones, Kabir Ali, Tomlinson

2012: Rouse, Kabir Ali, Riazuddin, Griffiths, Katich, Bates, Ervine, Mascarenhas, Wood, Vince, Adams, Balcombe, Carberry, S Terry, Tomlinson, Bilal Shafayat, Dawson

APPENDIX ONE

CRICKET IN HAMPSHIRE IN THE EIGHTEENTH CENTURY (SOME KEY MOMENTS)

1729   Combined Hampshire, Surrey *and* Sussex side v Kent.

1733   Married Men beat Batchelors [sic] twice at Stubbington & Titchfield – reported in the 18 June edition of *Parker's Penny Post*. See the *Cricket Statistician* no 137, Spring 2007.

1745   Hambledon Women v Bramley Women played nr. Guildford.

1749   Portsmouth Common beat Fareham & Titchfield at Milldam, Portsmouth.

1753   The first recorded match at Broadhalfpenny Down in which Hampshire defeated Surrey (*Salisbury Journal* 13 August 1753). See the *Cricket Statistician* no 154, summer 2011.

1756   The 'lost dog' newspaper advertisement in the *Reading Mercury*, which for some time appeared to be the first confirmation of cricket on Broadhalfpenny Down.

1765   Women's cricket at Upham.

1766   Sussex v Hampshire at Racedown.

1767   Hampshire v Sussex at Broadhalfpenny Down.

1768   Hampshire v Kent at Broadhalfpenny Down.

1769   First record of cricket in Basingstoke.

1771   First match between 'Hambledon' and England, Gentlemen of Hampshire v Gentlemen of Sussex, two matches at Broadhalfpenny Down and Goodwood.

The following matches are listed in full in the ACS Book *Great Cricket Matches 1772–1800. Those in italics were identified separately as The 'Lost' Great Matches, as complete scores are not available.*

1772:   Three matches between Hampshire and England at Broadhalfpenny Down, Merrow Down, Guildford, and Bishopsbourne, *two matches between Hampshire and Kent at Broadhalfpenny Down and Guildford, Hampshire v Surrey at Guildford.*

1773:   Three matches between Hampshire and England at Sevenoaks Vine, Finsbury and Broadhalfpenny Down, two matches between Hampshire and Surrey at Laleham Burway and Broadhalfpenny Down, *Hampshire v England at Laleham.*

1774:   Two matches between Hampshire and England at Broadhalfpenny Down and Sevenoaks Vine, Surrey v Hampshire at Merrow Down, Guildford, Hampshire v Kent at Sevenoaks Vine, *Hampshire v Kent at Broadhalfpenny Down.*

1775:   Two matches between Hampshire and Kent at Sevenoaks Vine and Broadhalfpenny Down, two matches between Hampshire and Surrey at Laleham Burway and Broadhalfpenny Down, *Hampshire v Kent at Guildford.*

1776:   Five matches between Hampshire and Kent at Molesey Hurst, Sevenoaks Vine (x 2), Broadhalfpenny Down, Chidden Holt, Hambledon, two matches between Hampshire and Surrey at Laleham Burway and Broadhalfpenny Down.

1777:   Six matches between Hampshire and England at Sevenoaks Vine, Broadhalfpenny Down (x 2), Laleham Burway, and Merrow Down, Guildford. In the first match v England, Aylward scored 167 in a total of 403 as Hampshire won by an innings.

1778:   Two matches between Hampshire and England at Sevenoaks Vine and Stoke Down, Alresford, two matches between Hampshire and Surrey at Broadhalfpenny Down and Laleham Burway.

1779:   Four matches between Hampshire and England at Stoke Down, Alresford, Sevenoaks Vine, Broadhalfpenny Down and Molesey Hurst.

1780:   Two matches between Hampshire and England at Bishopsbourne and Stoke Down, Alresford.

1781: Four matches between Hampshire and Kent at Stoke Down, Alresford, Bishopsbourne (x 2) and Broadhalfpenny Down. After this, Hampshire left Broadhalfpenny Down and played their major matches at Windmill Down, Hambledon or Stoke Down, Alresford.

1782: Three matches between Hampshire and Kent at Sevenoaks Vine, Stoke Down, Alresford and Bishopsbourne, Hampshire v England at Windmill Down, Hambledon.

1783: Two matches between Hampshire and Kent at Windmill Down, Hambledon and Bishopsbourne, Hampshire v England at Windmill Down, Hambledon.

1784: Hampshire v England at Sevenoaks Vine.

1786: Two matches between Hampshire and Kent at Sevenoaks Vine and Windmill Down, Hambledon.

1787: Three matches between Hampshire and Kent at Star Inn Coxheath, Bishopsbourne and Windmill Down, Hambledon. Formation of the Marylebone Cricket Club (MCC).

1788: Hampshire *and* Kent v England at Lord's Old Ground, Marylebone, three matches between Hampshire and Surrey at Molesey Hurst and Ludgershall and Windmill Down, Hambledon, two matches between Hampshire and England at Stoke Down, Alresford and Sevenoaks Vine.

1789: Two matches between Hampshire and England at Lord's Old Ground Marylebone and Sevenoaks Vine, two matches between Hampshire and Kent at Windmill Down, Hambledon and Bishopsbourne, Hampshire v Surrey at Molesey Hurst.

1790: Hampshire v Kent at Lord's Old Ground, Marylebone, two matches between Hampshire and England at Sevenoaks Vine and Burley-on-the-Hill, Hampshire *and* Surrey v Kent at Ludgershall, Hampshire *and* MCC v England at Lord's Old Ground, Marylebone.

1791: Four matches between Hampshire and England at Burley-on-the-Hill, Sevenoaks Vine, Windmill Down, Hambledon and Ludgershall, Hampshire v Surrey at Wrecclesham. Richard Nyren moved to London.

1792: Two matches between Hampshire and Surrey at Windmill Down, Hambledon and Ludgershall, two matches between Hampshire and Kent at Cobham Park and Dartford Brent. Hampshire *and* MCC v Brighton at Prince of Wales Ground, Brighton.

1794: Hampshire *and* Kent v MCC at Lord's Old Ground, Marylebone. Two matches between Hampshire and Surrey *and* Kent both at Stoke Down, Alresford.

1795: Two matches between Hampshire and England both at Dartford Heath.

1797: Two matches between Hampshire and MCC at Stoke Down, Alresford and Lord's Old Ground, Alresford.

1798: Two matches between Hampshire and MCC at Stoke Down, Alresford and Lord's Old Ground, Marylebone.

The preface to the ACS publication observed:

> In the 1770s the game's rural origins were still dominant and the greatest force on the cricket field was celebrated club based at Hambledon in the Hampshire Downs. By 1800 however the focus of the game had shifted emphatically to London and in particular to the Marylebone Cricket Club. (p. 12).

APPENDIX TWO

HAMPSHIRE CRICKET: 1800–1863

A selection of key events and matches, many of which can be found on *Cricket Archive*. Matches in UPPER CASE are those listed as first-class in the 1996 ACS publication *Complete First-Class Match List Volume One 1801–1914*. Throughout, the team is Hampshire, unless otherwise stated (e.g., South Hants Club or Gentlemen of Hampshire).

1803   v NOTTS & LEICS at LORD'S OLD GROUND.

1804   v MCC & HOMERTON at LORD'S OLD GROUND.

1805   v ENGLAND at LORD'S OLD GROUND (two matches).

1806   v ENGLAND (two matches) at LORD'S OLD GROUND and at STOKE DOWN, ALRESFORD.

1807   v ENGLAND at LORD'S OLD GROUND (two matches). The fashionable 'dandy' Beau Brummell played in the second match for Hampshire, his only first class match. He scored 23 & 3.

1811   Hampshire Ladies beat Surrey Ladies at Newington (2 October).

1816   v MCC at LORD'S (two matches),
        v EPSOM at EPSOM DOWN.

1817   v MCC AT LORD'S.

1818   v MCC AT LORD'S (two matches).

1819   v ENGLAND at LORD'S (two matches),
        v EPSOM at EPSOM DOWN.

1820   v ENGLAND AT LORD'S.

1821   v MCC at LORD'S. Hampshire's Thomas Beagley scored 113* for the Players, the first century in Gentlemen v Players matches.

1823   v ENGLAND at BRAMSHILL HOUSE the first of four Hampshire matches there (near Hartley Wintney).

1825   v GODALMING at BRAMSHILL HOUSE
        v SUSSEX at BRAMSHILL HOUSE,
        v SUSSEX at PETWORTH PARK,
        v GODALMING at GODALMING.
        Hampshire's William Ward scored 102*, the first century for the Gentlemen in matches v the Players. In the same year he purchased the lease of Lord's Ground, securing its future. Winchester College played their first match v Harrow at Lord's, winning by 139 runs.

1826   HAMPSHIRE & SURREY v SUSSEX at BRAMSHILL HOUSE
        HAMPSHIRE & SURREY v SUSSEX and at Petworth Park.
        Winchester College played and beat Eton for the first time.

1827   Southampton v Lyndhurst at the Marsh, Southampton.

1828   v ENGLAND AT LORD'S, a 12-a-side match and the last *major* Hampshire match until 1842.

1829   Hambledon v Midhurst at Midhurst.

1830   Gentlemen of England v Gentlemen of Hampshire at Lord's. It appeared that Gentlemen of England won by seven wickets but the scorebook showed one run short.

1831   East Hampshire v Midhurst at Midhurst.

1832   Thomas Lord (Lord's Ground) died and was buried at West Meon, his last home.

1833   Publication of John Nyren's *Young Cricketer's Tutor and The Cricketers of My Time*, the latter recounting the tales of the great players of the previous century. This publication had a key role in establishing the reputation of Hambledon as a centre of 18th century cricket, which has been republished many times – most recently by Ashley Mote.

1838   Gentlemen of Hampshire v MCC at Lord's.

1839   Hampshire v Stonehenge at Thomas Chamberlayne's Ground, Cranbury Park. Luff (37*) carried his bat in Hampshire's first innings. Gentlemen of Hampshire v MCC at Lord's and also at Thomas Chamberlayne's Ground, Cranbury Park. In the first of those two matches, GB Townsend scored 72 & 130. North Hampshire v South Hampshire at Day's Antelope Ground Southampton.

1840   Gentlemen of Hampshire v MCC at Lord's and at Day's Antelope Ground, Gentlemen of Hampshire v Gentlemen of Sussex at Day's Antelope Ground and at Royal New Ground, Brighton.

1841   Gentlemen of Hampshire v MCC at Day's Antelope Ground, Southampton v Alresford, South Hants Club v Clapton at Day's Antelope Ground, Southampton. The Duke of Wellington ordered cricket grounds to be established in every English barracks, including a number that were in Hampshire.

The ACS notes, from 1842, "Hampshire is briefly revived as a major county side".

1842   v MCC at LORD'S, Hampshire 49 all out in the first innings won by 235 runs – in MCC's second innings four men were absent hurt.
v ENGLAND at SOUTHAMPTON, ANTELOPE GROUND. Daniel Day was Manager of the Antelope Ground, the main Hampshire ground until 1884.

1843   v NOTTINGHAMSHIRE (two matches) at TRENT BRIDGE
and DAY'S ANTELOPE GROUND, SOUTHAMPTON,
v MCC (two matches) at LORD'S
and DAY'S ANTELOPE GROUND,
Gentlemen of Hampshire v Players of Hampshire at Day's Antelope Ground.

1844   v MCC (two matches) at LORD'S
and DAY'S ANTELOPE GROUND,
Gentlemen of Hampshire v Gentlemen of Sussex (two matches) at the New Royal Ground Brighton and Day's Antelope Ground, Gentlemen of Hampshire v Players of Hampshire at Day's Antelope Ground, South Hants Club v Hambledon (two matches) at Day's Antelope Ground and Broadhalfpenny Down.

1845   v MCC (two matches) at LORD'S
and at DAY'S ANTELOPE GROUND,
v PETWORTH (two matches) at PETWORTH
and at DAY'S ANTELOPE GROUND,
South Hants Club v Hambledon at Broadhalfpenny Down. Daniel Day took over the Woolston Hotel on the River Itchen near Southampton and created another cricket ground in the adjoining field.

1846   Hampshire v Petworth at Petworth, South Hants Club v Petworth at Day's Antelope Ground, Gentlemen of Hampshire v Players of Hampshire at Day's Antelope Ground

1847   Portsmouth & East Hants Club v South Hants Club at Day's Antelope Ground, which the latter won "by a concession". The Portsmouth & East Hants Club included E Taswell and their home ground (East Hants) was where Taswell Road now stands in Southsea. South Hants Club v Surrey Club (two matches) at the Oval and Day's Antelope Ground, South Hants Club v Bramshill (two matches) at Day's Antelope Ground and Bramshill Park. Hampshire

(John and Jas Llliywhite, D Day, Hervey-Bathurst etc) v Portsmouth (inc J Wisden & Taswell) at Day's Antelope Ground.

1848 v ENGLAND at DAY'S ITCHEN GROUND. William Clarke's All England XI, played in the county for the first time v XIV (14) of Hampshire in a benefit match for Daniel Day. George Deane scored 0 and 0 for Hampshire in his only county match but he did reach his personal century in December1928, his 100th birthday.
Hampshire v Henfield (two matches) at Henfield Common and East Hants Cricket Ground, Gentlemen of Hampshire v Players of Hampshire at Day's Antelope Ground.

1849 v ENGLAND (the All England XI) at DAY'S ITCHEN GROUND,
GB Buckley identified from *Bell's Life* (15 April and 6 May) a meeting held at the Woolston Hotel on 3 April to form "The Hampshire Cricket Club" (*n.b.* not "county"). The 36 men attending included Sir F Hervey-Bathurst, T Chamberlayne, C Beauclerk and Sir JB Mill. Henry Pearce was elected secretary and the meeting adjourned to 18 April at Day's Ground. The "first practice day of the club" was on 4 May and "several matches with various clubs have been arranged". Hervey-Bathurst and Chamberlayne are next recorded as playing for the Gentlemen of South Hampshire in their victory over the Gentlemen of Dorset at Day's Antelope Ground on 30 and 31 May. Two weeks later, Chamberlayne "bagged a pair" as Dorset had revenge in Weymouth, although this match is listed by *Cricket Archive* as the South Hants Club. In addition to the England match at the end of June, there was a South Hants Club match v South Wilts and in September a thrilling seven-runs victory for the Gentlemen of Hampshire over the Players of Southampton.

1850 XIV (14) of HAMPSHIRE v ENGLAND XI at DAY'S ITCHEN GROUND,
Gentlemen of South Hampshire v Players of Hampshire at Day's Antelope Ground.

No further first-class matches until 1861.

1851 Middlesex XI v Hampshire XI at Lord's, Farnham v North Hants Club at Wrecclesham, South Hants Club v Players of Hampshire at Day's Antelope Ground, 20 of Hampshire v All England XI on Day's Antelope Ground on 6, 7 and 8 October. Daniel Day took on the East Hants Cricket Ground in Southsea; it is no longer the site of a ground. Day only stayed there for two years.

1852 Hampshire *Cricket Archive* holds the original poster advertising The United Eleven of England v 19 Gentlemen of Hampshire at Portsmouth's East Hants Cricket Ground. The visitors – a breakaway side from Clarke's – are now commonly described as the United England Eleven and in fact they played 20 Gentlemen of Hampshire, South Hants Club v Players of Hampshire at Day's Antelope Ground.

1853 18 of Hampshire v United England Eleven at Day's Itchen Ground.

1854 South Hampshire v United England XI at Day's Antelope Ground.

1855 Gentlemen of Hampshire v Players of Hampshire at Day's Antelope Ground. The first match was played on the ground that became May's Bounty, Basingstoke.

1856 No matches listed involving Hampshire sides.

1857 Gentlemen of Hampshire v Gentlemen of Kent (two matches) at Canterbury and Day's Antelope Ground, Gentlemen of Hampshire v Gentlemen of Sussex (two matches) at Royal Brunswick Ground, Hove and Day's Antelope Ground, Gentlemen of Hampshire v I Zingari at day's Antelope Ground.

1858 Gentlemen of Hampshire v Gentlemen of Sussex (two matches) at Royal Brunswick Ground, Hove and Day's Antelope Ground, Gentlemen of Hampshire v Gentlemen of Kent (two matches) at Canterbury and Day's Antelope Ground, South Hants Club v South Wilts at Day's Antelope Ground.

1859 Gentlemen of Hampshire v Gentlemen of Sussex (two matches) at Royal Brunswick Ground, Hove and Day's Antelope Ground.

1860 Gentlemen of Hampshire v Gentlemen of Sussex (two matches) at Hove and Day's Antelope Ground, Gentlemen of Hampshire v MCC at Lord's, Gentlemen of Hampshire v Gentlemen of Berkshire at Day's Antelope Ground, Gentlemen of Hampshire v I Zingari at CG Taylor's Ground, Weston, Southampton, Gentlemen of Hampshire v Players of Hampshire at Day's Antelope Ground. Twenty-two Gentlemen of Hampshire v United Eleven of England at Day's Antelope Ground.

1861 v MCC at LORD'S with equal sides (11 each), which MCC won by an innings.
Gentlemen of Hampshire v Gentlemen of Sussex (two matches) at Hove and Day's Antelope Ground, Southampton v Westbourne at Day's Antelope Ground, East Hants Club v United England XI at East Hants Ground, Southsea, Gentlemen of Hampshire v United England XI at Day's Antelope Ground, Hampshire v United England XI at Roebuck Cricket Ground, Winchester.

1862 All England XI v Southampton Union at Day's Antelope Ground and v East Hants Cricket Club at East Hants Cricket Ground, Southsea, East Hants Cricket Club v New All England XI at East Hants Cricket Ground, Southsea, East Hampshire v South Hampshire at Day's Antelope Ground, Gentlemen of Hampshire v Gentlemen of Sussex (two matches) at Hove and Day's Antelope Ground, South Hants Club v South Wilts (two matches), venue unknown and Day's Antelope Ground, Gentlemen of South Hampshire v Players at Day's Antelope Ground, East Hants Club v United England XI at East Hants Ground, Southsea, 22 Gentlemen of Hampshire v United Eleven of England at Day's Antelope Ground, Hampshire v United England XI at Roebuck Ground, Winchester, Isle of Wight v United England XI at Trafalgar Rd, Newport, IOW.

1863 Twenty-two of Southampton Union v All England XI at Day's Antelope Ground, 22 of Basingstoke v All England XI at Hackwood Park, Basingstoke, Southampton Union v Hampshire Colts at Day's Antelope Ground, Hampshire v Surrey at Kennington Oval, Gentlemen of Hampshire v Gentlemen of Sussex (two matches) at Hove and Day's Antelope Ground, South Hants Club v Hampshire Colts at Day's Antelope Ground, South Hants Club v South Wilts at Day's Antelope Ground, East Hants Club v United England XI at East Hants Ground, Southsea, Gentlemen of Hampshire v United England XI at Day's Antelope Ground.

On 10, 11, 14 September 1863, 14 of Hampshire v Surrey at Day's Antelope Ground on the second day of which was held the Meeting to approve formally the establishment of Hampshire County Cricket Club. The match was not first-class. The Hampshire side: J Southerton, CF Lucas, JS Frederick, H Maturin, GM Ede, GH Case, HT Frere, H Stewart, H Holmes, EL Ede, NW Wallace, W Humphrey, CV Eccles, S Tubb.

APPENDIX THREE

HAMPSHIRE'S CRICKETERS

1. HAMPSHIRE'S CAPTAINS

This is a list of Hampshire's official, appointed captains. There have been many deputies.

1864 George Ede
1875 Clement Booth
1879 Arthur Wood
1880 Russell Bencraft
1883 Arthur Wood
1887
1888 Francis Lacey
1890 HW Forster
1893 Russell Bencraft
1896 'Teddy' Wynyard
1900 Charles Robson
1903 Edward Sprot (to 1914)

1919 Lionel Tennyson
1934 Geoffrey Lowndes
1936 'Dick' Moore
1938 Cecil Paris
1939 George Taylor (one season)

1946 Desmond Eagar
1958 Colin Ingleby-Mackenzie
1966 Roy Marshall
1971 Richard Gilliat
1979 'Bob' Stephenson
1980 Nick Pocock
1985 Mark Nicholas
1996 John Stephenson
1998 Robin Smith
2003 John Crawley
2004 Shane Warne
2008 Dimitri Mascarenhas
2010 Dominic Cork
2012 James Adams (Mascarenhas captain for T20)

2. 150 OR MORE FIRST-CLASS APPEARANCES FOR HAMPSHIRE

CP Mead (700 matches), AS Kennedy (596), PJ Sainsbury (593), D Shackleton (583), G Brown (539), JA Newman (506), RE Marshall (504), GS Boyes (474), HAW Bowell (473), JR Gray (453), DR Turner (416), H Horton (405), J Arnold (396), L Harrison (387), NT McCorkell (383), G Hill (371), MCJ Nicholas (361), Lord Tennyson (347), TE Jesty (340), OW Herman (321), DW White

(315), EDR Eagar (311), ACD Ingleby-Mackenzie (309), WH Livsey (309), RA Smith (307), DA Livingstone (299), VP Terry (288), NH Rogers (285), WCL Creese (278), HM Barnard (276), CG Greenidge (275), J Stone (274), AE Pothecary (271), EM Sprot (267), GR Stephenson (263), NG Cowley (257), RJ Parks (253), SD Udal (250), J Bailey (242), VHD Cannings (230), CL Smith (222), CA Connor (221), RMC Gilliat (220), AN Aymes (215), RJ Maru (213), MD Marshall (210), BSV Timms (208), BA Richards (204), KD James (204), TM Tremlett (201), AWH Rayment (198), 196 CB Llewellyn (196), AD Mascarenhas (194), RMH Cottam (188), MD Burden (174), JM Rice (168), CJ Knott (166), JW Southern (164), DA Steele (163), AJL Hill (161), H Baldwin (150).

3. 150 OR MORE LIMITED-OVERS APPEARANCES FOR HAMPSHIRE

DR Turner (377), SD Udal (356), RA Smith (347), MCJ Nicholas (346), TE Jesty (310), VP Terry (304), CA Connor (300), NG Cowley (288), CG Greenidge (274), 244 RJ Parks (244), GR Stephenson (237), KD James (227), AD Mascarenhas (226), AN Aymes (221), MD Marshall (216), TM Tremlett (202), CL Smith (200), BA Richards (186), JM Rice (178), RMC Gilliat (165), PJ Sainsbury (165).

4. HAMPSHIRE'S CAPPED PLAYERS 1895–1939

We do not have a clear record of every capped player pre-war or the years in which caps were awarded. This list was agreed by a Committee of Hampshire Cricket, with occasional additions over the past ten years:

Abercrombie C, Aird R, Altham H, Arnold J, Bacon F, Badcock J, Bailey J, Baldwin H, Baring G, Barrett E, Barton V, Bencraft R, Bowell A, Boyes S, Brown G, Brutton C, Budd L, Creese L, Day H, English E, Fry CB, Fynn CG, Greig J, Harfield L, Harrison G, Heath G, Herman O, Heseltine C, Hesketh-Pritchard H, Hill AJL, Hill G, Hosie A, Jameson T, Jacques A, Jephson RV, Jephson W, Johnston A, Judd A, Kennedy A, Knott C, Lacey F, Langford W, Lawson H, Livsey W, Llewellyn C, Lowndes W, McCorkell N, McDonell H, Mead P, Moore R, Newman J, Paris C, Parker J, Persse H, Poore R, Pothecary A, Quinton F, Raikes GB, Remnant E, Robson C, Soar T, Sprot E, Steele D, Stone J, Taylor G, Tennyson L, Walker DF, Webb A, White W, Wynyard E.

5. HAMPSHIRE'S CAPPED PLAYERS 1946–2013

For this period we have a complete record of caps and the years awarded.

Adams J 2006, Ayling J 1991, Aymes A 1991, Bakker PJ 1989, Balcombe D 2013, Baldry D 1959, Barnard M 1955, Blake D 1953, Bridger J 1954, Briggs D 2012, Brown M 2007, Bruce J 2006, Burden M 1955, Cannings V 1950, Carberry M 2006, Clark S 2007, Clarke M 2004, Connor C 1988, Cork D 2009, Cottam R 1965, Cowley N 1978, Crawley J 2002, Dare R 1954, Dawson G 1948, Dawson L 2013, Eagar D 1946, Ervine S 2005, Gilliat R 1969, Gower D 1990, Gray J 1951, Greenidge G 1972, Harrison L 1951, Hartley P 1999, Hayden M 1997, Heath M 1957, Herman R 1972, Holt A 1946, Horton H 1955, Imran Tahir 2009, Ingleby-Mackenzie C 1957, James K 1989, Jefferies S 1989, Jesty T 1971, Johnson N 2001, Katich S 2003, Kendall W 1999, Kenway D 2001, Knott C 1939, Laney J 1996, Livingstone D 1961, Lumb M 2008, McLean N 1999, Marshall M 1981, Marshall R 1955, Maru R 1986 Mascarenhas D 1998, McKenzie N 2010, Middleton T 1990, Morris A

2001, Mullally A 2000, Nicholas M 1982, Parks R 1982, Pietersen K 2005, Pocock N 1980, Pothas N 2003, Ransom V 1949, Rayment A 1952, Reed B 1967, Rice J 1975, Richards B 1968, Roberts A 1974, Rogers N 1947, Sainsbury P 1955, Shackleton D 1949, Smith C 1981, Smith R 1985, Southern J 1978, Stephenson J 1995, Stephenson R 1969, Stevenson K 1979, Taylor B 2006, Taylor M 1973, Terry P 1983, Thorneley D 2006, Timms B 1963, Tomlinson J 2008, Tremlett C 2004, Tremlett T 1983, Turner D 1970, Udal S 1992, Vince J 2013, Walker C 1949, Warne S 2000, Wassell A 1963, Watson S 2005, White D 1960, White G 1998.

6. *WISDEN'S* CRICKETERS of the YEAR

The year of nomination follows that of significant performance so, for example, Poore's 1900 refers to his batting in 1899. Those in brackets played for Hampshire but not when nominated.

(1895: CB Fry), 1900: Major RM Poore, 1911: CB Llewellyn, 1912: CP Mead, 1914: Hon LH Tennyson, 1933: AS Kennedy, 1959: RE Marshall and D Shackleton, 1969: BA Richards, 1974: PJ Sainsbury, 1975: AME Roberts, 1977: CG Greenidge, (1979: DI Gower), 1983: TE Jesty and MD Marshall, 1984: CL Smith, 1990: RA Smith, (1993: Wasim Akram), (1994: SK Warne*), (1996: DG Cork), (2003: ML Hayden), 2006: KP Pietersen and (SP Jones), (2010: MJ Clarke).

*Warne was one of the five Cricketers of the Century in 2000.

7. HAMPSHIRE & ENGLAND

In chronological order, the following represented England in Test Matches while with Hampshire:

AJL Hill, C Heseltine, EG Wynyard, CP Mead, CB Fry, Hon LH Tennyson, G Brown, AS Kennedy, J Arnold, D Shackleton, DW White, RMH Cottam, CL Smith, VP Terry, RA Smith, DI Gower, AD Mullally, JP Crawley, KP Pietersen, SD Udal, CT Tremlett, MA Carberry.

In alphabetical order, the following who played for Hampshire, represented England in Test Matches before or after their Hampshire career:

K Ali, VA Barton, DG Cork, NG Cowans, AJ Evans, LH Gay, ES Giddins, SP Jones, JP Stephenson.

In chronological order, the following represented England only in limited-overs and/or T20 matches while with Hampshire:

TE Jesty, AD Mascarenhas, MJ Lumb, DR Briggs.

APPENDIX FOUR

PRESIDENTS of HAMPSHIRE & MCC

HAMPSHIRE PRESIDENTS

This section is the product of research by Stephen Saunders and amends some previous lists. The first year of office is shown.

1863	Thomas Chamberlayne
1868	WWB Beach
1885	The Earl of Northesk
1887	AH Wood
1888	F Ricardo
1890	AF Jeffreys MP
1891	AF Jeffrys
1892	RG Hargreaves
1894	The Duke of Wellington
1895	Captain EG Wynyard
1897	Lord Abedare
1899	LG Bonham-Carter
1901	Sir George Meyrick
1903	WG Nicholson
1905	CAR Hoare
1909	Sir GA Cooper
1911	Dr R Bencraft
1913	JC Moberly (to 1914)
1919	Lord Swaythling
1921	Sir Godfrey Baring
1923	The Earl of Northbrook
1925	Lt-Col C Heseltine
1927	Sir Francis Lacey
1929	AJL Hill
1931	Major-Gen the Rt Hon JEB Seely
1933	Sir George Meyrick
1935	Sir Russell Bencraft
1936	Col C Heseltine
1937	Lt-Col C Heseltine (to 1944)
1946	JG Grieg
1947	Major HS Altham
1966	Lord Porchester
1968	Sir Reginald Biddle
1971	R Aird
1984	CGA Paris
1990	WJ Weld
2002	ACD Ingleby-Mackenzie*
2007	BA Richards
2009	NEJ Pocock

*ACD Ingleby-Mackenzie died in March 2006 and as a mark of respect, the position of President was left open until the following year.

MCC PRESIDENTS

The following Hampshire cricketers, officials or associates of Hampshire cricket have also been President of the MCC.

1826	The Rev. Lord Frederick Beauclerk
1827	HR Kingscote
1828	AF Greville
1831	W Deedes
1845	Thomas Chamberlayne
1857	Sir Hervey-Bathurst
1927	Sir Francis Lacey
1959	HS ('Harry') Altham
1968–1969	Ronnie Aird
1975	Cecil Paris
1996–1998	ACD (Colin) Ingleby-Mackenzie

BIBLIOGRAPHY

Stephen Saunders (1996, updated 2010) has published the full bibliography *Cricket in Hampshire*. His first version appeared in the 1996 *Hampshire Handbook*.

The bibliography below lists those books and sources which were particularly informative in compiling this publication.

Allen D (2007) *Hampshire County Cricket Club 1946–2006: Entertain or Perish*, Phillimore.

Altham HS, Arlott J, Eagar EDR, Webber R (1957) *Hampshire County Cricket: the Official History*, Phoenix.

Ashley-Cooper FS (1924) *Hampshire County Cricket*, George W May.

Association of Cricket Statisticians (1981) *A Guide to Important Matches Played in the British Isles 1707–1863*.

Association of Cricket Statisticians (1982) *Hampshire Cricketers 1800–1982*.

Association of Cricket Statisticians (1988) *Cricket Grounds of Hampshire*.

Gannaway N (1990) *A History of Cricket in Hampshire*, Hampshire Books.

Hampshire Cricket Society (1983) *Milestones of Hampshire Cricket*.

The Hampshire Cricketers Guide, various publishers: 1885–1890, 1892–1914, 1920–1939.

Hampshire Handbook, various publishers: 1950–2013.

Isaacs V (1996) *Hampshire CCC One-day Records 1963–1995*.

Isaacs V (1997) *Hampshire CCC First-Class Records 1864–1996*.

Jenkinson N (2001) *Here's the Hambledon Club*, Downed Books.

Jenkinson N, Allen D, Renshaw A (2000) *Images of Sport: Hampshire County Cricket Club*, Tempus.

May Lieut-Col J (1906) *Cricket in North Hants, Records and Reminiscences*, Warren & Son.

Midwinter E (1987) *The Lost Seasons: Cricket in Wartime 1939–1945*, Methuen.

Murrell RJ (2008) *Hampshire Cricket First Class "Top Tens"*.

Simons J (1993) *A History of Cricket in Hampshire, 1760–1914*, Hampshire CC Papers no. 4.

Wynne-Thomas P (1988) *The History of Hampshire CCC*, Christopher Helm.

Also, from the Hampshire Records Office at Winchester:

Hambledon Club Account Book

Hambledon Club Minute Books 1772 onwards

Hambledon County Club Book

INDEX

Hampshire players, major administrators, officers, opponents/teams, clubs and grounds by year, from the chronological section only: 1863–2013.

Abdul Razzaq, 2010
Abel R, 1897
Abercrombie, CH, 1913, '14, '15/18, '81
Aberdare, Lord, 1897
Accrington, 1910, '34, '36, '38
Adams GCA, 1998
Adams JHK, 2000, '02, '06, '07, '09, '10, '11, '12, '13
Advisory County Cricket Committee, 1968
Ageas Bowl, see Rose Bowl
Aird R, 1922, '24, '43, '45, '52, '58, '70, '84
Aldershot, 1905, '06, '10, '40, '51
Aldershot & District, 1941
Aldershot Services, 1940, '45
Allan JM, 1954
Allen DR, 2008
Alsop T, 2013
Altham HS, 1900, '08, '12, '21, '26, '46, '49, '56, '57, '58, '59, '61, '65
Alton, 1904, '05
Anderson JA, 2002
Andrew SJ, 1983, '84, '85, '87, '89
Andrews CJ, 1943, '45, '48
Antelope Ground (Day's), Southampton, 1864, '65, '68, '74, '75, '76, '79, '81, '84, '96
Antelope Inn, 1863, '66
Antigua, 1994
Aqib Javed, 1991
Arkwright FGB, 1942, '45
Arlott LTJ, 1939, '57, '58, '61, '77, '91
Army The, 1906, '53
Arnold ACP, 1915/18
Arnold J, 1928, '30, '31, '32, '33, '34, '35, '36, '37, '38, '39, '40, '43, '46, '47, '48, '50, '83
Arnold WJ, 1950
Arsenal FC, 1936, '52
Artistics, 1915/18
Arundel, 1962
Atherton MA, 1996
Australia, 1910, '28, '58, '91, '98.
Australians, 1877, '80, '82, '95/6, '96, '99, 1905, '09, '10, '12, '21, '30, '32, '34, '38, '40, 43, '48, '53, '56, '64, '68, '70, '72, '83, '85, '89, '93, '97, 2001, '05, '07, '09, '13

Australian Aboriginals, 1868
Australian Imperial Forces, 1919
Ayling JR, **19**85, '88, '91, '92, '93, **20**11
Aymes AN, **19**53, '84, '86, '89, '91, '98, '99, **20**00, '02

Bacon FH, **18**84, '95, **19**05, '15/18
Badcock J, 1906, '07, '08
Bailey, Sir DTL, 1951
Bailey GJ, 2013
Bailey J, 1927, '28, '31, '32, '33, '34, '36, '38, '39, '46, '48, '49, '50, '71, '81, '88
Bailey MJ, 1981
Baker AF, **19**85, **20**00
Bakker PJ, 1985, '86, '89, '90, '92
Balcombe DJ, **19**21, **20**01, '12, '13
Balderstone JC, 1975
Baldry DO, 1959, '61, '63, '81
Baldwin H, **18**77, '90, '91, '92, '94, '95, '96, '98, '99, **19**00, '01, '04, '05
Banerjee SN, 1936
Bangladesh, 2005, '10
Bannerman C, 1877
Barbados, **19**84, '88, '99, **20**10, '11
Barclay JRT, 2008
Bardsley W, 1912
Baring AEG, 1930, '31, '32, '34
Baring, Sir G, 1921
Barnard HM, 1951, '53, '54, '55, '57, '58, '61, '62, '63, '64, '68, '69
Barrett EIM, **18**96, **19**01, '02, '03, '12, '13, '20
Barrett P, 1983
Bartley LD, 1931
Barton CG, **18**91, **19**01
Barton VA, **18**92, '92, '93, '94, '96, **19**00, '01, '02, '03
Bashley (Rydal), **19**86, **20**06, '12
Basingstoke, **18**84, **19**06, '35, '44, '69, '72, '93, **20**00, '06
Basingstoke & North Hants, 1956
Bat & Ball Inn, The, 2008
BAT Sports, 2001, '02, '03, '05, '06
Bates MD, 2012, '13
Batty JN, 2007

153

Bath, 1903, '11, '14, '48
Beach WWB, 1868, '75
Beatrice, Princess, 1945
Bedfordshire, 1968
Bedi BS, 1973, '76
Bedser AV, 1946
Belcher G, 1915/18
Belgium, 1967
Bencraft, Sir HWR **18**79, '80, '85, '88, '89, '92, '95, **19**01, '03, '05, '10, '12, '15/18, '35, '36
Benham CC, 2001, '02, '04, '06
Benjamin WKM, 1994, '95, '96
Berkshire, 1991
Bethune HB, 1897
Bichel AJ, 2005
Bicknell MP, 1991
Biddle, Sir R, 1968, '70
Bignell GN (aka 'Newcombe'), 1905, '19
Binny RAW, 1948, '51
Blake DE, 1944, '49, '50, '53
Blake JP, 1944, '45
Bloefeld H, 1965
Blythe C, 1904
Board of Control, 1938, '68
Bodington CH, 1915/18
Bolus JB, 1963
Bombay, 2006
Bond SE, 2008
Bonham-Carter LG, 1899
Boon DC, 1988
Booth C, 1875, '79
Booth R, 1964
Border AR, 1985
Botham IT, **19**74, '81, **20**12
Botham LJ, 1993, '96
Bournemouth, **19**85, **20**03, '10, '11
Bournemouth Ground, see Dean Park
Bovill JNB, 1993, '95, '97
Bowell HAW, 1902, '04, '05, '07, '08, '09, '10, '11, '14, '20, '21, '26, '27, '28, '30, '43
Bowell NH, 1925, '26, '43
Bowley EH, 1935
Bowyer BG, 1947, '49
Boyd-Moss R, 1984
Boyes GS, 1921, '22, '23, '24, '25, '26, '27, '29, '31, '32, '33, '34, '35, '36, '38, '39, '40, '43, '45
Bradford, 1922, '47, '50, '55
Bradford, Sir ER, **18**96, **19**15/18

Bradman DG, 1930, '34, '38, '39
Bransgrove RG, 2000, '01, '06, '12
Bray C, 1939
Brent A, 1922
Bridger JR, 1941, '47, '54
Briggs DR, 2008, '09, '10, '11, '12, '13
Brighton, 1894
Bristol, **19**09, '11, '14, '53, '64, '72, '82, '88, **20**04
British Empire XI, 1943, '44, '45
Broadhalfpenny Down, **19**08, '99, **20**08
Brockwell W, 1897
Brodhurst BML, 1915/18
Brodhurst AH, 1944
Broomfield S, 1940
Brown FR, 1945, '49
Brown G, 1907, '08, '09, '10, '11, '13, '14, '19, '20, '21, '22, '23, '24, '26, '27, '28, '29, '30, '31, '32, '33, '34, '37, '83
Brown MJ, 2004, '07, '08
Brown W, 1934
Bruce JTA, 2003, '07, '08
Brunnschweiler I, 2001, '03, '11
Brutton CP, 1915/18, '21, '23
Brutton S, 1915/18
Buckinghamshire, 1865
Buckland EH, 1895
Budd WL, 1934, '35, '41, '43, '45
Buller JS, 1945
Burden MD, 1947, '51, '54, '56, '61, '63, '71
Burnett JP, 1960
Burton-on-Trent, 1955, '58
Bury L, **18**79, **19**33
Butt HR, 1901
Byng AM, 1915/18

Calmore Sports, 1989
Calthorpe, Hon FS, 1922
Cambridge University, **18**75, '79, '82, '93, **19**22, '30, '32, '41, '44, '68
Cambridgeshire, 1994
Campbell AK, 1943
Canada, **19**07, **20**11
Cannings VHD, **19**46, '50, '51, '53, '54, '55, '56, '57, '59, **20**12
Canterbury, **18**77, **19**08, '21, '23, '26, '27, '47, '55, '58, '64, '83, '84, **20**02, '05, '10
Caple RJ, 1962, '63, '64, '65
Carberry MA, 2006, '07, '09, 10, '11, '13

Cardiff, **19**32, '35, '66, '74, '75, **20**00, '12
Caribbean, 2011
Carter NM, 2012
Carty R, 1949, '54
Case GH, 1864
Castell AT, 1962, '63, '64, '66, '67, '69
Catisfield nr. Fareham, 1872
Ceylon, 1969
Chamberlayne T, 1863, '68
Charrett ?, 1945
Charterhouse School, 1915/18, '78
Chelmsford, **19**88, '91, **20**00, '12
Cheltenham, **19**07, '29, **20**05
Cheshire, **19**81, '89, **20**04
Chesterfield, 1938, '51
Chester-le-Street, 2007, '08
Chichester, 1908
Chippenham, 1964
Christian DT, 2010
Civil Service, 1943, '44
Clacton, 1958
Clark SR, 2007
Clarke MJ, 2004
Clay JC, 1948
Clifton, 1920
Club & Ground, **18**86, '92, '93, **19**37, '41, '47, '51, '54
Colchester, 1947
Collins TH, 1935
Combined Services, 1947, '48
Combined Universities, 1995
Compton DCS, 1941, '47, '57
Compton LH, 1941
Connor CA, 1984, '85, '86, '89, '92, '94, '95, '96, '98
Constantine Baron LN, 1945
Cook SJ, 2000, '02
Cooper Sir GA, 1908, '10
Cork DG, 2009, '10, '11
Cornwallis OW, 1921
Cornwallis WS, 1921
Cottam RMH, 1931, '62, '63, '64, '65, '66, '67, '68, '69, '70, '71, '72
Court RCL, 1936, '40, '47, '51
Coventry, 1912, '73
Cowans NG, 1994
Cowdrey MC, 1964
Cowes, IOW, 1938, '56, '61, '62
Cowie AG, 1915/18

Cowley NG, 1974, '77, '78, '81, '86, '88, '89
Cox GF, 1945
Cox RMF, 1986, '88, '90, '94
Crapp JF, 1953
Crawley JC, 2002, '03, '04, '05, '06, '07
Creese WLC, 1926, '27, '33, '34, '35, '36, '38, '39, '45
Cricket Council, The, 1968, '97
Cronje H, 1999
Cropper W, 1885
Currie CE, 1885

Dare RA, 1951, '52, '54
Darley Dale, 1975
Davis WW, 1984
Dawkes GO, 1955
Dawson GW, 1947, '48, '49, '50
Dawson H, 1947
Dawson, LA, **19**05, **20**06, '07, '11, '12, '13
Day HLV, 1922, '23, '24
De Freitas PAJ, 1994
Dean TA, **19**39, '47, '50, **20**12
Dean Park, Bournemouth, **18**69, '80, '97, '98, **19**02, '03, '04, '05, '06, '07, '09, '12, '13, '15/18, '25, '26, '27, '30, '33, '35, '36, '37, '38, '39, '40, '45, '46, '47, '48, '49, '51, '52, '54, '55, '59, '60, '61, '62, '63, '64, '65, '66, '68, '69, '72, '73, '74, '76, '78, '80, '83, '84, '88, '90, '92, '93, '98
Deane GO, 1964
Deane MW, 1895
Deanery, **18**86, '92, **19**51, '78, '80, '82
Debnam AFH, 1950, '51
Delve G, 2006
Derby, **18**76, '98, '99, **19**02, '04, '05, '83
Derbyshire, **18**76, '77, '78, '92, '93, '94, '95, **19**03, '05, '06, '12, '29, '32, '36, '38, '54, '55, '58, '60, '61, '63, '64, '66, '75, '76, '78, '80, '81, '88, '90, '93, '94, '99, **20**00
Devonshire, 1880, '84, '93
de Wet F, 2011
Dibden RR, 1998
Dible WG, 1883, '85
Dodds TC, 1941
D'Oliveira BD, 1968
Dominions The, 1915/18
Doran F, 1922, '48, '60
Dorset, **18**80, '84, **19**74, '92, '98
Dover, 1913

Drake EJ, 1931, '33, '34, '36, '41
Dravid R, 2000, '02
Duckworth/Lewis, 2010
Durham, **18**70, '95, 1992, '95, **20**00, '01, '07, '08, '09

Eagar EM, 2013
Eagar EDR, 1944, '45, '46, '47, '48, '50, '52, '54, '55, '57, '58, '60, '61, '77
East Hants Ground, Southsea, 1868
Eastbourne, 1950, '55, '58
Eastleigh, **19**94, **20**12
Eccles CV, 1868
Ede EL, 1863, '64, '80
Ede GM, 1863, '64
Edgbaston, Birmingham, **18**84, '93, '94, **19**15/18, '22, '25, '84, '87, '91, '94, '99, **20**00, '02
Edinburgh, Duke of, 1949, '54
Edrich WJ, 1947
Emery KD, 1981, '82, '83, '84
Empire XI, The, 1943
England, **18**77, '95/6, **19**02, '05, '08, '10, '12, '15/18, '21, '22, '30, '31, '33, '48, '50, '61, '77, '83, '88, '91, '93, '94, '99, **20**02, '04, '05, '06, '07, '09, '10, 11, '12, '13
England & Wales Cricket Board (ECB), **19**97, **20**00, '06, '10
England Women, 2013
English EA, **18**98, **19**64
English XI, 1864
English Women's Cricket Association, 1971
Ervine SM, **19**89, **20**05, '09, '10
Essex, **18**76, '87, '90, '92, '93, '94, '95, '96, '99, **19**13, '33, '36, '39, '61, '72, '74, '79, '81, '83, '84, '85, '86, '88, '89, '90, '91, '92, '94, '95, '96, '97, '98, **20**04, '05, '06, '08
Eton College, 1915/18, '22, '40, '59, '73, '82
Evans AJ, 1911, 1921
Evans DM, 1911
Evans J, 1920
Exton RN, 1945, '48

Faber MJJ, 1975
Fagg AE, 1941
Fareham, 1951
Faulkner P, 1969
Faversham, 1876

Fellowes, J, 1883, '85
Fenley S, 1935
Fielder AE, 1911
Fletcher KWR, 1985
Flint DPJ, 1989, '95
Flood RD, 1951
Ford BG, **19**85, **20**00
Ford G, 1981, '85
Ford P, 1985
Forster HT, 1911, '15/18
Forster HW, 1890, '92
Francis JD, 2001, '02, '03
Francis SRG, **19**97, **20**00, '01
Fraser ARC, **19**89, **20**02
Frederick J St J, 1864
Frere HT, 1864
Frome, 1961
Fry CA, 1931, '60
Fry CB, **18**95/6, **19**03, '08, '09, '10, '11, '12, '13, '14, '15/18, '60, **20**08
Fry J, 2008
Fry SH, 1931, '60
Fulham FC, 1930
Fynn CG, 1930

Gannaway N, 1945
Garaway M, 1993, '95
Geary G, 1926
Gentlemen v Players, **18**73, **19**04, '05, '07, '11, '12, '13, '27, '28, '32, '46, '50, '55, '63
Gentlemen of Devon, 1871
Gentlemen of England, 1919
Gentlemen of Hampshire, 1868, '71, '72, '73, '79, '84, '86, '89
Gentlemen of the South, 1903
Gentlemen of Sussex, 1872
Gibb PA, 1960
Gibbons HG, 1925, '28
Gibbs LR, 1988
Gibson O, **18**70, **20**07
Giddins ESH, 2003
Giles RJ, 1938
Gilliat RMC, 1966, '67, '69, '70, '71, '72, '73, '74, '75, '76, '77, '78, '81
Glamorgan, **18**95, **19**21, '22, '32, '35, '48, '59, '64, '66, '67, '69, '70, '73, '74, '75, '76, '81, '83, '89, '93, '96, '97, '99, **20**00, '02, '03, '04, '05, '06

Gloucestershire, **18**94, **19**03, '07, '09, '11, '14, '20, '26, '27, '45, '47, '53, '61, '64, '68, '72, '73, '75, '77, '82, '83, '90, '93, '96, '99, **20**03, '04, '12
Gomes HA, 1984
Gooch GA, 1984, '85, '96
Gornall JP, 1945
Gosport, 1978, '80, '82
Gover AR, 1941, '46
Gower DI, 1990, '91, '92, '93
Grace GF, 1880
Grace WG, 1903, '08
Graf SF, 1980
Graveney TW, 1953
Gravesend, 1867, '84
Gray JR, 1945, '49, '50, '51, '52, '53, '54, '55, '56, '57, '58, '59, '60, '61, '62, '63, '64, '65, '97, '98
Gray N, 2011, '12
Greenidge CG, 1905, '67, '69, '70, '71, '72, '73, '74, '75, '76, '77, '78, '79, '80, '81, '82, '83, '84, '85, '86, '87, '88, '90, '91
Greenwood FE, 1931
Gregory JT, 1905, '12, '15/18
Greig AW, 1977
Greig JG, 1901, '02, '03, '05, '14, '22, '46
Grierson HK, 1888, '93
Griffin GM, 1960
Griffiths DA, 2006, '09
Gross FA, 1924
Grundy J, 1865
Guard DR, 1948
Guildford, 1946
Gunner JH, 1915/18
Guptil MJ, 2013

Haggarth E, 1933
Haigh S, **18**65, **19**24
Hake HD, 1923
Hall PM, 1924
Hambledon, **19**08, **20**08
Hamblin JRC, 2001, '04
Hammond WR, 1927
Hampden Park, 1933
Hampshire Academy, 2002, '03, '07, '10
Hampshire Colts (& Under-19), **18**73, '84, '93, **19**76, '82
Hampshire Cricket Board, 1997, '99
Hampshire Hogs, 1951

Hansen TM, 1997
Hardinge HTW, 1913
Hardy JJE, 1983, '85
Harfield L, 1924, '25, '27, '28, '29, '30, '32
Hargreaves RG, 1892
Harper RA, 1985
Harris, Lord, **18**84, **19**13
Harrison BRS, 1957, '59, '61
Harrison L, **19**24, '39, '40, '47, '48, '50, '51, '52, '53, '55, '57, '59, '60, '61, '63, '66, '67, '81, '86, **20**12
Harrogate, **18**96, **19**76
Hartley PJ, 1999
Harvey IJ, 2008
Haskell R, 1941
Haslop PJ, 1962, '72
Havant, **19**51, '78, '80, '91, **20**01, '02, '03, '04, '07, '08, '09, 11
Hawke, Lord, 1932
Hayden ML, **19**01, '21, 97, **20**01
Hayes EG, 1909
Hayling Island, 1951
Hayter E, 1936
Hayward AJ, 1925, '26
Hayward M, 2008
Hayward RE, 1981, '91
Hayward T, **18**95/6, **19**12
Headingley, Leeds, **19**04, '20, '32, '81, '84, '99, **20**07
Hearne T, 1865
Heath GEM, 1936, '37, '38, '39, '40, '46, '47, '49, '50, '52
Heath M 1951, '54, '55, '58, '59, '63
Hebden GL 1945, '48
Hedley WC, 1898
Hemp DL, 1997
Hemstead E, 1865
Herath HRMB, 2010
Herman OW, 1927, '28, '29, '31, '32, '33, '34, '36, '38, '39, '43, '45, '46, '47, '48, '49, '67
Herman RS, 1967, '72, '73, '74, '76
Hertfordshire, **18**86, '87, **19**83
Hervey-Bathurst, FH, 1863
Heseltine C, **18**95/6, **19**00, '03, '24, '36, 43, '44
Heseltine CCP, 1943
Hesketh-Pritchard HV, 1902, '03, '04, '05, '07, '12
Hick GA, **19**97, **20**00
Hickton W, 1870

Hill, AJL, **18**93, '95, '95/6, '97, '98, **19**00, '02, '03, '04, '06, '07, '08, '21, '24, '29, '51, **20**06
Hill AEL, 1915/18
Hill C, 1905
Hill G, 1934, '35, '36, '38, '40, '46, '48, '49, '54
Hindley RJ, 2003
Hirst GH, 1924
Hilsum I, 2001
Hoare CAR, 1905, '08
Hobbs JB, 1909, '15/18, '20, '27
Hodges WF, 1945
Holder JW, 1967, '70
Holland, 1988
Holmes H, 1864, '67
Holmes P, 1920
Holt AG, 1935, '40, '41, '43, '45, '49, '54, '59, '65, '81
Hopkins FJ, 1904, '22, '25, '30
Hornsey, 1959
Horsham, 1921
Horton H, 1953, '55, '56, '57, '58, '59, '60, '61, '62, '62, '63, '64, '65, '66, '67
Hosie AL, 1921, '28
Hotham AG, 1901
Hove, **18**75, **19**45, '67, '84, '93, **20**04
Howell H, 1922, '25
Huddersfield, 1911
Hughes PJ, 2010
Hull, 1931, '70
Hulse Sir E, 1893
Humphrey W, 1864
Humphreys WA, 1885
Hungerford, 1990
Hunt J, 1863
Hutton, Sir L, 1947, '55
Hursley Park, 1982, '84, '85, '92
Hussain M, 1983
Hussain N, 1983
Hythe, 1941

Imran Tahir, 2008, '09, '11
India, 1951, '61
Indians (& All India), **19**36, '52, '71, '74, '83, '96, **20**06, '07, '11
Indian Premier League (IPL), 2007, '08, '09, '13
Ingleby-Mackenzie ACD, **19**46, '51, '52, '55, '56, '57, '58, '61, '62, '63, '64, '65, '66, **20**02, '06

Intikhab Alam, 1962
Ireland, **19**65, **20**09
Irfan Shah, 2001, '02
Isherwood LCR, 1921
Isle of Wight, 2006, '09, '12
Islington, 1865

Jackman RD, 1982
Jackson FS, 1915/18
Jackson HL, 1958
Jacques A, 1912, '13, '14, '15/18
Jacques PA, 2004
Jamaica, 1932
James AK, 1978, '85
James KD, 1985, '86, '88, '89, '91, '92, '96, '97, '98, '99
Jameson TO, 1925
Janmohamed F, 2001
Jardine DR, 1915/18
Jean-Jacques M, 1994
Jefferies SJ, 1988, '89
Jefferson WI, 2004
Jeffrys AF, 1890
Jephson WV, 1908
Jesson RWF, 1915/18
Jessop GL, 1907, '09, '11
Jessop GLO, 1933
Jesty TE, 1966, '67, '69, '72, '74, '75, '76, '77, '78, '79, '80, '81, '82, '84, '85
Jewell GAFW, 1945, '50, '56
Johnson NC, 2001, '02
Johnston AC, 1904, '06, '10, '11, '12, '13, '14, '41
Johnston WA, 1953
Jones SP, 2010, '11
Joseph LA, 1990
Judd AK, 1933

Kabir Ali, 2010, '11, '12
Katich SM, 2003, '12
Keech M, 1995
Keith GL, 1962, '63, '64, '65, '71, '75
Kendall WS, **19**93, '95, '98, **20**00, '02, '03, '04, '08
Kennedy AS, 1907, '09, '10, '11, '12, '13, '14, '19, '20, '21, '22, '23, '24, '25, '26, '27, '28, '29, '30, '31, '32, '33, '34, '35, '36, '37, '55, '58, '67

Kent, **18**67, '75, '76, '77, '78, '84, '92, '94, **19**01, '04, '05, '06, '07, '09, '10, '11, '12, '13, '14, '20, '21, '27, '32, '35, '38, '47, '48, '50, '52, '55, '57, '58, '65, '66, '67, '68, '70, '72, '73, '74, '75, '77, '78, '80, '83, '84, '89, '92, '94, '95, **20**01, '04, '05, '06, '07, '10

Kent Cricket Board, **19**99, **20**00

Kenway DA, **19**93, **20**01, '05, '08

Kenya, 1999

Kenyon D, 1955

Kidderminster, 2007

Kingston-upon-Thames, 1946

Kitchener FG, 1896

Knight AE, 1912, '33

Knight NV, 2002, '05

Knights E, 1947, '71, '75

Knott CJ, 1938, '40, '43, '45, '46, '47, '48, '49, '50, '51, '52, '53, '54, '81

Lacey FE, **18**80, '82, '84, '85, '87, '89, '92, '98, **19**27, '29

Laker JC, 1950

Lamb AJ, 1984

Lamb GA, 2004

Lancashire, **18**70, '88, '94, '95, '97, '99, **19**01, '03, '04, '10, '14, '20, '21, '26, '27, '28, '30, '34, '35, '47, '50, '57, '65, '67, '68, '69, '70, '71, '72, '75, '82, '84, '89, '90, '91, '92, '95, '96, '98, '99, **20**02, '04, '06, '09, '11, '13

Lancashire League, 1910, '15/18, '34, '39

Laney JS, **19**89, '95, '96, '99, **20**01, '02

Langford WT, 1903

Lara BC, 1994

Latchman AH, 1974

Latouf KJ, 2006

Lawrence DV, 1990

Lawrie PE, 1923

Lawson HM, 1935, '41

Lawson MB, 1935

Lee AM, 1945

Lee GM, 1913

Lees H, 1863

Leewards Islands, 2011

Leicestershire, **18**91, '92, '93, '94, '95, '96, **19**00, '26, '48, '53, '54, '55, '67, '69, '72, '74, '75, '76, '78, '80, '85, '88, '90, '94, '96, '98, **20**00, '02, '04, '06, '11, '12

Leicester, 1899, 1907, '38, '50, '53, '76, '77, '94

Lewis AE, 1911

Lewis RV, 1967, '69, '70, '71, '73, '81

Leyton, **18**93, **19**03, '13

Light, E, 1893

Lillee DK, 1988

Lillywhite J, 1864

Lincolnshire **18**75, **19**66, '67

Lipscomb, FW, 1881

Lipscomb WH, 1866

Liverpool, **19**01, '20, '21, **20**10

Livingstone DA, 1959, '61, '62, '63, '64, '65, '67, '68, '70, '72, '88

Livsey WH, 1914, '19, '20, '21, '22, '24, '27, '29, '30

Llewellyn CB, **18**95/6, '99, **19**00, '01, '02, '03, '04, '05, '06, '08, '09, '10, '11 '15/18, '21, '23

Lloyd CH, 1968

Lock GAR, 1963, '67

Lodge LV, 1933

Logan RJ, 2005

Lohmann GA, 1885, '95/6

London Counties, 1941, '43, '44

London Police, 1945

Longparish, 1980, '87

Lord JC, 1864

Lord's, **18**65, '66, '77, '78, '79, '95/6, **19**07, '15/18, '19, '31, '34, '35, '46, '48, '50, '60, '63, '70, '74, '75, '76, '83, '84, '88, '89, '91, '92, '95, '98, **20**06, '09, '10, '12

Loughborough University, 2002, '13

Lowndes WGLF, 1915/18, '34, '35

Luard AJH, 1901

Lucas CF, 1864, '65, '66

Lumb MJ, 2007, '09, '10, '11

Lymington, 1983, '85

Lyndhurst, 1874, '76

Maartensz, SGA, 1919

Macey RE, 1947

Mackenzie PA, 1936, '38, '39, '40, '43, '45

Malone SJ, 1980

Mann D, 2012

Manners JE, **19**36, '45, '47, **20**12

Marlborough College, 1915/18

Marshall MD, 1976, '79, '80, '81, '82, '83, '84, '85, '86, '87, '88, '89, '90, '91, '92, '93, '96, '99

Marshall P, 1979

Marshall RE, 1950, '53, '55, '56, '57, '58, '59, '60, '61, '62, '63, '64, '65, '66, '67, '68, '69, '70, '71, '72, '76, '92
Martin E, 1895, 1904
Maru RJ, 1984, '85, '86, '88, '89, '90, '95, '98, 2008, '12
Mascarenhas, AD, 1996, '98, 2000, '01, '03, '04, '05, '07, '08, '09, '10, '12, '13
Massey S, 1981
Masters DD, 1999
Maxwell GJ, 2012
May PBH, 1982
McArdle T, 2012
McBride WN, 1926
McCorkell D, 1951
McCorkell NT, 1930, '33, '34, '35, '36, '37, '38, '39, '40, '45, '47, '48, '49, '50, '51, '52, 2012
McDonell HC, 1909, '19
McKenzie ND, 2010, '11
McLaren AC, 1901
McLean NAM, 1998
McLeod A, 1936, '40
McMillan CD, 2005
MCC, 1863, '65, '66, '69, '72, '75, '76, '77, '78, '79, '80, '81, '86, '87, '90, '91, '93, '98, 1906, '07, '11, '12, '13, '21, '22, '25, '47, '50, '51, '52, '53, '58, '59, '68, '69, '74, '98
Mead CP, 1903, '05, '06, '07, '08, '09, '10, '11, '12, '13, '14, '15/18, '19, '20, '21, '22, '23, '24, '25, '26, '27, '28, '29, '30, '31, '32, '33, '34, '35, '36, '37, '56, '58, '72, '83
Mead W, 1876
Melbourne, 1877, 1977
Melle BG, 1914, '15/18, '19, '51
Melle MG, 1951
Merry L, 2001
Meyrick Sir George, 1901, '03, '33
Middlesborough, 1965
Middlesex, 1864, '65, '75, '94, '97, 1900, '02, '03, '07, '19, '20, '21, '23, '25, '34, '35, '47, '48, '49, '55, '57, '59, '60, '66, '67, '70, '76, '77, '78, '79, '80, '81, '82, '83, '84, '85, '86, '88, '89, '90,
'91, '92, '93, '96, '98, 2000, '02, '04, '06, '07, '08
Middleton TC, 1980, '83, '85, '86, '88, '90, '91, '92, '95
Midwinter E, 1940
Milburn SM, 1997

Miller DA, 2012
Miller KR, 1943
Minor Counties, 1981
Minor Counties South, 1973
Misselbrook H, 1869
Mitchell TB, 1938
Moberley JC, 1912, '13
Moody TM, 1997
Moore RH, 1905, '31, '33, '34, '35, '36, '37, '38, '45, 2004, '05
Moreton-in-the-Marsh, 1972
Morris AC, 1998, 2001, '03
Morris RSM, 1989, '94, '95
Morris ZC, 2001
Mottram TJ, 1970, '71, '72, '73, '75, '76, '77
Muir GH, 1915/18, '24, '31
Mullally AD, 1988, 2000, '01, '02, '04, '05
Muralitharan M, 1999
Murtagh AJ, 1970, '71, '73
Mustard P, 1901
Myburgh JG, 2011
Mycroft W, 1876

National Cricket Association, 1968, '97
Nayudu CK, 1936
New Zealand, 1906, '31, '58, '83, '99
New Zealand Expeditionary Force, 1940
New Zealanders, 1931, '43, '49, '73, '94, 2004, '13
Newcastle United FC, 1952
Newman J, 1951
Newman JA, 1906, '07, '08, '09, '10, '11, '12, '13, '14, '19, '20, '21, '22, '23, '24, '25, '26, '27, '28, '29, '30, '37, '58
Newport, IOW, 1938, '51
Newton E, 1900
Nicholas MCJ, 1978, '82, '83, '84, '85, '86, '88, '89, '90, '91, '92, '94, '95, '99, 2000, '01
Nicholson WG, 1903, '05
Noble MA, 1905
Norfolk, 1880, '86, '87, 1965, '84
Norfolk, Duke of, 1958, '62
North MJ, 2009
North v South, 1928
Northampton, 1927, '68, '86, 2009, '12
Northamptonshire, 1895, 1905, '06, '08, '27, '35, '38, '45, '46, '72, '73, '76, '80, '84, '85, '86, '88, '90, '92, '93, 2013

Northbrook, Earl of, 1923

Northlands (& Banister) Road, Southampton **18**67, '83, '84, '85, '91, '94, '96, '97, '98, **19**00, '03, '04, '05, '08, '09, '10, '11, '12, '20, '21, '22, '23, '24, '25, '26, '27, '29, '30, '32, '33, '34, '35, '36, '38, '40, '41, '45, '46, '48, '49, '50, '52, '62, '64, '65, '66, '67, '68, '71, '72, '74, '76, '77, '83, '84, '85, '88, '89, '90, '92, '93, '94, '96, '98, '99, **20**00

Nottinghamshire, **18**94, **19**07, '13, '21, '23, '29, '30, '32, '34, '35, '38, '46, '57, '68, '71, '72, '73, '81, '87, '89, '90, '91, 2004, '05, '06, '09, '10, '11

O'Connor M, 1988

Old Tauntonians, 1951, '78, '82

Old Trafford, **18**70, **19**57, '65, '69, '70, '74, '76, '84, '89, '92, **20**06, '09

Oldroyd E, 1921

Olympic Games, 1912

O'Sullivan, DR, 1970, '71, '73, '74

Oval The, **18**64, '66, '80, '83, '84, '85, '97, '98, **19**02, '03, '09, '11, '27, '31, '36, '51, '61, '69, '84, '86, '95, **20**00, '04, '05, '07

Oxford, 1907, '54

Oxfordshire, 1892

Oxford University, **18**75, **19**04, '12, '13, '19, '26, '45, '50, '54, '56, '61, '66, '68, '71, '88, '89

Packer KFB, 1977, '78

Pakistan, **19**61, '68, **20**13

Pakistanis, 1954, '62, '06

Palairet LCH, 1896

Palmer Charles H, 1953

Palmer Cecil H, 1904, '15/18

Palmer RH, 1945

Panesar MS, 2002

Parfitt PJ, 1963

Paris CGA, 1936, '38, '40, '43, '61, '81, '84, '90

Parker FAV, 1940

Parker JP, 1926, '33, '45

Parks JM, 1974

Parks RJ, 1953, '80, '81, '86, '89, '91, '92

Parks, The (Oxford), 1919

Paultons, 1988

Pawson HA, 1940

Pearce WK, 1945, '50, '53

Perkins GC, 2012

Persse HW, 1907, '15/18

Petersfield, 1951

Philadelphians, 1884, '89, '97

Piachaud JD, 1960

Pietersen KP, 2001, '05, '08, '10

Pike NS, 2001, '03

Pitman RWC, 1951

Players, The, see Gentlemen v Players

Players of the South, 1903

Playfair Cricket Monthly, 1960

Pocock NEJ, **19**78, '80, '82, '84, **20**09

Pollard KT, 2010

Poore RM, **18**95/6, '98, '99, **19**00, '01, '02, '03, '04, '06

Porchester, Lord, 1965

Port Elizabeth, 1970

Portsmouth, 1978

Portsmouth & Southsea, 1951

Portsmouth Sub Committee, 1946, '47

Portsmouth FC, 1904, '12, '57

Portsmouth Ground – see United Services

Pothas N, 2004, '05, '06, '07, '08, '09, '10, '11

Pothecary AE, 1926, '27, '32, '33, '36, '37, '38, '41, '45, '46

Pothecary SG, 1927

Powell DBL, 2007

Powell E, 1884, '85

Prittipaul LR, 2000, '01, '05, '12

Procter MJ, 1972, '77

Proud RB, 1938, '44

Prouton RO, 1945, '50, '52, '53, '54

Public Schools XI, 1915/18

Pullar G, 1957

Quaife WG, 1922

Querl RG, 2013

Quinton FWD, **18**95, '96, **19**00

Quinton JM, 1896

Rae AF, 1948

Raikes Rev GB, 1900, '33

Raising the Standard (ECB), 1997

Ransom VJ, 1947, '48, '49

Rayment AWH, 1949, '50, '52, '55, '56, '58

Reed BL, 1958, '65, '66, '67, '68, '69, '70, '71, '81

Reifer EL, 1984

Relf R, 1925, '26, '30

Remnant ER, 1911, '19, '20, '21, '22

Rest, The, 1911, '13, '15/18

Rest of the World, 1968, '70
Rhodes W, **18**65, **19**13, '20, '24
Ricardo F, 1888
Rice JM, 1974, '75, '76, '80, '82
Rich D, 1985
Richards BA, **19**68, '69, '70, '72, '73, '74, '75, '76, '77, '78, '86, **20**06, '09
Richards IVA, 2013
Richardson A, 2002
Richmond TL, 1922
Ridding CH, 1864
Ridley AW, 1875, '76, '77
Roberts AME, 1973, '74, '75, '76, '77, '78
Roberts W, 1889
Robertson J, 1957
Robertson-Glasgow RC, 1915/18
Robins RWV, 1949
Robinson A, 1943
Robinson DJ, 1998
Robinson LG, 1919
Robson C, **18**95, '97, **19**00, '01
Rochdale, 1939
Rock DJ, 1977, '78, '80
Rogers FG, 1924
Rogers HJ, 1915/18
Rogers NH, 1940, '46, '47, '48, '49, '50, '51, '52, '53, '54, '55
Romsey, 1951
Roper C, 1957
Roper DGB, 1945, '52
Rose/Ageas Bowl, **19**66, '94, '98, '99, **20**00, '01, '02, '03, '04, '05, '06, '07, '08, '09, '10, '11, '12
Rouse AP, 2011
Rowe A, 1993
Royal Air Force, The, 1940, '41, '43, '45
Royal Navy The, 1913, '31
Russell AI, 1886
Ryan FP, 1919
Ryan P, 1971
Rylott A, 1878

St Luke's, 1880
Sainsbury PJ, 1951, '54, '55, '56, '57, '58, '60, '61, '62, '63, '64, '65, '67, '68, '70, '71, '72, '73, '74, '76, '90, '91
Salisbury IDK, 2007
Sandeman GAC, 1915/18
Sandham A, 1933

Santall FR, 1922
Scarborough, **19**11, '75, '76, '86, '87, '90, **20**10
Schofield JEK, 2001, '02
Scotland, 1933, '92
Scott RJ, **19**83, '86, '88, '90, **20**08
Scott WEN, 1989
Seeley Rt. Hon JEB, 1931
Sexton AJ, 2001
Seymour C, 1883, '85
Seymour J, 1907
Shackleton JH, 1998
Shackleton D, **19**36, '47, '48, '49, '50, '51, '52, '53, '54, '55, '56, '57, '58, '59, '60, '61, '62, '63, '64, '65, '66, '67, '68, '69, '98, **20**07
Shafayat BM, 2012
Shahid Afridi, 2012
Sharp J, 1910
Shaw A, 1887
Sheffield, **18**95, **19**21
Sheffield United FC, 1936
Shepherd DJ, 1966
Shield INR, 1945
Shine KJ, 1989, '92, '93
Shirazi D, 2001
Shirley WR, 1915/18, '22, '23
Shirreff AC, 1944, '48, '50
Shropshire, **19**99, **20**05
Singh Y, 2007
Slaney C, 1999
Small MA, 1984
Smart CC, 1935
Smith CL, 1980, '81, '83, '84, '85, '86, '87, '88, '89, '90, '91
Smith EJ, 1922
Smith RA, **19**05, '81, '83, '85, '88, '89, '90, '91, '92, '93, '94, '96, '98, **20**00, '01, 02, '03
Smith RC, 1944
Smith CH, 1864
Soames H, 1867
Soar T, **18**87, '92, '93, '95, '96, **19**00, '02, '03
Sobers GS, 1971
Sohail Tanvir, 2013
Solly A, 1935, '36
Somerset, **18**80, '81, '83, '84, '85, '91, '95, '96, '98, '99, **19**01, '05, '10, '11, '13, '14, '23, '27, '30, '36, '55, '57, '61, '74, '75, '78, '79, '81, '82, '83, '89, '92, **20**01, '05, '08, '10, '11
South Africa, **19**13, '68, '96, '99, **20**00, '05, '06, '12

South Africans, **18**92, '94, '95/6, **19**01, '04, '05, '10, '12, '22, '32, '51, '55, '60, '70, **20**03, '11, '12
South Hants Touring Club, 1978, '86, '93
Southampton, **18**65, **19**51, '78
Southampton & District, 1941, '45
Southampton FC, **18**96, **19**04, '30, '43, '53
Southampton Grounds – see Antelope or Northlands Road
Southampton Park, 1891
Southampton Police, 1943, '44, '45
Southampton Touring Club, 1940, '41, '44, '45
Southampton Union, 1864
Southend, 1936, '83
Southern JW, 1974, '76, '77, '78, '80, '81, '83
Southern League, The, 1988, '91
Southerton J, 1864, '65, '66, '69
South Hants Club, 1864, '66
South Wilts, **18**64, **20**04, '05, '08, '09, '12
Spens, J, 1882
Sprankling WL, 1940, '45, '46, '47
Sprot EM, 1901, '03, '04, '05, '07, '08, '11, '15/18, '19
Squires HS, 1949
Sri Lanka, **19**81, '99, **20**04, '06, '11
Staffordshire, 1993
Staples SJ, 1939, '45, '49
Stares J, 1980
Steele DA, 1894
Steele JWJ, 1938
Stephenson GR, 1973, '79, '80, '81
Stephenson JP, **19**95, '96, '98, **20**01, '08
Stevenson K, 1978, '79, '81
Stewart AJ, 1996
Stoats, The, 1951
Stokes MST, 2006
Stone J, 1903, '05, '07, '08, '12, '14, '19
Stratford-upon-Avon, 2005
Streak HH, 1995
Studd HW, 1901
Suffolk, 1999
Surrey, **18**63, '64, '65, '66, '83, '84, '85, '88, '90, '91, '92, '94, '95, '97, '99, **19**04, '05, '06, '09, '12, '24, '27, '29, '31, '33, '35, '36, '37, '46, '50, '52, '53, '54, '55, '56, '57, '58, '59, '61, '62, '66, '69, '71, '72, '74, '81, '82, '83, '84, '86, '89, '91, '94, '96, '97, '99, **20**01, '01, '02, '03, '05, '06, '07, '08, '10, '11

Sussex, **18**63, '64, '73, '75, '80, '82, '83, '85, '90, '92, '93, '94, '96, **19**03, '04, '05, '08, '09, '11, '27, '35, '36, '45, '50, '51, '54, '61, '63, '64, '69, '75, '78, '81, '82, '86, '92, '93, **20**00, '01, '03, '04, '06, '07, '08, '09
Sutcliffe H, 1920, '32
Sutcliffe JF, 1915/18
Sutherland T, 1898
Swansea, 1922, '46, '57, '77
Swaythling, Lord, 1919
Sydenhurst Ramblers, 1951
Sydney, 1983

Tancred AB, 1904
Tasmania, 1932
Tate E, 1898
Tate F, 1870, '76
Tate HW, 1869, '76
Tate MW, 1927
Taunton, **18**95, '99, **19**01, '13, '30, '78, '83, '85, '92, **20**08, '11
Taylor BV, 2000, '04, '06, '09
Taylor GR, 1939, '40, '81
Taylor JD, 1947, '50
Taylor JMR, 2013
Taylor MNS, **19**73, '74, '76, '80, '89, **20**00
Taylor NR, 1990
Taylor RW, 1953
Taylor W, 1974
Tendulkar SR, 2002
Tennyson LH (Hon/Lord), 1913, '14, '15/18, '19, '20, '21, '23, '25, '26, '27, '29, '31, '32, '33, '34, '37, '44, '51
Terry VP, **18**96, **19**78, '81, '83, '84, '85, '86, '87, '88, '89, '90, '91, '92, '93, '94, '95, '96, **20**02, '08
Test & County Cricket Board, 1968, '97, '98
Test Trial, 1913, '46, '50
Thorneley D, 2006
Thorpe GP, 1996
Thresher P, 1866, '69
Thursfield MJ, 1995
Timms BSV, 1959, '60, '63, '64, '68
Titmus FJ, 1955, '63, '64
Tomlinson JA, 2006, '08, '10
Tonbridge, **18**67, **19**04, '07
Torquay, 1871
Toynbee GPR, 1915/18
Transvaal, 1932

163

Treagus G, 1995
Treherne J, 1941
Treherne RJ, 1941
Tremlett CT, 2001, '03, '04, '05, '06, '07, '09, '11
Tremlett TM, **19**74, '78, '80, '81, '83, '84, '85, '86, '87, '90, '91, **20**01, '02
Trent Bridge, Nottingham, **19**22, '35, '50, '66, '76, '87, '89, '93, **20**01, '04, '05, '09
Trinidad & Tobago, 2011
Trojans, 1905, '51, '69, '85
Trumper VT, 1905
Tubb S, 1864, '65, '66
Tulk DT, 1957
Turner IJ, **19**86, '93, **20**08
Turner DR, 1966, '67, '69, '70, '71, '72, '73, '74, '75, '76, '78, '81, '82, '84, '87, '88, '89
Tyson ? (Colonel), 1863
Tyson CT, 1921
Ubsdell G, **18**64, '65, **19**64
Udal S, **18**95, **19**86, '92, '93, '94, '95, **20**00, '01, '02, '03, '05, 06, '08
Underwood D, 1984
United Services Ground, Portsmouth, **18**82, '95, '96, '98, '99, **19**01, '04, '05, '06, '11, '13, '14, '20, '23, '27, '29, '35, '36, '46, '47, '48, '50, '53, '56, '57, '59, '61, '64, '65, '66, '69, '70, '71, '73, '74, '81, '83, '93, '99, **20**00
United Services Portsmouth, 1983
United States of America (USA), 1907
Utley RPH, 1928
Vass WPUJC, 2003
van der Gucht CG, 2001, '03
Verity H, 1939
Vince JM, 2008, '09, '10, '13
Waldron ANE, 1942, '45
Walford MM, 1947
Walker C, 1947, '49, '50, '51, '53, '54
Walker DF, 1936, '37, '38, '39, '41
Walker G, 2001, '03
Walsh CA, 1990
Walsh JE, 1953
Waqar Younis, 1991
Ward HF, 1894, '96, '97
Ward JM, 1975
Warne SK, **19**99, **20**00, '01, '03, '04, '05, '06, '07
Warner PF, 1915/18
Warwickshire, **18**78, '84, '89, '94, '95, '97, '99, **19**02, '06, '11, '12, '14, '20, '23, '25, '27, '30, '37, '51, '60, '64, '65, '66, '67, '68, '71, '72, '80, '87, '89, '93, '94, '95, '97, '99, **20**01, '02, '04, '05, '07, '09, '10, '12
Wasim Akram, 2003
Wassell AR, 1959, '61, '63, '64, '65
Waterlooville, 1978
Watkins LC, 1945
Watson SR, 2004, '05
Watson W, 1963
Webb AS, 1901, '03
Webber R, 1957
Weekes E deC, 1950
Weld WJ, **19**90, **20**00, '02
Wellington, The Duke of, 1894
West Indians, **19**00, '23, '32, '48, '50, '63, '64, '73, '76, '79, '81, '83, '84, '88 '91, '94, '97, '99, **20**04, '07, '12
West Indies, 1912, '25
Weston-Super-Mare, 1927, '47, '55
Wheater AJ, 2013
Wheatley KJ, 1966, '67, '70
Whitaker PR, **18**95, **19**94, '95, '98
White C, 2011
White DW, 1957, '59, '60, '61, '62, '63, '64, '65, '66, '67, '68, '69, '70, '72
White GW, **19**98, **20**02, '08
White WN, 1909
Wildeman F, 1960
Wilson A, 1953
Wilkinson AJ, 1865
Willis RGD, 1981
Wilson R, 1913
Wiltshire, 1964, '72, '73
Winchester, **18**91, '92, **19**88
Winchester College (& Ridding Field Ground), **18**66, '72, '75, '84, **19**12, '15/18, '40, '41
Winchester St Cross/Greenjackets, 1875
Windward Islands, 2011
Winslow OE, 1874
Wisden Cricketers' Almanack, 1909, '10, '13, '32, '46, '59, '63, '68, '84, '89
Wood AH, 1868, '85, '87
Wood CBJ, 1954
Wood CP, 2011, '12
Wood JR, 1986, '89, '90, '93
Wood MDF, 1915/18
Woodroffe KHC, 1915/18

Woods SMJ, 1895/6
Woolley FE, 1915/18
Wootton G, 1865
Worcester, **18**99, **19**05, '12, '27, '35, '74, '75, '88, '94, **20**07
Worcestershire, **18**95, '99, **19**04, '05, '06, '19, '22, '25, '39, '46, '52, '56, '62, '64, '65, '66, '71, '74, '80, '87, '88, '89, '91, '93, '94, '96, '97, **20**01, '07, '09, '10
Worrell LR, 1973
Worthing, 1951, '54
Wyatt FJC, 1908
Wynne-Thomas P, 1900
Wynyard EG, **18**79, '87, '90, '93, '94, '95, '96, '97, '98, '99, **19**00, '01, '02, '03, '05, '06, '07
Yaldren CH, 1915/18
Yorkshire, **18**88, '93, '94, '95, '96, '98, **19**00, '01, '02, '03, '04, '05, '06, '11, '12, '13, '19, '20, '21, '22, '23, '24, '25, '27, '31, '32, '33, '35, '37, '38, '39, '46, '47, '49, '54, '55, '59, '60, '62, '63, '65, '66, '67, '68, '69, '72, '74, '75, '76, '80, '82, '83, '86, '87, '90, '94, '97, '98, 2000, '01, '02, '06, '07, '11, '12
Yorkshire United, 1874
Young C, 1867, '78, '80
Zimbabwe, **19**83, '95, **20**03, '05, '13